THE YEAR OF AFFECTIONS.

The Year of Affections

Jean-Baptiste Avrillon
Translated and Adapted by E.B. Pusey

Cover design by Ben Jefferies

Published by Nashotah House Press
Nashotah, Wisconsin
2022

Print on Demand

Available at Nashotah House Press

www.Nashotah.edu

THE

YEAR OF AFFECTIONS;

OR, AFFECTIONS

ON THE LOVE OF GOD,

DRAWN

FROM THE CANTICLES,

For every Day in the Year.

BY AVRILLON.

TRANSLATED FROM THE FRENCH, AND ADAPTED TO THE USE OF THE ENGLISH CHURCH.

LONDON:
WILLIAM JONES CLEAVER, 80, BAKER STREET,
PORTMAN SQUARE;
& J. H. PARKER, OXFORD.

1847.

CONTENTS.

ON THE UNITIVE LIFE.

EDITOR'S PREFACE.

This beautiful book needs, in itself, no introduction. The few suggestions which are needed as to its use in the holy season before us, are supplied in the Author's Preface. There was moreover scarcely a word in it, in its original form, about which any one, educated in the true principles of our Church, could have the slightest doubt. Expressing throughout a fervent love of God in an expansion of the language of the Canticles, it scarcely touches upon any subject in which Christians are not one. And so it is hoped that it will be a happy accession to our devotions in this our most solemn season, cheering us amid our self-denials and penitence, by fostering that love which hallows them. For thus must our whole inward man be formed together, and habits, now too often disunited, be healthfully joined: a fearing love and a loving fear. Love, without continued penitence and present strictness, will be weak and unreal; penitence and strictness without or with little love, is a body without a soul. Love must sweeten, and soften, and hallow penitence; penitence must chasten our love, give it purpose, and solidity, and strength, and character. Penitence, without love, were no Christian penitence; love, without abiding penitence, were not a sinner's love: but love lifts up penitence, penitence deepens and strengthens love; and penitent love at once ascends to and reaches the Throne of God Who is Love, and remains on earth, "the humble and contrite spirit," wherein He Who filleth heaven and earth, cometh down to "dwell." And so, during these days also, love shall cheer our penitence, in itself austere and cheerless, giving it a brightness and gladness of its own, almost above our Easter joys, when it is cherished and practised out of love to Him Who redeemed us, but against Whom we have sinned; so may we come with joy to that Great Easter-Day, when "the days of penitence" being over, the Lord will indeed "appear unto salvation" to all true penitents, who, in His absence, have, from love, "wept bitterly," and who have longed and looked for His Coming, not because it shall put off their sackcloth and gird them with gladness, but because it shall be His full Presence, Whose presence, in their soul, sin has darkened.

One subject only should perhaps be touched upon, as connected with the structure of this book, although not entering very deeply into its substance, the division into the Purificative, Illuminative, Unitive Life. This division, which pervades the most searching and deepest practical books of the Continent, has, (it is interesting to observe,) together with the whole subject of meditation, and the practice connected with it, been recognized by that great practical writer of our own, who is most deeply acquainted with the human heart, and, perhaps, most unites penitence and fervid love.

The chapter of Bishop Taylor, however, "upon Meditation," in which he touches on this subject, takes in so much besides of extreme value for the formation of habits of devotion which we much need, that it seemed well to add the whole as a distinct witness. It exhibits, in a remarkable degree, the characteristics of that great writer; his large grasp of mind, with the minute knowledge of the details essential to his subject; his union of solidity and fervour, his deep perception of our varied wants and their varied remedies, and the shortcomings to which we are liable in their application; his vivid appreciation and power of appropriating and condensing to our use whatever is excellent, wherever it is found. The whole chapter, as any one will see who is at all familiar with the great moral writers of the later Continental Church, is founded upon them, uses their very words and turns of expression, gives their advice and their cautions. It is a remarkable recognition by a Bishop of our Church, of the practical teaching of one who commonly has been known among us as a bye-word only.

As a supplement to what has been said by Bishop Taylor, it may here be added, the distribution into the Purificative, Illuminative, Unitive Life, is founded on the course prescribed in the celebrated "Spiritual Exercises," for the solid conversion of the soul to God: a course which was most wonderfully blessed in the conversion of tens of thousands; of late, that it has, it is believed, been uniformly contracted into the fourth of the space allotted by its author, its fruits, although still considerable, have been very much diminished, both in depth and extent.

The course was originally adapted for a temporary retreat from the world, in which, for a month, the soul was separated as much as possible from the business and distractions of the outward world, and occupied with itself and its End, God. This period was ordinarily distributed into four divisions, which thus came to be called "weeks;" yet not in any such mechanical way, as though the same effects would, in the same time, be produced in minds of various spiritual states and characters. It is expressly provided in the "Exercises" themselves, that each period should be lengthened or shortened according to the proficiency of each. Nor again was it thought that any habits could, in so short a space, be permanently formed. Rather it was a sort of prelude and foretaste of what was to be carried on during the whole subsequent life. By the grace of God a good foundation was laid, good seed sown in the heart by God, to be treasured up and guarded faithfully, as the gift of the love of the Lord God. Those who used these Exercises were especially warned at their close, that as heat is easily lost by one passing into the cold, so all the fervor and light thus gained might readily be lost on the return to ordinary life, being as yet something whereby the soul had been affected, not strengthened and annealed into a habit. Daily meditation for half an hour, or, if it could be, for an hour, daily self-examination for a quarter of an hour, weekly Communion, with confession, a spiritual guide with whom to communicate on all which concerns the soul, the frequent reading of pious books, the conversation of the good and avoidance of the evil, daily advance in virtue, especially in humility, patience, and charity, and a continual aim at the highest perfection which any could attain in his state of life, according to the measure of Divine Grace, was the outline of the course recommended, in order to preserve that which any had received. It was also made a special subject of warning, that persons were not to think that they had done with any one stage, because they passed on to another; "as if, the first period being finished, any were fully and perfectly 'purified,' or the second and third ended, were perfectly 'illumined,' or at the close of the fourth, had attained to a full 'union' with God; for that all these needed long time, labour, and practice, in extirpating sins, subduing passions, acquiring virtues." Nor again, if any had some earlier foretaste of the "Unitive Life," were they to abide continually in it, but to return to the former, and long and steadily bind themselves to the mortification of passions and the practice of virtues.

With these limitations, the course thus entered upon was a sort of compendium, a mirror, of the whole Christian life; such as it would be, were we what we should. Its commencement, "the Purgative Life," corresponding with "Conversion;" the "Illuminative Life," wherein the cleansed soul receives "light" from above, being the increased insight and growth in Christian graces and duties; the "Unitive way" being that full union of the soul with God which wills only what He willeth, loves only what He loveth, and findeth in the love of CHRIST its sole End, and Support, and Reward, and satisfying Fulness. But since, to the end, there will be, in all, faults yet to uproot, shortcomings still to mourn, graces yet to deepen, the two former "lives" will never be at an end, while "the Unitive Life" is not to be sought for as a reward, but is in its fulness "hidden with CHRIST in GOD," to be revealed at His Appearing to those who love Him.

Of these first two portions, then, with which most, here below, have most to do, the order is founded on the words of Holy Scripture, "Cease to do evil, learn to do well." The first "week," or period, was accordingly employed in strict self-examination, and a survey of the whole life; its end was the rejection of sinful habits, "exterminating the vices and evil habits in their very sources and first principles," to gain a great hatred of sin, and great confusion and penitence for having sinned against GOD. This was the object on which prayers, meditations, sifting of self, for the time, were concentrated. "Shame and confusion of face" were the object of prayer; the subjects of meditation were the infinite hatefulness of sin, as being against the Infinite Goodness of GOD, and so righteously deserving eternal punishment; or as shown in the hopeless fall of angels, the damnation of others for less sins than ours, man's whole fallen state, the pains of hell as brought before the soul through all the senses, the sight of its vast fires wrapped round the body and closing in the soul, the hearing of the groans, howlings, and blasphemies against CHRIST, the overpowering smell of corruption, the bitter taste of tears and the worm of conscience, the touch of those fires which burn the very soul; and, again, as giving these their terror, the sense of our own individual corruption as obtained by the gradual recollection of the sins of the whole life, in its several years and portions, the careful weighing of our sins in their own intrinsic foulness, even had they been unforbidden, until we came to view ourselves as one ulcerous sore, out of which flows forth all this corrupted virus of sin. Yet all this could not be borne without continual intercourse with CHRIST; and so each meditation began with prayer to Him, and closed with converse with Him, beholding Him on the Cross, and pouring out the heart before Him; accusing self before Him, or asking grace or counsel of Him; thinking what we have or can do, in return, to Him; praying Him to give us detestation of ourselves, self-correction, recovery from this world's vanities; thanking Him that we are not among the damned, but have until now His exceeding mercy and pity.

With these meditations were united outward aids, which might either hinder distraction, or strengthen their efficacy. The imagination (in cases where GOD had given it) was used to place the soul in scenes harmonizing with the thoughts, as a criminal is placed, bound hand and foot, before the judge; or as a deserter, who had been loaded with benefits, before the king and the whole heavenly court. Thoughts, even of religious joy, such as of the Resurrection of our LORD, were withdrawn; much more, every thing which might lead to laughter was carefully excluded; the light of day, except as far as was actually needed, was shut out; the eyes, except for courtesy, were not to meet others; penitence was practised, both within and without; within, in sorrow for sin; without, in such acts of "revenge" as the flesh might bear without great weakness or injury to health (strict care of this being taken, so that diminution of sleep, as most affecting it, is expressly excepted). By all, the soul was "brought" as "into the wilderness," that after she had abode there for a time, GOD might "speak to her heart."

This whole course, which in "the Exercises" was the exclusive occupation of a week, except for such intervals of bodily refreshment as were necessary, and which was lengthened or abridged as any one obtained more slowly or more speedily the end proposed,—a deep "contrition, grief, and tears for his sins," was the commencement of Conversion; or, in a more restricted sense, Conversion itself, as the act of turning away from sin unto GOD, to be carried on and completed and bound fast in subsequent life. It was closed by a general Confession and the reception of the Holy Eucharist, this being "an exceeding aid both to the avoidance of sin, and for the conservation and enlargement of the grace received."

This period was called "the Purificative way," or "life," in that its object was, that the soul should be cleansed of its sins.

"The end and scope, proposed in all the exercises of the first week, is chiefly this, that we should know that we have gone astray from that way which was to lead us to that ultimate end for which we were created; and should, consequently, sorrow for this sad and so grievous wandering, and conceive an intense desire of returning into that way, and ever persevering in it."

"In the second week the end is, to set before us CHRIST our LORD and SAVIOUR as the True Way, as He Himself said, 'I am the Way, the Truth, and the Life,' and 'No one cometh unto the Father but by Me.'"

"For He is the Exemplar given by the Father to men, by imitating Whom we may amend our corrupted manners, and direct our feet in the way of peace. Wherefore, since the Life of CHRIST is the All-perfect Life, and the very Ideal of virtue and holiness, it follows that the nearer our life approaches, by imitation, to His, the more perfect is it also, yea, and cometh nearer to its ultimate end, and so also is the more blessed."

"Wherefore this second week corresponds to the 'Illuminative' way, because CHRIST is the Sun of Righteousness, Who illumineth every man that cometh into the world, and came to this end, that He might shed light on [illumine] those who sit in darkness and the shadow of death. And since sins and evil affections darken the soul, and hinder it and withdraw it from the imitation of CHRIST, therefore these were to be first uprooted out of the heart by these first exercises and meditations."

This second period was distributed into two weeks, the second of which was chiefly occupied in strengthening the purposes formed in the first. The characteristic of this whole period might perhaps be designated by one chief occupation of it, "the choice of life," i. e. the settled purpose that it should be, according to the circumstances of each, "to the greater glory of God." If that state were already fixed, as with those who were in any office of the Church, or were already married, then that state was to be reviewed in all its several relations, "with no other object than what should advance the glory of God and his own salvation, withdrawing from love of self, and any private end." The same rule was applied to all details in which choice was to be used. In those who were wholly free, and to whom a more devoted life seemed open, the choice, although with great discretion, was to be laid before them; yet with the special caution, that any of great fervour, especially if naturally excitable, were to be prohibited from binding themselves while in the midst of those sensible consolations, lest they should afterwards repent. But this choice, whether of the whole of life or of details, was to flow entirely from "the contemplation of our Lord and of His Kingdom; that so the mind might be raised from things earthly and transitory, to desire to imitate Him." The subject, then, of meditation at this first period was, the "Life of Christ;" that in contemplation of this, the soul might enquire and long for that life in which He would have it serve His Majesty, that it might conceive the desire of being likened unto Him, and the deepest thankfulness it could towards Him Whose Gifts to us and Deeds for us were so boundless; and "learn the frame of mind needed, that we be perfected in that state which His Divine Goodness should suggest to us to choose."

This "choice," then, related not to high things

chiefly (which would be for the few), but in all things to "set before us our Saviour CHRIST, and to follow Him," "to do all things to the greater glory of God." To this end, all mankind were conceived as ranged under the two "standards" of Satan or of CHRIST: Satan inviting his to the love of riches, worldly honour, and to pride; our LORD, "beautiful exceedingly in form, and All-lovely to gaze upon," calling His to the spiritual love of poverty, (and if called of GOD, to actual and real poverty,) to love of reproach and contempt, and to humility. Or they were exhibited under the three classes of persons, all in possession of the same sum, gained not unlawfully, yet with some other end than of the Love of GOD; whereof the first would wish to lay aside its affection towards its treasure, but would, all life through, use no means; the second would use means, but its own, and would draw GOD over to itself, rather than go to GOD; the third would retain or part with what it had, out of no respect to itself, but "out of the desire of the Divine Glory."

The whole object, then, of this week, as summed up by the author in what he wished to be the waking thoughts, is "to call forth the longing to know more clearly the Eternal Word Incarnate, that I may serve Him, and cleave to Him the more intensely, as I the more see His most incredible goodness towards me." The meditation of the Passion was to fix the choice thus made, as the inexhaustible storehouse of His bounties, the special food of the soul.

The soul having thus formally renounced all sin, and been bent to the study of its Divine Master, was now yet further to be strengthened against the seductions of created goods, by the contemplation of the blessedness flowing from the Fountain of all blessing. Divine Love was the crown of this course. "For since there are two things, which most commonly withdraw us from the chief good, i. e., the knowledge and love of God and the Lord Jesus, and the imitation of Him; first, the fear of evil; second, the love of created goods; in the third week, we set before us Christ crucified; in the fourth, His Life in glory. For all the evils of the world, since they have passed through His sacred Heart, have lost their force of evil, and if they flow to us from His Side, have no longer any power to harm, but rather are a means to profit. But by His state of glory, the Lord hath the disposal of all goods, as He saith, 'All power is given unto Me in heaven and in earth.' And so in His Hand they lose their poisoning influence. The right use, then, of good or evil dependeth on this, that we receive them from the Hand of the Lord Jesus, and pour them back into His All-loving Bosom, i. e., to His Glory."

But although perfect love be the crown of our life, love there must be, in the very outset of conversion, adapted to our state. At first, a sorrowing love, because we have sinned much; then, a sympathizing love, because for our sins He hath suffered much; a love also, founded (as it is given in the Exercises themselves) on the thoughts of the extreme hatefulness of sin, which was so atoned for; "the infinite goodness and wisdom of God, which devised so apt a means to melt the hearts of men by His love, and draw them to Himself;" the confirmation of our hope, that He Who hath given the greater, the Blood of His Only-begotten, will give eternal glory also, which is assuredly the less; in one word, "the enkindled love of God, from the consideration of so great goodness, so great a benefit given us, and so given."

And when the soul has long laboured to purify itself from sin, and by Divine Grace to conform itself wholly to the will of God, then those writers[1] who have known that blessed state, speak of one yet higher, the foretaste of future bliss, in which it "liveth in perfect union and intimate communion with God, is occupied with God Alone, and finds no hindrance to this Divine intercourse; in which, continually abandoning itself to the Hands of God, placing itself with unreserved confidence in the Hands of God, it enjoyeth a perfect repose, both in itself, by a deep recollectedness, wherein it tastes the Presence of God, and gives itself unceasingly to Him; then, too, in the Heart of Jesus Christ, where it makes its constant abode; then, also, in the Bosom of Providence, where it reposeth softly, so that no accidents can disturb its tranquillity:" a state "in which it hath Christ ever present, and tastes the sweetness of His Presence, holding delightful and soothing converse with Him, with as much ease as our very breathing; has truly no interests but His; exists and lives only by Him, as if it were but one thing with Him." "The soul thus 'transformed into the image of the glory of

[1] Surin, Catechisme Spirituel, c. 7. Compare, as far as belongs to the passive part of the gifts of this life, the wonderfully glowing words of Bishop Taylor below.

the Lord,' gains, as it were, a new being; it has new desires, new inclinations; its powers are repaired, as it were, and perfected by the gifts of God, which overflow the whole soul—the life is thenceforth all heavenly. The imagination is full of supernatural ideas; the appetite has only holy transports; the understanding but heavenly wisdom; the memory only Divine objects; the will is filled, as it were, with a furnace ever burning, which giveth freedom of motion to the body also, that it may follow the spirit." "Such," this writer sums up, "is the state of one transformed: his faith is sublime; his hope lively; his charity burning; all his moral virtues are then, as it were, Divine; there is nothing in him which holdeth to the earth."

It need only be added here, that this high spiritual life was the less exposed to delusions, because, as the Holy Eucharist sealed and established that first stage of the cleansing of the soul, so It was "its nourishment in this its highest, and along the whole road of perfection." "It is the Divine Eucharist which carries on this great work, through the graces of which It is the source, and the singular strength which It communicates to the spirit. All who aspire to perfection ought to regard this Sacrament as the chief means of succeeding in their undertaking, and they ought to receive It often, according to their frame of mind; at first, twice in the week; then some three times; at last, daily, when they have reached this state whereof we speak. The frame of mind they should bring to the reception of the Eucharist is reverence, founded on the greatness of God Whom they receive, and their own nothingness; contrition, to purify themselves of the least spot; and love, to unite and incorporate them for ever with JESUS CHRIST."

Full also and overflowing with spiritual joys, as the "Unitive" life is exhibited to be, not joy or even love alone, but perfect conformity and union with the will of GOD, is its characteristic. The preparations for it, as given by the same experienced writer [2], are, "1. an inward death to self by an entire abnegation of self, so as to renounce all, even the most refined and the purest pleasures, such as the very pleasure in virtues, and ease in practising them, whereof GOD sometimes deprives souls for a time, that they may detach themselves from all which is the object of sense, and abandon themselves, without reserve, to the designs of His Providence: 2. to seek GOD purely, accustoming the soul to look to Him Alone in all things: 3. to purify and enlarge more and more in the heart the fire of love, taking occasion of all things to increase in the love of GOD, so as henceforth to love Him Alone, and all things in Him Alone, and for Him Alone, without allowing the soul to be drawn by any other less perfect motive. By these holy exercises, the soul, completing its purification, is prepared for the union with GOD."

It can, indeed, only be from this entire oneness of the will with that of GOD, that its deep, full, all-pervading, all-encircling, enrobing peace has its source. It is a *state* into which the soul is brought, not an

[2] C. 6. fin.

occasional access of feeling; nor, again, a mystic state only, in which the soul is passive, but only receives impressions. It interferes with the exercise of no faculties, but sets them wholly free from self, desires, and fears; the peace which it imparts "is given to the spirit, not to the senses," "making it in such wise master of itself, that nothing can disturb it:" "in the midst of occupations, it is as self-possessed as if it had nothing to do." It is "a light accompanying the soul everywhere;" guiding it, in simple and uninstructed people, ever to discern what is right. The infused desire for the glory of God makes it desire fervently to win souls to Him, so that it cannot be inactive: "it loves suffering through its love to its Saviour, and desire to be likened to Him," so that it cannot be a relaxed love. It changes no employment, but amidst all lives in God Alone; "prayer is its element," as God is the Centre to which, in all its occupations, it tends.

Having thus given the high experience of others, it becomes necessary to give their cautions also; cautions the more necessary, because a class, still containing many earnest persons, out of the Church, looks to something resembling, in a faint degree, these transports and sensible consolations, as the essential evidences and tokens of the Divine favour. The first is against any impatient longing for the sweetnesses even of Divine love, instead of patiently following that course of cleansing the soul which He allots it. "If[3] any were to aspire hastily to that

[3] Directorium in Exercit. Spirit. c. 39.

'unitive' way, there would result great confusion, which would hinder altogether all spiritual progress; and, moreover, it would be exposed to perils and illusions. It were as though one would pass from the lowest school to the highest, without passing through the intermediate; or, as though from the lowest step of a ladder any would, by a spring, transport himself to the highest, omitting those which lie between. So, then, before any professedly practise himself in this, which we have called the 'unitive' way, he ought first to be well cleansed by the exercises of the purgative life, and, thereafter, also to have made good progress in the 'illuminative' way. From neglect of this, it happeneth that many, not walking, but overspringing in the way of the LORD, after long time and various trials, are found devoid of virtues, impatient, and irritable, and with other like imperfections. Nay, rather, this advance to a higher way hangeth not so much on our choice, or will, or effort, as on the direction of the HOLY GHOST, Whose wont it is to place these ascents in the soul, that it may go from strength to strength."

The second is of the like sort, even after having been admitted to some foretaste of Divine love, not to be discouraged by dryness of spirit, nor to seek anew for sensible consolations, but to be content to be as He wills. "Do not seek for deliciousness and sensible consolations in the actions of religion," says our own Bishop Taylor, "but only regard the duty and the conscience of it. For, although in the beginning of religion, most frequently, and, at some other times, irregularly, GOD complies with our infirmity, and encourages our duty with little overflowings of spiritual joy, and sensible pleasure, and delicacies in prayer, so as we seem to feel some little beam of heaven, and great refreshments from the Spirit of consolation; yet this is not always safe for us to have, neither safe for us to expect and look for: and when we do, it is apt to make us cool in our inquiries and waitings upon CHRIST, when we want them: it is a running after Him, not for the miracles, but for the loaves; not for the wonderful things of GOD, and the desires of pleasing Him, but for the pleasures of pleasing ourselves. And as we must not judge our devotion to be barren or unfruitful, when we want the overflowings of joy running over: so neither must we cease for want of them. If our spirits can serve GOD choosingly and greedily, out of pure conscience of our duty, it is better in itself and more safe to us." It is but a weak love, which cleaves to the object of its love, only in His presence, and when He visibly pours His favours upon it; it is often to prove and strengthen love, that He withdraws Himself for a while from the soul, that "loving" Him "unseen, it may the more, though now it see Him not, yet believing, rejoice with joy unspeakable, and full of glory." "The[4] best remedy for obtaining devotion of GOD, is to humble oneself under the mighty Hand of GOD, and subject and resign oneself to His Divine will; for often that displeasure and bitterness cometh not so much from fervor, as from a certain secret pride, whereby a person trusts

[4] Direct. c. 7.

in his own pains-taking, or because he would excel herein, or out of self-love, which loveth consolation. Wherefore he should rather hold to this; having done what in him lieth, let him leave all besides to the will and the love of GOD, and trust that this very dryness is therefore permitted by GOD, because it is best thus. And this very feeling of humility and submission towards God is often more effectual to gain from Him the grace of praying well."

And since the soul is so naturally eager after refreshment, and the school through which GOD most usually carries it, if it will not outrun His guidance, must often be felt very tedious and dreary to ardent souls, there shall yet be added the result of the experience of one, to whom heavenly consolations were so largely afforded, and which was pointed out to the editor, as remarkably bearing out the advice of Bishop Taylor [5], which will occur afterwards.

"It [6] is a most important caution, that no man apply himself to the interior exercises of prayer, with the expectation or desire of the least extraordinary favour; but deeming himself evidently most unworthy of the least, he must beg only the necessary virtues of a penitent and servant of GOD. Such desires expose to certain dangerous illusions, and banish not only such favours, but, what is of greatest importance, all the fruits of Divine grace. If any one receive extraordinary favours, let him never dwell upon, or much

[5] Holy Living, c. 4. sect. 7. On Prayer, Remedies against tediousness of spirit. § 5.

[6] Abstract of St. Teresa's Interior Castle of the Soul. Note to Butler's Life of St. Teresa, Oct. 15, Vol. ii. p. 684.

consider them; but endeavour, with the greater fear and ardour, to improve in his soul true humility, patience, compunction, and charity, in which alone sanctity consists, and which the servants of God best improve by trials."

Even in those Exercises which are classed under the "Purgative" life, and which are both adapted to the solemn season whereupon we are entering, and to most of ourselves, as being but in the outset, if even in the outset, of the spiritual life, we must recollect that humility is needed. Even in so far as they are here imperfectly touched upon, they furnish rather some analogy to the course best for us, than a direct absolute guide. In the wonderful book from which they are taken, a spiritual guide is throughout presupposed, who should apply, and temper or modify, this course according to the temperament, bodily or mental strength, sex, capacity, age, previous instruction, acquirements, trials at the time itself, and other incidental circumstances of each. And, perhaps, in combination with the great wisdom and purified desire for the glory of God Alone, manifested in the "Exercises," scarcely any thing strikes us at first sight more than the tender care and sympathy with the minds who should be so trained, not to discourage, or weary, or strain, or force them on, or allow them to be hurried on by natural excitement, or to interfere any way with the work of God. The instructor is specially and repeatedly[7] warned, that his only office

[7] Direct. c. 24, § 1. c. 5, §§ 4, 5. c. 19, § 2. "That such deliberations may be made the more solidly and without man's

is "to remove hindrances, guard against what might injure," (as errors, deceits, disorderly affections, and inclinations,) "to follow, not to forestall, the Divine motions;" "not to attribute any thing to himself, but to ascribe all to God;" to "add nothing of his own, but leave to God to dispose of His own creature, according to the good pleasure of His goodness; lest, if he mingle aught of his own, that be to be apprehended which the Lord said, 'Every plant which My Heavenly Father hath not planted, shall be rooted up.'" It might hardly be safe, either for body or mind, to attempt to follow these Exercises out, alone and continuously, in their austerer form. Yet the truth they presuppose is common to all, may be acted upon by all; that detailed knowledge of, and contrition for, past sins, must be the foundation of our whole spiritual building; that the eye must be cleansed in order to receive the light of Divine truth; and that the more we labour to cleanse our souls by contrition, confession, at least to God continually, (when that to man may, to the unbiassed conscience, seem Christianly inexpedient,) and such self-chastise-

persuasion, it is much better to permit that God Alone should treat with His own creature, and no third person interpose." 24, § 1. "Let him look and desire this only, that the will and good pleasure of God be fulfilled, adding nothing of his own spirit; for this is to thrust his sickle into God's harvest." Ib. § 2. "It is best during the 'exercises' to seek and await for the will of God, until our Creator and Lord Himself communicate Himself to the soul devoted to Him, and embracing it, dispose it to His love, praise, and service, as He knoweth to be most expedient." Exercit. Adnot. 15, ex 20.

ment as the health may surely bear and as may evidence real indignation at our sins, the more we may hope that He will cleanse them, Who Alone can, and that being cleansed, He will, in His time, fill anew with the fire and glow and light of His Spirit, the vessels which He had made and re-made, and we had marred.

E. B. P.

CHRIST CHURCH,
Septuagesima,
Feast of the Conversion of St. Paul, 1845.

THE

YEAR OF THE AFFECTIONS.

AUTHOR'S PREFACE.

THE Song of Songs is an excellent fountain, a plenteous source, where the heart finds the substance and the power of the purest and most touching feelings, the most fit to inspire, to nourish, and to augment Divine love. In this book, GOD and the soul, under the mysterious and sacred names, now of Lover and beloved, now of Brother and sister, oftener of Bridegroom and bride, speak a language of the heart which it is difficult to hear without being sensibly touched by the feelings they express, except to those whose sad estate the Prophet Isaiah deplores when he says, that "None considereth in his heart, neither is there knowledge nor understanding" for divine things: Non recogitant in mente suâ, neque cognoscunt, neque sentiunt. (Isa. xliv.)

This pure and holy converse between the Heart of GOD and that of His bride, this loving and sublime flow and refluency of affections, full of Heavenly ardour, inspires the timid soul with holy boldness to speak the same language. When it sees the earnest desire of Almighty God for the heart of a creature formed by His Adorable Hands, sees Him Whose Majesty is dreadful, tender and caressing, desiring its love, calling it His fair one, His love, His dove, His sister, and His spouse, it is inflamed with holy desire of becoming worthy of these lovely and ennobling titles; it puts itself in the place of this happy bride, first thinks, then speaks, and lastly feels like her.

The heart of man is subject to variableness, weariness, dryness, and is not always ardent nor stored enough to commune with God. Now carried away by its natural fickleness and lightness, a sententious truth, full of unction, has power to arrest and fix it; now weary of the most delicious food, because accustomed to it, a new affection gives new point to its love; now fainting and overcome by weariness whose cause it knows not, a loving expression presented to it has power to arouse it from its langour. It is the voice of its Beloved that knocketh: Vox dilecti pulsantis. (Cant. v.) The bride hears, she rises, she quickly opens her whole heart to Him, and executes what He ordains.

Indeed, the reading of something lively, distinct, and touching, has power to supply the indigence and barrenness of the mind and heart. The mind finds a thought which fixes, a truth which strikes it; and the heart an expression which touches it, an affection which it embraces. This affection is impressed on the heart as the seal on wax, it remains engraven upon it, and strengthens it against the wanderings to which it is but too subject.

Affections are the voice and the nourishment of the heart, and it cannot obtain them from a purer source than the Holy Canticles, which consist only of affections expressed by the Heavenly Spouse Himself, or put by Him in the heart and on the lips of a bride whom He has carefully instructed in the most excellent secrets, and the most tender expressions of the Divine love. The heart forms its affections on this excellent model; it discerns the sublimity of this Divine language, which, though approaching to that put into the mouth of impassioned men by profane love, is yet altogether wise, pure, and sacred; and it easily perceives the character of Divinity spread over this whole book; it reads it with profound respect, and it makes use of it with precaution.

To speak to God by affections, is to speak to Him heart to Heart. By affections the heart calls God to the assistance of its weakness, and God calls it tenderly to commune with it; He renders it attentive, and touches it. The more the heart speaks, the more it loves to speak; the more it feels, the more it desires to feel; the more it hears the voice of God, the more it wishes to hear it. Now it is a secret voice which, though not articulated, makes itself heard by Him to Whom it speaks; now the fulness of the heart relieves itself by sighs, and by short and ardent prayers. It says, like the bride, "Let me hear Thy Voice, O Heavenly Spouse, for sweet is Thy Voice:" Sonet vox tua in auribus meis, vox enim tua dulcis. (Cant. ii.)

Affections are also the most exquisite food of the heart of the spiritual man. To it they are what air and ordinary viands are to the body of the natural man. By them he breathes, is supported, and acquires new strength. An affection, now of suffering, now of strong, and now of tender, love, is for him a feast of delicious dishes variously seasoned, which God presents to him to nourish his love. If he is careful from time to time to substitute one affection for another, as soon as he perceives that that which occupied him begins to be weakened, worn out, and effaced, this harmless novelty hinders him from falling into weariness and sloth. By this pious industry he overcomes his natural fickleness, and learns at length to attach himself without difficulty to the only Object Which he ought to love. Nourished daily by this food, which may be found in this Year of the Affections, he will more easily detach himself from the earth to rise to God. Our steps to approach Him, indeed, says St. Gregory, are as many as the affections and feelings which we put forth: Ante Dei oculos tot gressus ponimus, quot affectus movemus. (D. Greg. Moral. xxiii. 5.) If love is a fire, affection is its flame; and this pure and light flame is always in agitation, till it has reached the Heart of God, the Adorable Principle from whence it emanated, and the loving Centre to which it aspires. When the heart is afflicted, it finds means to temper the bitterness of its sufferings by the sweetness of its affections. Like the bride, it makes a sweet mixture of these pleasant spices with the myrrh which it is obliged to gather. (Cant. v.) It endures the strength of that healing wine which would intoxicate it, through the milk of these heavenly consolations. When the heart is sorrowful, the affections console it; when wandering, they recall it; when hard, they soften it; when dejected, they raise it up; when empty, they fill it; when dry, they moisten it; when cold, they warm it; when fainting, they give it new vigour; the affections, in short, says one, are to our souls as a spiritual Spouse, filled with Heavenly sweetness; and from their chaste union result very considerable benefits. (Hug. Card. sup. Prov. c. 2.) Thence proceeds that spirit of compunction, thence those frequent sighs towards Heaven, thence those sweet and salutary tears; thence that contempt for earthly things, thence that pure and fervent devotion; thence, lastly, those delightful transports towards God, which render all the false joys of the world insipid.

I know that the solidity of love is rather to be sought than its tenderness; I know that feelings alone, devoid of practice, are but a sweet and pious delusion, which favours the weakness of some temperaments, feeble and easily moved, now melted by a sacred, now by a profane subject, thus substituting an imaginary love for that heroic charity which, far from making sensible pleasures a principal object, is always ready to sacrifice them.

They are, nevertheless, of very great utility, and when we know how to use them as holily as the bride, they infallibly lead to true love. Indeed, when the heart is sensibly penetrated with a feeling of tenderness for God, it soon resolves to labour for His glory and for its own salvation, and it does this far more easily than if it felt nothing. These feelings, then, are not necessary only to penitents to soften the rigour of their labours, but they also sustain the most perfect, who have till their death a heart of flesh, and consequently sensible to this sort of impressions; and we shall never find delusion in them, if we strive to conform our life to the tenderness and nobleness of our feelings. As a soul that loves God assiduously and with perseverance, is always rising, says St. Augustine, so that one feeling of love contributes to render the next more pure, more perfect, and more ardent, we have been careful in this work, which is, properly speaking, only a paraphrase for the affections, on the most beautiful passages of the Canticles, to follow closely the different degrees of Divine love, of the Purificative, the Illuminative, and the Unitive Life, from penitential love, its beginning, to love of union, its end and consummation. It is divided into fifty-two weeks, each of which contains seven affections, so that the heart will find one for every day in the year, whereon to converse with God.

It may be used as a journal of affections for the heart, which will thus render a daily tribute to the Heart of God.

AFFECTIONS

FOR

THE PURIFICATIVE LIFE.

First Week.

PENITENT LOVE.

IN the religion of JESUS CHRIST no one can be a lover without being a penitent, nor a penitent without being a lover. Both repentance and love show themselves in tears; the one pours forth tears of grief, and the other pours forth tears of affection; and these tears blend harmoniously, because the offended GOD and the beloved GOD, before Whom they fall, is still the Same GOD. Love without repentance is a flower without fruit, which has but an outside show, and produces nothing; and repentance without love is a wild fruit, which has nothing but bitterness, and cannot nourish.

The penitent spouse who had but just forsaken the world, has, nevertheless, the boldness to begin her song by asking of her GOD and her Lover a kiss from His Mouth: osculetur me osculo oris sui. (Cant. i.) This chaste kiss was at once the seal of her reconciliation, and the token and pledge of her love; but is it not strange that a penitent soul, who ought only to pour out herself in tears, should at once aspire to this familiar nearness to the God she has offended? And yet it is not so, for if she loves, she has a right to claim every thing from His Infinite Goodness.

Thus, too, she excuses her boldness by the motive which gave rise to this feeling, " because," says she, "the sacred breasts of Thy Mercy are better than wine;" quia meliora sunt ubera tua vino. (Ibid.) This wine is understood, according to the holy Fathers, either of pleasure, which, like ordinary wine, says the Wise Man (Prov. xxiii. 31), as a serpent, insinuates itself softly, in order to spread the poison of its deadly drunkenness; or of the terrible wine of the wrath of God, which this spouse would avoid, by furnishing herself with a penance wherein love and sorrow are equally marked. Thus hardly is she entered upon the career of penitence, than she enters also upon that of love, and she produces the one simultaneously with the other.

She says afterwards, in the same chapter, that she is black, but she is comely: nigra sum, sed formosa. (Cant. i.) The painful exercise of penance has blackened her flesh, and tanned her complexion; but the practice of love has beautified her soul. These are the first sentiments of penitence and love in the spouse of the Canticles, and in imitation of which we may frame the following.

AFFECTIONS.

FIRST DAY.

Osculetur me osculo oris sui. (Cant. i.)

Grant, Lord, to my sinful soul the holy Kiss of Thy Mouth, as a token of perfect reconciliation. Do Thou sanction Thyself the boldness of my demand, by the gift of a sincere penitence and of a true love, which Thou alone canst give, to make me worthy of the true Kiss of Thy Mouth, even Thy Grace. Overwhelmed with offences, confounded by my iniquities, I deserve not to approach to Thy adorable Feet; nevertheless, Thou permittest me to approach to Thy Mouth, provided that I love Thee: what goodness is this! My mouth is defiled, Thine is Purity Itself: mine has often given a false account of my heart when it told Thee that I loved Thee, and Thine has ever been the sincere organ of a Heart burning with love for me. But, O celestial Spouse, if I deserve not yet to be admitted to the chaste kiss of the bride because my soul is sinful, Merciful Father, I ask for that of the prodigal son, in the guise of a penitent (St. Luke xv. 20), until I become, by my love, worthy of the other.

SECOND DAY.

Osculetur me osculo oris sui.

Thy adorable Mouth, O celestial Spouse, has often declared to me Thy love. Thou hast given me such tender and true instances of it, that my soul, sinful as it is, dares to make to Thee the petition of the spouse, and to pray Thee that by a chaste and awestruck kiss, I may touch that Mouth Which has been so gracious to me. Bend down Thy lips, O Lord, draw Thou nigh to mine, and sanctify my mouth by penitence and love. May I feel by this holy channel the movements, the breathings, and the Divine tenderness of Thy Heart, and may these communicate themselves to mine, to purify and to consecrate it. May the Heavenly Fire, which proceeds from this pure Mouth, take possession of my heart, and for ever inflame it. May the all-powerful Breath, which comes out from this Divine Organ, inspire me with a new spirit and a new heart. It is the Breath of Thy adorable Mouth which has formed me, which has made me come out of nothingness; it is also by the Breath and by the Kiss of Thy Mouth that I hope to be reformed, and that I shall come out from the nothingness of my sins to live by vivifying grace. Kindle in my heart, by the sweet breath of Thy Mouth, a pure and holy fire, which may never be extinguished; form there Thyself a sincere horror of the sins with which I have defiled my innocence, and a strong resolve to expiate them by my tears, in order that I may have grace to die, as the Saints, in the Kiss[1] of the Lord.

THIRD DAY.

Osculetur me osculo oris sui.

Thou hast made known to me, Lord, by a happy trial, the wondrous steps by which Thy Infinite and All-powerful Mercy leads a sinful soul from the abyss of her disorders to penitence, and to the chaste Kiss of Thy Mouth. This Mercy waiteth with patience, it kindly overlooks, suffers long with charity, it forecomes, it calls, it importunes, finally it converts, it sets on fire and makes us worthy of the Divine Kiss of Thy Mouth. Thou hast long waited for me, Lord, and but for this invincible patience, I was running to my destruction; Thou hast overlooked my offences, and Thou hast loaded me with favours as though I was not offending Thee; Thou hast borne with me whilst I outraged Thee; Thou hast called me, and I have not replied to Thy voice; Thou hast sought me with the eagerness of a mother, whilst I was flying from Thee; and, finally, Thou hast offered me the Kiss of reconciliation: give It me, Lord; behold me ready to receive It. I ask It with the more confidence, because it is Thyself Who inspirest me to ask: but support Thou me, that I may not fall. Give tears to my eyes, and groans to my heart; and trace on it in

[3] See S. Cyprian, Ep. vi. § 3. p. 15. n. 9. Oxf. Tr.

characters of fire the most lively feelings of penitence and love, in order that I may love Thee, and that I may punish myself for not having always loved Thee.

FOURTH DAY.

Quia meliora sunt ubera tua vino. (Cant. i.)

Yes, LORD, the sacred Breasts of Thy Mercy are better far than the wine of Thy wrath. Alas! I have but too well deserved to drink to the dregs the terrible cup which Thou didst in times past put into the hands of sinful Babylon. Thy justice might blast and crush me; and stern as it might be, I could, in perishing, only adore the awful Hand that struck me. Dreadful justice, terrible wine, I fear thee: I know well that my head is not strong enough to support thee; but I shall find a sure covert from thee in the Bosom of the Divine Mercy. I will run thither as a child to the breasts of its mother; I shall there find a holy milk, which is better than wine. My GOD is just, it is true, but He is full of Goodness; sinner though I be, He permits my heart to love Him; He presents me with the breasts and the milk of His Grace, although I have only presented Him with the gall and bitterness of my sins. Yes, celestial Spouse, I will love Thee; but I will never cease to make amends for my sins.

FIFTH DAY.

Quia meliora sunt ubera tua vino.

What shall I do, LORD, to avoid the wine of Thy wrath, and to deserve the life-giving milk of Thy Mercies? Sorrow, groans, sighs, tears of grief, tears of tenderness, from henceforth ye shall be my portion; this is the price, Divine Spouse, with which I will buy the Kiss of Thy Mouth, and the milk of Thy Grace. Thou hast offered me both ever since my infancy, and I have made myself unworthy of them by running after the poisoned milk of a deceitful world, which I have unhappily preferred to Thine. In spite of my unfaithfulness, which deserved eternal punishment, Thou with infinite goodness still offerest me the Kiss of reconciliation; Thou hast added to that, not only the milk of Thy sacred Breasts, but yet more, all the Blood that Thou hast shed for me. Should I not, therefore, shed torrents of tears? Should not my flesh be torn by the severities of penance, as Thine has been by the barbarity of the tormentors? Should my heart be whole? Should it not rather be broken by contrition, melted by tears of grief, or reduced to ashes by the fire of my love?

SIXTH DAY.

Quia meliora sunt ubera tua vino.

Faithless creatures, flattering and seducing pleasures, ye are the false and intoxicating wine which has made my heart but too giddy; ye have made me lose my reason as often as ye have made me lose the Grace of my God; ye have been the amusement and delight of my seduced heart; henceforth ye will call forth my groans and tears. I now discover that ye have only given me poison embodied in a sweet and deadly draught; all that ye have left me is bitterness, which will last until death. Now I run, to be healed, to the Divine Breasts of Thy Mercy, O my Saviour! I am a child who am but beginning to be born to Thy Grace by penitence and by love: I have no want but this milk; it is the only nourishment that can be necessary to me, and that I can desire. I know that this liquor, so white and sweet, is formed by Thy Blood, which is its source; I know that Thou hast merited for me this milk of Thy grace, by nothing less than the Blood that Thou hast shed at Thy death; I know, in short, that it is only through the excess of Thy Love that Thou hast shed this Blood. To reply to these favours as I ought, it is necessary that I should love Thee, and should do penance, though it should cost me my life, and so I now resolve.

SEVENTH DAY.

Nigra sum, sed formosa. (Cant. i.)

Happy would it be for my soul, O Divine Spouse, if she could say with as much truth as the Bride of the Canticles, I am black, but comely. Alas! I became black and misshapen amidst sinners; but I am about to make amends for my past unfaithfulness with such unflinching zeal, that my flesh will become yet more black amidst penitents, so that at last I shall acquire true whiteness and true beauty amidst holy men and women who love Thee. Let this unhappy body perish, which tends only to corruption; let this flesh perish that I have so much loved, albeit the foe which I had most to dread. I only ask, Lord, that Thou shouldest adorn the soul which Thou hast redeemed. Wash her in the milk of Thy mercies; wash her again in the Blood which Thou hast shed for her, that she may become lovely in Thy sight; inflame her with the fire of Thy love, in order that she may keep herself in unswerving purity. The more my body shall be marred by the wholesome sternness of penance, the more beautiful will it be in the sight of my celestial Spouse, and Him Alone do I desire to please.

Second Week.

LAMENTING LOVE.

A Christian, when once he has embraced the rigours of penance, if it be joined with love, full soon sheds tears over himself, full soon breathes sighs and groans towards heaven. It is difficult for a true penitent, in the bitterness of his soul, to go over the life which he has dragged on in sinfulness, without groaning and sighing from the bottom of his heart. But happy are these groans, happy these sighs, happy these sobs, since they flow from the influence of grace, and from the breath of the Holy Spirit, Who Himself in an ineffable manner groans in us and with us, and Who forms these groans in our hearts by penitence and love!

But as the violence of both, that is, of penitence and of love, cannot but burst the narrow limits of a penitent heart, it must make a vent for itself by the eyes and mouth. The eyes shed tears, and the mouth sends forth sighs and groans, which it can no longer restrain, because they are driven on by the fire of Divine love, and so these lamentations frame themselves into words, and intelligible sentences. I acknowledge that the lamentations of a penitent soul are not without bitterness and grief; so it must be to make up for the sinful sweets which, with the loss of its innocence, the heart has tasted; but this bitterness is always really soothing, because it is not without love. "The penitent soul," says St. Gregory, "leans and feeds upon his own lamentations;" luctu suo anima pascitur (Moral. v. 7); and at the same time that they increase her love, they assist her to endure with greater ease the burden of penance, which she has imposed upon herself.

The Spouse says, speaking to her beloved, "the voice of the turtle is heard in our land:" vox turturis audita est in terrâ nostrâ. (Cant. ii.) This voice, says St. Bernard, is more like a mournful sighing than a song of joy, and serves to remind us of our miseries and of our pilgrimage, and makes us long after our country.

This mourning bride, then, quits this figure; and feeling that she has compelled her Beloved to forsake her by forsaking Him, she says, or rather cries out: Turn, my well beloved: revertere, dilecte mi. (Cant. ii.) It is thus that the penitent soul ought to raise up lamentations, and to call to God unceasingly to succour her weakness.

AFFECTIONS.

FIRST DAY.

Vox turturis audita est in terrâ nostrâ. (Cant. ii.)

The voice of the turtle dove is heard in our land, says the spouse. Ah! the plaintive voice and cooing of the turtle dove is not enough for this barren land, even my heart; it ought rather to pour forth either the roarings of lions, or the wailing cry of ostriches, and make the most frightful solitudes resound with her sobs, because she has a thousand times offended her God. The turtle dove is innocent, and I am sinful; to be faithful is her wont, to be faithless is mine; she loves to moan in lonely spots, and I am always restlessly seeking the vain joys in a sinful world; she has only a natural life to lose, and I may lose a life of grace and glory: is not this matter enough for tears tears? over what I have lost through my fault, and which I might have kept: tears over what I have committed against my God, and which I might have avoided: tears over what I am now, and what I should be, if I had been more faithful: tears over the uncertainty of my penitence, my grace, my love, and my estate: tears over the Heaven I hope for, and which I may lose in a moment: tears, in short, over the eternal torments of hell, which I fear, and which I have deserved.

SECOND DAY.

Vox turturis audita est in terrâ nostrâ.

Let my soul, like a lonely and mourning turtle dove, water the earth with her tears, and be only heard through the noise of her sighs and groans. So long as one is in this world, it is always a time to lament that we have sinned, and that all that is left us is only fear or hope. Let her, with penitent Augustine, continually mourn; let her find no comfort but in tears and lamentations, in penitence and love, and let her mourn that she has not always mourned, for she has always deserved to mourn. Let her feed only upon the bread of affliction; let her quench her thirst but with the water of her tears; let her have no other language than that of her sighs, no other harmony than that of her sobs, no other pleasure than that of self-mortification, no joy but in having nothing in which to rejoice. Provided she loves, she will be happy, because she will find an innocent joy in her own lamentations. She ought to taste no other so long as she shall be in this mortal body; she must weep and lament in this vale of tears, if she would be plunged in a torrent of delights in her heavenly country.

THIRD DAY.

Vox turturis audita est in terrâ nostrâ.

It is for Thee, Lord, to form in me the true moanings of penitence and love, because, though without Thee I can do Thee wrong, without Thee I cannot weep or moan. Enlighten and inflame me, O Divine Sun! grant me the grace which St. Augustine begged of Thee; show me myself: ostende meipsum mihi (Aug. Conf.); that penetrated by my true miseries, I may draw from them subjects for tears and moanings. What have I been? What am I? What shall I be? What have I done? What have I merited? What have I gained? What have I lost? and what can I do? What have I been? alas! a mere nothing. (Isa. xli.) What am I? a sad mass of corruption, filth, and iniquities. What shall I be? the food of worms. What have I done? nothing for Thee, and sin alone is my work. What have I deserved? to groan for ever in hell. What have I gained? not a single virtue, but sorrowful treasures of crimes and of wrath. What have I lost? Thy graces, O my God, and the fruit of the Blood Thou hast shed for me. In short, what can I do? Nothing without Thy help. What motives for tears and lamentations! I feel it, O celestial Spouse, and yet happy should I be if these feelings were lasting, sincere, and steadfast, and if they produced in me works of penitence and love!

FOURTH DAY.

Vox turturis audita est in terrâ nostrâ.

"The winter is passed," says the Spouse: happy if it were passed for me as well as for her! My heart was all ice whilst I was a rebel to His graces, and insensible to His love. This Divine Sun has just risen upon my soul, and it must be, in this ungrateful land, heretofore hardened by the frost of mine unfaithfulness, I must needs lift up the voice of the turtle dove, and my tears must flow from a lamenting love. But can I still, reconciled as I may appear, flatter myself that I love my God, and am loved by Him? Ah! this uncertainty makes me groan. How can I, without confusion and horror, depict what I am, and recount what I am not? I am defiled, even after what my God has done to purify me: nevertheless, I feel that I hate that which I am, and I have a horror for that which I have been. Let us then blot out what once we were by our tears and groans; let us wash us in the Blood of Jesus Christ, and stain ourselves no more. Let us begin to groan now, and never cease till death: it is not too much in order to avoid eternal groaning.

FIFTH DAY.

Revertere, dilecte mi. (Cant. ii.)

"Turn Thou, my well Beloved," and draw near to my fainting soul, to give her the life that she has lost by forsaking Thee. I lament, Lord, and I feel that all is wanting from the moment that Thou forsakest me. Turn, then, celestial Spouse; hearken to my moaning voice, which calls Thee to mine aid: listen to the feelings of love, which Thou Thyself dost form in my heart. As often as Thou wert tempted, on the subject of Thy doctrine, Thou didst answer only by words; and whenever Thou wert tempted on the score of Thy mercy, Thou didst answer by acts of love. Thou didst incline Thy heart to the lamentations and sobs of the adulterous woman, to the tears and penitence of Peter, to the love and devotion of Magdalene. Thou art ever the Same God, that is to say, a God of mercies; Thou hast the same power, the same goodness, and the same heart. Turn, then, to me, and grant this return to my moaning, my sobs, my tears, my penitence, and my love: I would weep, I would love, that I might never quit Thy side.

SIXTH DAY.

Revertere, dilecte mi.

Can any one, O my God, fix his thoughts on his estrangement from Thee without groaning over it? Can a man think how richly he has deserved this estrangement and not be drowned in tears? Thou didst draw near to me every day, and I did all I could to drive Thee away: I multiplied offences, and Thou didst overlook them. Thou didst keep back Thy justice, and when ready to crush me, as I deserved, Thy love did suspend and hold it in abeyance to spare me, and I did not restrain my sinful hand. I did run from Thee, and Thou didst lovingly pursue this rebellious and miserable nothing, which Thou couldst have blasted and reduced to ashes. Thou didst speak to me sometimes by inspirations, sometimes by the sting of conscience, sometimes by the fear of Thy Judgments, and I turned a deaf ear, or I stifled Thy voice by that of the world, whose pleasures enchanted me, and to which I gave all my attention. What else, then, can I do but increase my tears and groans until they reach the sum of my offences, to induce Thee to turn to me again, never to forsake me?

SEVENTH DAY.

Revertere, dilecte mi.

"Turn to me, my well Beloved," and give me strength to return towards Thee, since it is impossible for me to make the first step of my return, if Thou dost not take me by the hand. Too long have I forsaken Thee, and I cannot think of it without lamenting. But why did I not lament while I was in a situation so worthy of tears? I lamented not, because I was too blind and too hardened to see and feel the weight of my estrangement. Thou didst forsake me, because I persecuted Thee; and I did forsake Thee, because Thy Presence was a rebuke to my excesses. Thus Thy steps and mine were increasing each day the terrible distance that my sins had put between Thee and me. It is, then, necessary, that Thou shouldest give me now grace to feel my estrangement, that I may lament at having earned it, and never having felt it as I ought; but it is for Thee, LORD, to form in me lamentations worthy to efface my crimes which are innumerable, and to induce Thee again to draw near to me in order to restore life to me.

Third Week.

SUFFERING LOVE.

WE may say to GOD that we love Him with all our heart, we may repeat it over to ourselves, believe and feel it, yea, shed tears in this pious and sweet devotion; but if we have not yet passed through trial and suffering, or have only passed them in fretfulness and cowardice, all this is only doubtful love, proceeding much more from natural disposition than from grace. Here is a man who makes a thousand protestations of love and attachment to GOD, yet, at the least disappointment, is discouraged and grows cold: those same eyes which had just shed tears of an apparent and sensible devotion, now overflow with tears of vexation at finding themselves abandoned to affliction; this same mouth which had protested its love so loudly, complains yet more loudly of its sufferings; that heart which was apparently waiting upon GOD, now turns the tide of feeling in favour of its own daintiness, and puts all in practice to deliver itself from the pain it endures. Then let such a man be sure that this heart has had only an imaginary love for God, which, like a false and counterfeit coin, reddens under the hammer, and vanishes in smoke in the crucible; suffering, which is its touchstone, charges it with falsehood, because it finds no place there.

The spouse of the Canticles was too well tutored to fall into the snare of this false love; and she was so persuaded that suffering was necessary to true love, that she said to the daughters of Jerusalem, Despise me not if I am tanned, because it is the Sun which hath blackened this complexion, which was once of the lily and the rose: Nolite me considerare quòd fusca sim, quia decoloravit me sol. (Cant. i.) No one can be exposed to the burning heat of the Sun of Justice without losing happily the signs of daintiness.

Afterwards she says that her Beloved shall rest upon her bosom as a bundle of myrrh, esteeming herself too happy by this bitterness to pay for the privilege to love Him and to be loved of Him: Fasciculus myrrhæ dilectus meus mihi; inter ubera mea commorabitur. (Cant. i.) Finally, the Spouse says that her Beloved is as the lily among thorns: sicut lilium inter spinas (Cant. ii.); that is to say, the more she suffers, the more she gives out the sweet perfume of her love.

FIRST DAY.

Nolite me considerare quòd fusca sim, quia decoloravit me sol. (Cant. i.)

Do not despise me if I am black, says the spouse; it is the burning heat of the sun that has changed my complexion. What impression has the Sun of Justice made upon me since He has risen upon my soul? Alas! I flatter myself that I love my God, and it may be I have not yet begun to do so, because as yet I have suffered nothing for His love. Is then my heart more detached from creatures and from all sensible things? Is my spirit more obedient and more submissive? Is my flesh more mortified and less rebellious to the spirit? Does it carry through its macerations the marks of penitence and love? Is it crucified with the affections and lusts? (Gal. v. 24.) How far am I, then, from being able to say with the spouse, "I am black because the sun has looked upon me." What have I hitherto really suffered for Thee, O celestial Spouse! I bear about, alas! a flesh which starts aside at suffering, which takes alarm, which shudders, and rebels at the least mortification, which yields to the least stroke of pain, and which has no wish but for luxury and pleasure. When shall I master it, O my God? When for Thy love I shall wage a constant war upon it.

SECOND DAY.

Nolite me considerare quòd fusca sim, &c.

Do Thou, O Divine Sun, burn and consume in me all that is opposed to the pureness of Thy love. Thou canst at once harden and melt my heart; harden it against worldly objects which it loves with so much tenacity; and melt and soften it for Thyself alone, Whom Alone it ought to love. O that Thy Celestial rays might strike this sinful flesh, and so burn it up like that of the Spouse, that by means of suffering it may bear the glorious marks of Thy Divine Love. Do Thou extinguish those fires which are opposed to Thine; weaken this formidable enemy, lest it master my spirit; uphold its weakness, lest, being overcome, it make me lose the only good to which I aspire, which is to love and possess Thee: give me power to make it suffer even to death, lest it rebel against me; diminish its sensitiveness and daintiness; harden it to pain, to mortification, and suffering, in order that my whole being, that is to say, my heart, my spirit, and my flesh, may prove to Thee that I love Thee, and that I have no wish but to love Thee.

THIRD DAY.

Fasciculus myrrhæ dilectus mihi; inter ubera mea commorabitur. (Cant. i.)

"My Beloved," says the spouse, "from henceforth shall be to me a bundle of myrrh, which shall abide upon my bosom." Thy will, then, O Divine Spouse, is that I suffer, since Thou presentest to my soul, as to Thy bride, a bundle of myrrh, which is the emblem of suffering? Can I refuse Thee this testimony of my love? Thou hast suffered for love of me, very GOD as Thou art, and I am but a miserable creature. Thou wast innocent, even Innocence Itself; and I am sinful, and conceived in sin. (Ps. li.) It is then just that I suffer, and I consent to it; but Thou wilt also that I love to suffer, because that Thou commandest me to place the bundle of myrrh upon my heart, which is the seat of love. Ah, LORD! it is here that I feel my extreme weakness. I can suffer, but I cannot love to suffer unless Thou changest this heart, which has no wish but for pleasure. Put Thine in the place of mine; suffer in me and with me, as Thou hast suffered for me; Thyself fasten this bundle of myrrh upon my heart, for it is Thyself who art this mystic nosegay; and I shall triumph over all, or rather, Thou wilt Thyself triumph in me.

FOURTH DAY.

Fasciculus myrrhæ dilectus meus, &c.

Away with the sickly odour of those deadly flowers, which may infatuate and cannot strengthen; away, seducing and flattering pleasures, those poisoned sweets, which charm at first, and at last give death to the soul which allows herself to be corrupted by them. The myrrh which my Divine Spouse presents to me may indeed be bitter, but this bitterness brings a salutary balm that keeps off decay and death. Those sufferings which He exacts from me are the true myrrh which destroys self-love and supports Divine love. Sacred Spouse, I would carry Thee on my heart as a bundle of myrrh. I cannot love Thee unless I taste of the bitterness of the gall of which Thou hast drunk deep; and my soul would be unworthy the august character of Thy Spouse, if I refused the mystic posey which Thou presentest me. I will carry it upon my heart until death; the powerful odour of this spiritual myrrh shall be from henceforth the only perfume that I will inhale, and its salutary bitterness the only sweet that I will seek.

FIFTH DAY.

Fasciculus myrrhæ dilectus meus, &c.

Ah! gross is the blindness which dreams that we can love God, without, like the spouse, carrying the bundle of myrrh on our hearts, that is to say, without suffering, and loving to suffer for His love! How great that other blindness, which thinks that amid the bitterness of this myrrh no true sweets are to be found! But what a monstrous error is it to hope to taste of true pleasures apart from one's God! How many times, O my soul, hast thou experienced this truth! What innocent joys have you not tasted when you have suffered purely for His love! And what sorrows hast thou not undergone in the pleasures of the senses! What remorse in the soft and languid life thou hast led! What disgusts! What troubles, and what alarms! The love of the world is sweet and endearing in its first fruits, but in the end it is filled with bitterness. Thy love, on the contrary, O my God, presents at first some bitternesses, but they are sweetened because Thy Cross is never without unction, and the unction of Thy Cross is Thy love. The bitterness of this myrrh soon gives place to the sweetness of honey and milk. Ah! if I love true pleasure, shall I hesitate to devote my heart to Thee, and to suffer for Thy love?

SIXTH DAY.

Sicut lilium inter spinas, sic amica mea inter filias. (Cant. ii.)

"My beloved," says the Celestial Spouse, "is like the lily among thorns." She must therefore love and suffer at one and the same time. When the wind sways the thorns, they pierce the lily on every side, but how does this beautiful flower revenge herself for so many wrongs? It is by turning her wounds into so many mouths, from which she breathes forth a sweet perfume to embalm those thorns that have so cruelly torn her. Imitate this spouse, O my soul, and this lily among thorns: revenge thy sufferings only by increasing thy love for those who make thee suffer. A Christian who loves and suffers may, perhaps, appear miserable, but he can never really be so. This mysterious lily, though torn among the thorns, has ever in her heart her God, and He carries her by His Love. Let us then rather call suffering and desolation by the name of consolation and pleasure; let us suffer and let us love; there will rise in our hearts a perfume, of which the sweet smell will ascend unto the Throne and unto the Heart of God.

SEVENTH DAY.

Sicut lilium inter spinas, sic amica, &c.

I shall never preserve either the whiteness of innocence, or the fragrance of virtues, or the purity of my love, if I be not often exposed among thorns. As soon as my love shall begin to grow weak, I consent, O Celestial Spouse, to be exposed as the lily among thorns. Wound my heart with the chosen arrow of Thy love, to win me on to seek Thy Face, as the hart wearied by the chase seeketh water to refresh himself. (Ps. xlii.) Then shall I say with confidence, Come to me, LORD, since I am in suffering and since I am there by Thy order, or give me strength to go to Thee; uphold me in my affliction, lest I be overcome; be with me in tribulation, according to Thy Divine Word. I cry unto Thee with the prophet, deliver me, not from my affliction, for I consent to suffer, but deliver me from impatience, from murmuring, from faintheartedness, and from daintiness, and give me grace ever, among the thorns and sufferings that encompass me, to seek my consolation and repose in Thee Alone.

Fourth Week.

OBEDIENT LOVE.

THE Holy Fathers give the same praises to obedience as to love, only because it is its inseparable companion, and it is the spring of true love.

The word of GOD prefers it to sacrifice, (1 Sam. xv.) because that, in the ordinary victims, only a flesh, not our own, is offered up; but in obedience we offer up our self-will, and this great and noble sacrifice can be made only by the hands of love; without that, it would be beyond the power of nature. Thus, as that obedience which only comes from a servile and mercenary fear, and which is not animated by love, deserves no reward, so that love is false which is not accompanied by an unquestioning obedience.

Obedience ought to be received in the heart; it is its centre; when it is there, it joins itself to love which puts it in motion, and they act together to banish self-will, and to put God's will in its place.

It is thus by obedience that the Bridegroom delights to prove the love of His spouse; and to make this obedience easier, He promises that she shall be crowned. "Come," He says, "with Me from Lebanon; My spouse come from Lebanon; come, and thou shalt be crowned: Veni de Libano, Sponsa mea, veni de Libano; veni, coronaberis. (Cant. iv.) He repeats three times this word, come, to conquer, by these loving repetitions, all the resistance of her self-love and her weaknesses: again, this obedience was hard, because she had to forsake the grandeurs and pleasures of Lebanon, which is the type of the world, to follow the Spouse upon the mountain of myrrh, which is the symbol of Calvary.

When the bride has obeyed the first command of her Spouse, He says, "Open to me, My sister, My love, My dove:" Aperi mihi, soror mea, amica mea, columba mea. (Cant. v.) It is not enough, in fact, that she have ascended to this mystical mountain; it is necessary also that she open to Him her whole heart. So also she says, she rose at once to open to her Beloved, though her hands dropped with myrrh: Surrexi ut aperirem dilecto meo; manus meæ stillaverunt myrrham (Cant. v.); that is to say, that having opened her heart to Him, she has embraced from obedience, and for His love, the most rigorous mortifications.

AFFECTIONS.

FIRST DAY.

Veni de Libano, Sponsa mea, veni de Libano; veni, coronaberis. (Cant. iv.)

"Come from Lebanon, My spouse, come from Lebanon; and thou shalt be crowned." I hear, O Celestial Spouse, Thy voice which calls me, and bids me to come out from Lebanon to follow Thee upon the mountain of myrrh. Thou wilt then that I should love Thee, and show my love by obedience. I should be my own enemy if I disobeyed a precept so mild and so glorious, which asks my love, and which asks it for Him Who is the most worthy of all the affections of my heart. Let us obey without delay, whatever obedience may cost our weakness; let us come out from Lebanon, let us come out from the pleasures and false greatness of the world; let us come out from our own flesh and its lusts; let us boldly ascend the mountain of myrrh, where Love Himself has been crucified for us, and where out of obedience He is dead. Let us not strive for any other crown than that of thorns, which He has borne upon His head; it will be followed by a crown of glory, if we will love and obey unto death.

SECOND DAY.

Veni de Libano, Sponsa mea, &c.

Thou callest me, Lord, upon the mountain where Thou distributest crowns to Thy lovers; and my dainty will rises against it, because it is frightened at the combats it must endure to win it. Should I feel in my heart so much repugnance to obedience and love? Should I hesitate to come from Lebanon, and to sacrifice my inclinations when Thou dost promise to crown my obedience? My heart grows sick, and will have no yoke, when Thou wouldest lay one on her, though that yoke be mildness itself; and, on the contrary, she pretends to lay one on herself when Thou art willing to disburden her; and this yoke which she lays upon herself is severe and insupportable. Is not this a very hard yoke, to be the slave of the world, to groan under the tyranny of one's own passions? Ah! LORD, teach me to shake off this iron yoke, which costs me so many tears, which makes me commit so many sins, and which gives up my soul to so much remorse. It must be by taking that of love, which Thou dost offer me. Be then, O my soul, obedient to GOD, ascend with courage the holy mountain; the crown awaits you; change this shameful bondage, which thou hast endured so long, into an innocent and glorious bondage: it is only Divine love which can break your chains, and win for you the happy liberty of the children of GOD.

THIRD DAY.

Veni de Libano, Sponsa mea, &c.

I feel, O Celestial Spouse, that I am but too much wedded to the pleasures of Lebanon, which is the sinful world, and that the Holy Mountain, whither Thou callest me, alarms my self-indulgence. Help me then to come out, to obey, and love Thee; illuminate my blind spirit to know Thee, and induce it to submit blindly to Thy commands; give to this hard and dry heart feelings to take delight in Thee, to obey Thee, and by love to serve Thee all the days of my life. I will freely gather upon the mountain the bitterest myrrh, but let the sweetness of Thy Divine spices accompany it; show me the crown to aid my obedience, and to beckon on my love; since it is Thy will that I should love Thee, and Thou commandest it under pain of eternal damnation; Thyself give me what Thou dost command, and command what Thou wilt, because I can neither obey Thee nor love Thee without the help of Thy grace.

FOURTH DAY.

Aperi mihi, soror mea, amica mea, columba mea, immaculata mea. (Cant. v.)

Open to me thy heart, thou who art "My sister," because I have espoused thy flesh: "My love," because I have favoured thee with My graces, and that has gained thee My affection: "My dove," because by obeying Me thou shalt have the simplicity and innocence of a dove: "My spotless one," because I have washed thee in My Blood. Open to Me this heart; I have knocked at its door long enough without being heard. Awake, come from the bed of thy weakness; obey the voice of Thy Spouse, if thou wilt not hear that of Thy Judge: open this heart, which thou hast closed so long to My Word and to My Love: empty it of all worldly ties, close it to all creatures; I will enter there, I will fill it, I will dwell there, I will consecrate it: I ask thee for it, although it is Mine, and I have a right to exact it. I obey, O Celestial Spouse! my heart is ready, it is closed to all creatures, it is open for Thee Alone; enter there, be Thou its Master, dwell there, and never leave it.

FIFTH DAY.

Aperi mihi, soror mea, &c.

To whom could I more fitly open my heart than for Him Who made it, Who asks it of me, and Who only bids me open it for Him after having opened His Own to me whilst yet His enemy? To Whom ought it to be more faithful and more obedient than to Him Who is in such a manner its Master, that He can annihilate it, and punish its rebellions with eternal chastisements, and crown its obedience with immortal glory? Who more worthy to enter and repose there than He Who Alone is able to fill it, to sanctify it, to inflame it with celestial fire, and to hallow all its impulses and affections? Who more worthy of its love than He Who is supremely the Object of love, and Who is Love Itself? Let us, then, rise with as much promptness as the spouse; let us no longer lie softly in the midst of pleasures, nor be buried in the terrible sleep of indifference, of lukewarmness, and of luxury. I must obey when JESUS CHRIST speaks; I must open when He knocks, lest by shutting the heart to Him when He asks to be admitted, He abandon it for ever, so that from that time it be open to nothing but sensuality, the world, and the devil.

SIXTH DAY.

Surrexi ut aperirem dilecto meo. (Cant. v.)

"I arose," says the spouse, "to open to my Beloved as soon as I heard His voice." I must imitate this obedient spouse, and rise up quickly to open my heart the first moment that I hear the Voice of the Bridegroom. The least feeling, the least inspiration, shall from henceforth with me hold the place of an absolute command, and shall be followed forthwith by my obedience, and I will never defer, even for a moment, since the least delay may bring with it an infinite evil. I can obey Him, I can love Him; most unhappy were I if I did not! How deplorable would be my lot, O my GOD, if I was unable to open my heart to Thee, and if it were incapable of love to Thee! For, alas! what would it love? vain grandeur? sensual pleasures? the world? myself? Cruel love! wretched objects! unworthy to occupy my heart, and to fill its vast void. But I am able to love my GOD; He permits it, He orders it, and He helps me to do it. In bidding me love Him, He gives me the right to aspire to His Heart: why renounce so noble a privilege? why prefer cowardly sleep to the greatest of all goods? why not submit myself to a law which is all my safety, my happiness, and my glory?

SEVENTH DAY.

Surrexi ut aperirem dilecto meo.

Let me but obey the Voice of my God, and rise up as the spouse to open my heart to Him; in a word, let me but love Him, then have I nothing more to do; I have fulfilled the whole law. However manifold may be my duties, I have but one to fulfil, and that is to love; all others are reduced to this one alone: among the infinite objects which present themselves to my heart, I have but One Alone to love, and that is God. Ah! Lord, how simple is my religion! and how dastardly I am not to obey Thee! Can I complain of the multitude of laws, since I have but one alone, which is that of love? Can I be bewildered by the multitude of objects, when I have Thee Alone to love, and when it is Thou Who knockest at the door of my heart, and Who assistest me to open it to Thee? I will, then, love Thee, O Celestial Spouse! with all the ardour of which I am capable. I will love Thee supremely and without measure, with all my heart and without reserve, sincerely and without hypocrisy, unceasingly and without change; assist me to prove to Thee by this my obedience and love.

Fifth Week.

LOVE HUMBLED.

As the love of God is a creating love, it delights to work upon nothingness; there doth it operate with the most success, there it burneth with most ardour, there it triumpheth with the greatest glory. From whence it comes, that when a profound humility is joined to true love, this union is all-powerful to win the heart: for, if pride makes in the heart of man a criminal fulness, which prevents the entrance of the love of God, humility makes a happy void, which God soon fills with the out-pouring of His charity.

A man full of himself is incapable of loving God, because he is falsely puffed up with his own excellence; a Christian free from self-love, who knows himself, who despises himself, who counts himself nothing, and who consents to be counted as nothing, is much more susceptible of the impressions and feelings of Divine love, because he has no enemy in himself to fight against it; and this formidable enemy is pride.

It is very remarkable, that the first words which the Bridegroom addressed to His spouse, in the Holy Canticles, tend to make her know and humble herself. "If thou know not thyself," says He, "O thou fairest among women, go thy way forth by the footsteps of the flock:" si ignoras te, ô pulcherrima mulierum, egredere, et abi post vestigia gregum. (Cant. i.) The knowledge of our own nothingness is then the first step in a penitent life, to attain to the love of God.

Afterwards she says that the time to prune the vine is come, tempus putationis advenit. (Cant. ii.) She knows her faults, she therefore humbles herself, and labours to cut them off. In short, she weeps humbly and bitterly over her sins: she has, she says, washed her feet, that is to say, her faults, with the water of her tears, and she will no more put them in the filth and mire: lavi pedes meos; quomodo inquinabo illos? (Cant. v.) She has obtained pardon for her sins by the sacrifice of a contrite and humble heart; and she will take every precaution of which she is capable, not to defile herself anew.

AFFECTIONS.

FIRST DAY.

Si ignoras te, ô pulcherrima mulierum, egredere, et abi, &c. (Cant. i.)

If thou know not thyself, O thou fairest among women, go thy way forth by the footsteps of the flock. It is to my soul that Thou speakest, O Celestial Spouse! Give it then the beauty which Thou dost ascribe to it, and which it cannot gain but through Thy grace and Thy love, since I confess that it is become quite mis-shapen by pride. But can it really be that I knew not myself, and that I deserved to be driven from the presence of the God Whom I love? Can I be ignorant that I am kneaded with mire and filth, and that I am conceived in sin? (Psalm li.) All which surrounds me, and all which composes me, persuades me I am nothing: this weak flesh which only tends to corruption, this blind spirit which has no inheritance but ignorance, this frail heart which has no bent but for sin; this will, so weak for good, and which has no power but to rebel against my God: ah! I am persuaded, and I feel I am nothing. Lord, grant me grace never to forget it: instruct me more deeply in the knowledge of myself, in order that I by it may humble myself, and that this humility may produce in my heart true love.

SECOND DAY.

Si ignoras te, ô pulcherrima, &c.

I know, O my God, that I am only the dust of the earth, that I carry my humiliation in the midst of me, and that, nevertheless, I am proud and vain. I am only dust, how can I raise myself to Thee, Who art a pure Spirit? I feel that my love sometimes transports me towards Heaven; but I feel also that my flesh keeps me down, and makes me fall again immediately into the clay whereof it is kneaded: my soul would love Thee Alone, and my flesh desires only to love the world and pleasure: what strange humiliation for me! and how can I reconcile these two enemies, who make continual war? I will consider this flesh as a sink of filth; this view will humble my pride and my vanity. If I am obliged to nourish it, that it may not perish, I will subdue it that it may not rebel; and by the hard servitude to which my zeal shall reduce it, I will make it serve, in spite of itself, to prove my humility and love.

THIRD DAY.

Si ignoras te, ô pulcherrima, &c.

I cannot labour seriously to know myself perfectly, if I do not despise and humble myself: I cannot humble and abase myself before my God, if I do not love Him; I cannot love Him, if I do not please Him, and if I be not esteemed by Him. To please God, to be loved, to be esteemed by God, to partake of the favours and tenderness of the Heart of God, are the happy fruits of humility joined to love. But how is it possible that a being so miserable as I am, can possess all these treasures, of which the least portion is better than the whole of earth's treasures? It is possible in this way; I am sure to know God when I shall entirely know myself; I am sure to ascend unto Him, as soon as, by a profound humility, I shall descend often into the abyss of my own nothingness; I am sure to be loved by Him when I shall love Him, to please Him when I shall be displeasing to myself, to have His esteem when I shall despise myself, to partake of His Divine favours when I shall think myself the most unworthy. Self-knowledge, contempt, humiliations, from henceforth be ye the delights of my heart, since ye can make me love my God, and draw to me His esteem and love, and that is all I desire.

FOURTH DAY.

Tempus putationis advenit. (Cant. ii.)

"The time to prune the vine," the spouse says, "is come, the winter is passed," the approach of the Sun will soon give me light to know all my miseries, and by them to humble me; It will soon melt all the ice of my heart; soon warm it and encourage it to prune this mysterious vine of my soul, which has produced so much useless wood, and which is good for nothing but the fire. Ah, Lord, what barren branches have I to cut off from my vine! what sins have I to expiate, and bad inclinations to take away! To have lived so long without loving Thee, to have allowed my soul to put forth so many useless and criminal desires, to have suffered so many passions to grow up there; what a subject for humiliation! My soul was a choice vine, which was to have borne fruits worthy of eternity; and because I have neglected to prune it, it has only borne fruits of malediction. Thou couldest, Lord, either have plucked up this unfruitful vine, and cast it into the fire, or have deprived it of the hedge of Thy Divine protection, and it would have been trodden underfoot by its enemies: yet Thou hast spared it. Let me then cut these branches until it weeps, and tears of grief and compunction gush forth from it; let us cut them off by the sword and steel of a true contrition, that all may be consumed by the fire of Divine Love, and that there remain only what can bear fruits worthy of being presented upon the table of my Celestial Spouse.

FIFTH DAY.

Tempus putationis advenit.

If Thou hadst abandoned my vine as soon as I neglected to cultivate and to dress it, if Thou hadst punished me, O my God! at the first moment that I deserved it, it had been at most but an act of Thy Justice, clearing away a most miserable creature from the world, Christianity, and religion, where I did not deserve to hold my place; and Thou wouldest be neither less great, less just, or less happy. My vine produced nothing but sour and wild grapes, because I neglected to cut off from it the useless wood; and its fruits were not worthy of entering into Thy cellars. It is to Thee, O infinite Goodness! that I owe life after having deserved death. But for Thy mercy I should be even now consumed, and I should be burning in eternal flames without hope and without resource. This thought penetrates me, this truth confounds me. Could I then be so unhappy as not to humble myself and not to love Thee? I will do both, Lord: I will love Thee, that I may learn truly to humble myself; I will humble myself, that I may render myself worthy truly to love Thee.

SIXTH DAY.

Lavi pedes meos, quomodò inquinabo illos? (Cant. v.)

I have washed my feet, how shall I defile them anew? The spouse who spoke had need only to wash her feet, and she had done so already, O celestial Spouse! when Thou didst knock at her door: but, alas! I have need to wash all my body and all my soul, because both are filthy; and according to the language of the Prophet, "I stick fast in the deep mire, where no ground is." (Psalm lxix.) I have known it, and I am not humbled by it; I have seen it; I have perceived my stains, and I have not washed. Thou hast, O my God, with admirable charity taken care Thyself to wash me; Thou hast washed me upon Calvary with the Blood which Thou hast shed for me; Thou hast washed me in the waters of Baptism, and I have stained the whiteness which I had there acquired; Thou hast washed me often in the Baptism[1] of Penitence, and I have contracted fresh stains; Thou hast washed me in the Holy Communion, when Thou hast given me Thy Body and Thy Blood, and I am fallen again into the mire. Wash me still more; complete my purifying by humiliation and love, and grant me grace never to defile myself.

SEVENTH DAY.

Lavi pedes meos, quomodò, &c.

What cause have I to humble myself when I think of the different defilements with which my soul has been disfigured! Nothing less than the baptism of penitence, the abundant tears of love and the blood of God, was wanting to wash my soul, so much was it defiled: but I have much more cause to humble myself, when I consider how often I have fallen again into the mire, after having washed away my filth to approach my God. When, then, shall I have love and courage enough to say with the Spouse: "I have washed my feet, how could I soil them again? I have washed my pride by the humility of my tears, and I will fall into it no more. I have washed all my filth by penitence and love: rather let me die than stain my feet by any step contrary to my duties. I have washed myself completely in the blood of the immaculate Lamb; I ought to preserve the purity which it has procured me, though it should cost me my life."

[1] Dans le Sacrement. See on Surin, p. 228, and elsewhere.

Sixth Week.

GRATEFUL LOVE.

As insensibility is the mother of ingratitude, love is the principle of thankfulness; for though this virtue, which is hallowed by nature, policy, and religion, may be an act of justice, because every man who receives contracts with his benefactor a debt which he must pay, this gratitude is never perfect, if it is not accompanied with love: it is but a sorry gratitude which does not feel the favour it has received, and which would pay back a benefactor precisely what it has received, and because it has received, especially when love has been the principle of his liberality.

God heaps favours upon us only to excite in us at the same time love and gratitude: "His favours," says a celebrated doctor, "proceed from the furnace of His charity, and they are so many caresses, by which He designs to light in our hearts the fire of His love." (Hug. Card.)

The bride, sensibly touched by the gifts and favours which she has received from her Celestial Spouse, expresses her grateful love in terms of great energy. She makes, says St. Ambrose, three different declarations, the second of which exceeds the first, and the third is more perfect than the other two. She says, in the second chapter, "My Beloved is mine, and I am His:" Dilectus meus mihi, et ego illi. He is mine, that is to say, He has prevented me with His favours and His mercies, which I did not deserve, and which He has drawn from nothing but from the deep treasure of His goodness. I am His, that is to say, it is then very right that I show Him my gratitude, that I love Him, and that I should be all His, as He is all mine.

This Spouse binds herself still more closely to her Beloved, by a gratitude more earnest, more tender, and more devoted, when she says, in the sixth chapter: "I am my Beloved's, and my Beloved is mine:" Ego dilecto meo, et dilectus meus mihi. This expression, more bold because she begins with herself, adds over and above the other a more absolute consecration, and it thence appears that she is sure of her own heart. Finally, in the seventh chapter she says: "I am my Beloved's, and His heart turns towards me:" Ego dilecto meo, et ad me conversio ejus. Behold her sure of the Heart of her Divine Spouse; and see her gratitude, and love, and the reward of both one and the other.

AFFECTIONS.

FIRST DAY.

"My Beloved is mine;" He is my fortune, my heritage: in this world He is all mine, and I am all His; and He will still be "my Portion in the land of the living." What a treasure is this! but how is it possible that He can be mine? Am I not herein an ingenious self-deceiver, making myself a present of a possession which I do not possess? God, Who is all things, I, who am nothing; God, Who is Greatness Itself, I, who am meanness; God, Whose vastness fills both Heaven and earth, I, who occupy but a very little space, and that only through His mercy! Yet He is mine, because He has given Himself to me: that is the title which establishes my right, that the contract which justifies my possession. He has signed it with His Blood by dying on the Cross for me; He has ratified it in Heaven after His Ascension; He ratifies it again each day when He gives me His Body and His Blood at the Holy Communion: I can, therefore, no longer doubt that my Beloved is mine; but what I have now to do is to engrave it on my heart in indelible characters, to feel it every day of my life, and to be, by love and gratitude, entirely His, as He is mine.

SECOND DAY.

Dilectus meus mihi, et ego illi.

Thou art all mine, LORD, what then can I do to prove that I am all Thine? Thou art all mine, because Thou hast done all for me, and Thou hast given Thyself up entirely to me: Thou hast created me; Thou hast redeemed me; Thou hast preserved me; Thou hast heaped upon me an infinity of graces; Thou didst open to me the gates of Heaven whilst I was at those of hell. Alas! my gratitude is loaded and overburthened with so many favours; I feel my weakness, and I know that I cannot do for Thee what Thou hast done for me: but Thou hast loved me, and I can love Thee; that is my resource, my happiness, and my glory; that is my consolation. How happy am I to have a heart capable of this, since it is by love alone that I can make Thee a return, and Thou dost hold me acquitted of all my innumerable obligations, if I love Thee! Why then hitherto have I not done it? Happily for me, there is still time to be wholly Thine, and Thou art so merciful as to overlook all my former ingratitudes, if I now begin to love Thee with all my heart.

THIRD DAY.

Ego dilecto meo, et dilectus meus mihi. (Cant. vi.)

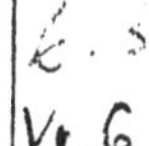

"I am my Beloved's, and my Beloved is mine,"

says the Spouse. May I hold this language, O my God? Ah! I perceive that it contains two propositions, of which the first makes me tremble because it is doubtful, and the second is all my happiness because it is sure. "My Beloved is mine," I cannot doubt it after what He has done for me, and is still doing every day. I am my Beloved's; ah! I dare not say it, until I have given Him more certain proofs than I have hitherto done. Is it true, O my soul, that thou art wholly God's? Is it true that thou canst, without fear, call Him thy Beloved? Thou dost belong to Him, and art His, because thou art the work of His Hands and the price of His Blood; but art thou His by a sincere change of mind and heart? Does thy mind refer to Him all its thoughts, aims, and enlightenings? Does thy heart consecrate to Him all its wishes, its affections, and feelings? Does it return Him the tribute of love and gratitude which it owes Him? Examine thyself upon this important point, and make haste to repair all thine ingratitude.

FOURTH DAY.

Ego dilecto meo, et dilectus meus mihi.

What a subject for shame and confusion, if I should not endeavour to be wholly my Beloved's, as He is wholly mine; and if I should refuse to return to Him what I only possess by His pure liberality. Whom can I love with more justice than Him Who has first loved me without my having deserved it? Whom ought I to love with more tenderness than Him Who has carried His tender love so far as to give me His Heart to win me to give Him mine? To whom should I with more justice consecrate my life than to Him without Whom I could not live, and Who came upon the earth only to give me, at the cost of His own, a life of grace? For whom could I suffer, for whom could I die more gloriously than for this generous Friend, Who has suffered, Who has shed His Blood, and Who died for me to prove the greatness of His love?

FIFTH DAY.

Ego dilecto meo, et dilectus meus mihi.

I am Thine, O Celestial Spouse, or at least I wish to be Thine in every moment of my life, whatever it may cost me. Take this heart, once so ungrateful, which has so often rebelled against Thy gifts and Thy most manifest favours; take this rebellious and wild heart, which has so often resisted Thee, notwithstanding Thy express commands and Thy most tender entreaties; take this slothful heart, which Thou hast loved with so much ardour, and which has served Thee with so much lukewarmness and listlessness. Alas! how comes it that Thou hast not punished my ingratitudes, which are so enormous and so innumerable? How hast Thou borne with me so long in this sin, this slothfulness and dissipation? I deserved long ago to be punished as a sinner, to be cast out of Thy adorable Mouth as cold and sickly; and Thou hast spared me, Thou hast preserved my place in Thy Heart, from which I deserved to be shut out and driven away for ever. I had rather die than not be Thine! rather die than forget Thy favours!

SIXTH DAY.

Ego dilecto meo, et ad me conversio ejus. (Cant. vii.)

"I am my Beloved's, and my Beloved is turned to me," says the Spouse. It is by this full and tender return that He rewards my love. Can it be that I am so happy as to draw towards me the Eyes, the Mind, and the Heart of this God of Majesty! What glory! I attach myself to a human being, and act kindly towards him, yet instead of thanking me, he often pays me only with contempt and ingratitude: I attach myself to my God, I give myself to Him, and He turns to me immediately; His Eyes look upon me with favour; His Spirit is attentive to my good; His great Heart bows Itself and stoops to my nothingness; He unites His Heart to mine; He heaps upon it new graces to attach it more strongly to Him. Devote thyself, O my soul, wholly to thy God, Whose Heart is so benevolent, that He pays a hundredfold all that thou givest Him: do what thou mayest, thou wilt never be in advance of Him. Love Him, then, as He has loved thee, and regulate thy gratitude by His.

SEVENTH DAY.

Ego dilecto meo, et ad me conversio ejus.

Can I, O Celestial Spouse, be wholly Thine, if Thou dost not first give Thyself wholly to me? Could I turn my heart towards Thee, if Thine were not first turned to me, to draw me to Thee? No, Lord; and indeed Thou hast made these first steps, and I have not profited by them. Hardly had Thy all-powerful Hand brought me forth out of nothing into being, than Thine Eyes looked upon me and Thine Heart loved me. If love is a natural affection, I cannot, without ingratitude and injustice, refuse to love Thee, because Thou art the Author of nature; my heart ought unceasingly to turn again towards Thee as towards the first principle of its natural being: but what ought it not to render to Thee, to Thee Who hast also turned towards it, to draw it by Thy grace and mercy from the annihilation of sin, Who hast saved it from hell, Who hast opened Heaven to it by dying for it? But, O my God, how great a thing it is for me to be able to discharge these immense debts with nothing but the mites of my love!

Seventh Week.

LOVE WHICH DENIES ITSELF.

To act and suffer contentedly for such a God, is not enough to prove to Him that we love Him, above all after having sinned against Him; it is further necessary to deprive ourselves, for His love, of all that we possess and love with too much affection. A great action has its merit before God, but a great self-denial has its own also; and it often even surpasses the action, because it costs incomparably more to the heart. Suffering comes most frequently from an external cause, which smites us with sorrow, and which only becomes meritorious when it is borne with patience and for the love of God: but self-denial proceeds from an inward cause; in this case it is the heart which breaks away from itself to please God alone, Whom it loves with greater ardour. In ordinary suffering man bows his head to receive the blow, when it pleases the Lord to strike: in self-denial, he runs to the altar, and is at once the sacrificing priest and the victim; he plunges the sword into his bosom, and strikes to the bottom of the heart, there to search for the secret idol to immolate, and to tear it in pieces with his own hands. Persons have been known to suffer for God the most poignant afflictions, and have borne the most painful labours for His glory; and yet when the time came to deny themselves some little darling inclination, they have felt an infinite repugnance. A voluntary privation is therefore a great witness of love.

The Spouse of the Canticles had put off her robe to take her rest, and she will no more resume it:

Exspoliavi me tunicâ meâ, quomodò induar illâ? (Cant. v.) She had, says St. Ambrose, forsaken all her earthly affections; she had laboured to put off the old Adam and his works; she had clothed herself with the new one, and she had now to uphold herself courageously in this resolution.

She complains a moment afterwards that the watchman of the city smote her while she sought her Beloved, and that they have taken away her robe: Tulerunt pallium meum. (Cant. v.) These watchmen, says St. Gregory, are the doctors, the preachers of the Gospel, and spiritual directors. The penitent Spouse is struck by their words; and they take away her robe when they induce her to strip herself of all earthly affections, to run more easily in the way of the Commandments and Evangelical Counsels, and to show her love by the privation of that which she loved more than her duties.

AFFECTIONS.

FIRST DAY.

Exspoliavi me tunicâ meâ, quomodò induar illâ? (Cant. v.)

"I have put off my coat," says the Spouse, "how shall I put it on?" Thy love, O Heavenly Spouse, is then a severe judge who condemns all true Christians to self-denial; it is a winning freebooter who takes the prey; it is a fire which separates; it is a mild tyrant who takes away and tears from the heart, with a kind and healthful violence, all its too tender ties: but it is a just judge, who only condemns to self-denial in order to put in the place of what it takes away an object infinitely more lovely than that which the heart loved; it is a friendly robber who despoils only to enrich; it is a holy fire which separates only to purify and to reunite; it is a mysterious sword which cuts off all gross and earthly affections only to procure blessings infinitely more precious; it is a gentle tyrant who only plucks from the heart the perishable object it loved to put Himself in its place: thus, there is much more to gain than to lose in self-denial. Why then, O my soul, dost thou delay to put off thy coat with the Spouse? Deprive thyself boldly of all which can put the least obstacle to thy love. It will at first cost some struggles to thy heart, but thou wilt be soon indemnified by the infinite blessings that thy Spouse prepares for thee.

SECOND DAY.

Exspoliavi me tunicâ meâ, quomodò, &c.

I am born, O my God, with the wretched coat of sinners, which is that of the old Adam; and this coat is made and woven of pride, of avarice, of sensuality and earthly affections, and of all the different sins of which a corrupt nature is capable. Thou hast stripped me of it by baptism, and there Thou hast clothed me with that of the new man, which is a robe of innocency, of justice, and of grace. I ought to have said with the Spouse, I have put off my sinful coat to repose under the shelter of the innocency which my Spouse has procured me; how can I resume it? I am, then, most unhappy so often to have put off the second to take up again the first, for which I ought to have such a horror, since it has cost Thee all Thy Blood, O my God, to take it from me. I have deprived myself of that possession to which I ought to cling; I have loved passionately what I ought to hate: let us, then, now change both language and conduct; let us courageously deprive ourselves of what we have loved too much; let us taste the joy of what we had given up by our own fault.

THIRD DAY.

Exspoliavi me tunicâ meâ, quomodò, &c.

No sooner do I put off my ancient robe for the love of my God, but He at once clothes me with the precious garments of His grace: no sooner do I empty my heart but He fills it, and puts Himself in the place of that which I shall have sacrificed for His love: I cannot tear from this heart the subject of its lusts without His making it up to me at once by a love more innocent and glorious: as soon as I have renounced a sinful pleasure, He makes me taste a pure and holy joy; so soon as I have detached myself from the creature, He binds me to Him by sweeter and more blessed ties. In short, I cannot prove to Him my sincere attachment, by denying myself what prevents my loving Him with all my heart, without His heaping upon me happiness and riches. Let us then boldly deprive ourselves of all which can be the least obstacle to His love; let us break our chains; let us wean ourselves from the poisoned milk of sensual pleasures; let us strip ourselves of the shameful garments of the old Adam, and never let us take them again.

FOURTH DAY.

Exspoliavi me tunicâ meâ, quomodò, &c.

Is it then really true that I have left the garments of the old Adam, to clothe myself with those of the new, who is Jesus Christ? Am I free from those sudden bursts of pride and self-love, of that desire to make a show, and to be esteemed, and to bear the palm from others? Have I begun to deprive myself, for the love of my God, of a constant self-seeking, of love of my own ease, and of desire of temporal things? Have I cut off superfluity in all things? Am I contented with necessaries which ought to satisfy me, and which I have never wanted. Have I sacrificed this false daintiness in my food, my dress, and my furniture? Have I cut even to the root my animosities, my pride, my haughtiness, my antipathies, my contemptuous airs, my coldnesses, and all which in me is opposed to true love? Have I stripped myself of that unevenness of temper, that opposition to advice, and that infinite repugnance to humiliations which I feel? Alas! if I have done it, it has been but for some days, and my inconstancy has soon made me take again my old garment, woven of all the wickedness and weakness of which I was beforetime guilty. If I had really loved my God, I should have stripped myself of all, and I should have done it for ever.

FIFTH DAY.

Tulerunt pallium meum. (Cant. v.)

While I sought my Beloved, says the Spouse, the watchmen of the city wounded me; they took away my robe from me. A man who seeks Jesus Christ, and desires to find Him, must expose himself to all, and deprive himself of all; without this precaution, He hides Himself, and none can find Him. The pastors and the men of God, who are the watchmen of the city, treat roughly every one who has not stripped himself of all that is inconsistent with this search; they are obliged to take away our veil; and by the sword of Thy Divine Word they cut away the things to which we are too much attached. Have I not rebelled when the Ministers of the Sacraments, or my superiors, have wished to deprive me of that of which I ought to have deprived myself? Have I been as faithful and as generous as the Spouse, who, though wounded and deprived of her veil, forebore not to run with the utmost swiftness after Him Whom her soul loved? Have I attributed to passion or to partiality that which I ought only to have attributed to their zeal and my indolence? Have I not been discouraged by it? and have not those privations so necessary to my love, occasioned in me complaints and murmurs? Ah! LORD, what cause have I not here to bewail over myself!

SIXTH DAY.

Tulerunt pallium meum.

It is absolutely necessary, either to strip ourselves of all which binds us to the creature, or to suffer those to deprive us of them who guide us, or wait till an irritated GOD shall violently cut them off at the moment of death. If privation appears now so rigorous, it will be much more so then, and perhaps it will be followed by the hardest and most cruel of all privations, which is that of GOD. If I deny myself now, I lose but very little, and GOD recompenses me for it abundantly. Indeed, what more advantageous than to purchase by some passing sacrifice the grace, the esteem, and the love of GOD! to earn a right to possess an eternal kingdom by the privation of some temporal delights! to purchase an infinity of glory by lowliness, and even the possession of GOD Himself by some slight pain! what a gainful merchandise is this! how harshly should I deal with myself if I did not consent to it!

SEVENTH DAY.

Tulerunt pallium meum.

How blind we are, not to bow down quietly to the orders of a severe Providence, when It takes off our garments, and when It takes care Itself to deprive us of what we have loved too much for our good! On the contrary, how tender and benevolent is this Providence! how healthful is its apparent rigour when it interests itself in these privations, and puts forth its hand to make them for us, when ours is too weak of itself to make a sacrifice of them to Him! When we labour of ourselves alone to restore to God's dominion a heart which has withdrawn itself from it by love for the creature, we then feel plainly that we are but weakness, and are subject to grievous relapses. We walk away, and then draw near again; we promise and we retract; we leave and we resume; to-day we deny ourselves an object, and the next day we regret our self-denial. How long will you, O weak heart, waver between happiness and eternal misery? Is it the severity of the sacrifice which stops and alarms thy daintiness? Begin but to love, and God will uphold your wavering courage, and thou wilt soon consent finally to deny thyself what thou didst love too highly, and with too much affection.

Eighth Week.

LOVE ACTING.

The love of God makes us not only feel, but also act; it is a sacred fire kindled in our hearts by the Holy Spirit, which, like a material fire, heats, purifies, and acts at the same time. It is true, it produces repose; but not an idle and slothful repose. In the centre of our heart it is a sovereign upon his throne; the virtues are on its circumference, it touches them, it puts them in motion, and they receive from it all their value and force, in such manner that without it they are only phantom virtues. As true love comes from God, it ought to bear the image of its adorable Author, Who is always in action and always at rest; it must, according to the words of a Holy Doctor, even in its actions, be an expression of the greatness, the infinity and the eternity of God (D. Thomas in quodlib.): that is to say, that all its actions ought to be great, and that by a profound humility it ought to think that they are very little; charitas operatur magna, et reputat parva: thus does it answer to the greatness of God. It ought to multiply them infinitely, as much as it is able; and it ought to think them very few in number: operatur multa, et reputat pauca; it is thus it answers to the infinity of God. It ought, in short, to labour unto death without wearying, and to think that it has worked but a moment for the Glory of God: operatur diu, et reputat breve; it is thus it answers to His eternity.

As Divine Love has its repose and its action, there are times wherein the Bridegroom forbids any one to awaken His spouse; but there is also a time wherein He says: "Arise, my love, my fair one, and come away:" Surge, amica mea, speciosa mea, et veni. (Cant. ii.) The bride rises up to action immediately, although her hands are dropping with the most sweet-smelling myrrh: Manus meæ stillaverunt myrrham, et digiti mei pleni sunt myrrhâ probatissimâ. (Cant. v.) Myrrh has two qualities: it is bitter, and it has a perfume; it marks a noble action, which is painful to nature, but which, warmed by the love of God, spreads around a most sweet smell.

AFFECTIONS.

FIRST DAY.

Surge, amica mea, speciosa mea, et veni. (Cant. ii.)

"The voice of the turtle-dove is heard," says the Spouse, "the winter is past, the flower of the vine has perfumed our fields; rise up, then, my love, my fair one, and come away." I have moaned as the turtle-dove, because I have offended my God; the winter is past, because through His Grace I am come out from the slough of my iniquities, and the sun of justice has melted the ice of my heart; my vine has already put forth some flowers; and I have begun to tell my Celestial Spouse that I love Him: I have felt it; but He asks me for fruit, and He wishes me to show that I love Him effectually by rising up to go to Him. Unite, O my soul, these two indispensable duties, which, if separated, cannot produce thee any blessing. Love with all thy heart the God for Whom thou dost work; and work without ceasing for the God Whom thou dost love: give Him thy heart and hands without reserve, and for ever; He desires, that by both of these organs thou shouldest show Him thy love: without love, thy works are thankless and unfruitful; and without works, thy love is a mere illusion.

SECOND DAY.

Surge, amica mea, speciosa mea, et veni.

Arise, My love, My fair one, and come to Me. Rise up, surge; long time hast thou been buried in the sleep of idleness and listlessness; and a heart asleep cannot love her God; it is not yet time to enjoy a repose which thou hast not yet earned. Thou hast tasted but too much the repose of sinners, which is a lethargic and deadly repose, and thou must watch, and work long before thou canst deserve that of the Saints, which is a Divine repose, and which nothing but active love can procure. My well-beloved, amica mea, this is a style which I give thee of My free grace; fulfil, then, its duties with vigilance, and by the laborious exercises which are enjoined thee; come, veni; it is not enough to rouse thee and to arise; to feel from time to time that thou dost love Me; that would be only a false feeling, if it were not sustained by action. Come, then, and come to Me, Who call thee; flee idleness and sloth; flee the world and its maxims; flee from thyself to come more surely to Me: walk courageously upon the footsteps I have marked for you; be not frightened to find there thorns and blood: if thou lovest Me truly, thou wilt overcome thy weakness.

THIRD DAY.

Surge, amica mea, speciosa mea, et veni.

I clearly see, that, if I would find my Beloved, I must rise up, I must walk, yea, and that unceasingly and without stopping. If I would not become worse, I must labour unremittingly to become better. Material fire fails not to become low and go out if care is not taken to feed it with new fuel to keep up its flames: the fire of the love of God soon languishes if we do not provide it with fresh fuel to support it in all its strength; and this fuel must be frequent acts of this love. Neglect, then, nothing, O my soul; if thou wouldest always love, make thyself familiar with the heart's language with thy God; speak to Him thy feelings over and over again; try to renew them as often as thou dost breathe: but, above all, obey whenever He speaks to thee; awaken as the bride; rise, up, walk and work; without that you run the risk of never loving Him, or of not loving for long.

FOURTH DAY.

Surge, amica mea, speciosa mea, et veni.

Whence comes it that formerly to my slothful and sluggish heart all was painful? Whence comes it that the least labour disgusted it? that penitence terrified it, and that mortification was like a rigorou punishment? Whence comes it, Lord, that, contented to have on my lips the words, "My God, I love Thee," I remained buried in a sleep of dreadful listlessness and real insensibility; and that, to drown my conscience, and to deceive it about the indispensable precept of Thy love, I tranquilly reposed under the shelter of some easy and merely natural virtues, which cost nothing to my heart. Alas! it is because I did not love Thee; and yet I was so blind as to believe that I loved Thee. Now I well know that the duties of piety are hard to fulfil for one who is destitute of true love; and that for one who loves Thee they are sweet in the keeping. I shall say, then, without fear and without presumption, that I am beginning to love Thee, as soon as I shall find pleasure in my duty, and that I shall earnestly overcome all the repugnance that I shall find to it: but, alas! LORD, when will that be?

FIFTH DAY.

Manus meæ stillaverunt myrrham, et digiti mei pleni sunt myrrhâ probatissimâ. (Cant. v.)

"My hands," says the bride, "dropped with myrrh, and my fingers with sweet-smelling myrrh." In order to open to my Spouse, and to give Him admittance into my soul, it is not enough that my heart be filled with some feelings of tenderness, I must further act and work: my hands ought to be full of myrrh, which is the symbol of action: this myrrh ought to be the most exquisite, that is to say, my actions ought to be accompanied by all the innocency and purity of which I am capable: this myrrh ought to be odoriferous; that is to say, the ardour of my love ought to send up an agreeable perfume, even to the Heart of my GOD: my love must, therefore, be active and laborious, and, without quitting my heart, it must spread itself over my mind, to purify all its thoughts; over my will, to regulate all its desires; over my eyes, to measure all their looks; over my mouth, to sanctify all its words; over my feet, to guide all their steps; and over my hands, to hallow all their actions. My love shall preside over my work, shall animate it, and make it meritorious; but my work will awaken my love, lest it become faint; it will sustain it, and will be the proof of it.

SIXTH DAY.

Manus meæ stillaverunt myrrham, &c.

The more I reflect upon my past life, the more I perceive with grief that my hands are emptied of that precious myrrh with which those of the bride were all filled when she opened to her Beloved. I see only sloth, listlessness, and lost time; I have yet done nothing for my God, Who has done all for me, and I have laboured only for the world, though it be my most cruel enemy.

I did, then, Lord, thoroughly mistake myself when I had the temerity to say to Thee, and to say to myself, that I loved Thee! In what strange illusion have I passed the best part of my life! I thought that I loved Thee, because my heart felt from time to time some sweetnesses and some natural tastes, which it took for true love; but, alas! my slothful and idle hands have not yet said so, because they have as yet done nothing either great or painful, nor pursued any thing for Thy love.

SEVENTH DAY.

Manus meæ stillaverunt myrrham, &c.

I cannot lawfully aspire to Heaven without loving God with all my heart; nor can I pretend to love without loving Him with all my powers of head and heart, and without fulfilling all the duties of that laborious and active love which labours unceasingly to destroy all the vices, and to gain all the virtues which compose the holiness of my estate. Love is not love when it is idle, and when it leaves all to flow on according to its natural temper and its sluggishness: it must either be holy or must labour seriously to become so, in order to be able to say, without self-deceit, that we love God truly, since active love is the basis, the nourishment, and the food of holiness. Thou hast, then, O my soul, still a long journey to make; but, nevertheless, be not disheartened; love by working for God and thy neighbour; work in love, and soon wilt thou arrive at the happy end to which thou dost aspire.

Ninth Week.

TRUSTING LOVE.

Trust in God is, of all the Christian virtues, that which appears to have the most intimate union with the Divinity. It is that which opens to us the Heart of God, and which makes us free to open ours to Him as we would to a true friend: it surpasses, in one sense, the three theological virtues, and it forms their ornament and their sweetness. (D. Th. ii. 2.)

Faith is its basis and support, because no one can trust in a person unless he is assured that he is sincere, that he will not deceive him, that he loves him, and can assist him.

It strengthens Hope, because, while Hope carries us up to objects infinitely above us, trust in God (which has more sweetness, being always accompanied by love,) makes Hope to love the blessings to which she aspires, and trust in the word of Him who has promised them. Finally, it very much increases Love, because it carries us towards God as to a friend, upon whose heart she binds a most strong affection. Hence it comes, that according to the counsel of the Apostle we ought to use all diligence, not to lose our trust, because that in losing it we lose our love and the rewards that await our love. (Heb. x. 35.) The title of Brother, Friend, and Spouse, which God gives Himself in the Holy Canticles, cannot but increase the love and trust of the spouse; and, indeed, she compares Him to a living tree, loaded with delicious fruits, and she says she has sat down under the shadow of Him Whom she had so much desired: Sub umbrâ illius quem desideraveram sedi. (Cant. ii.) Afterwards she adds, that the fruit she found there was sweet to her taste: Et fructus ejus dulcis gutturi meo. (Ibid.) Nourished by so delicious and beautiful a fruit, protected by so powerful a God, she will be much more the mistress of her passions, and she will fear much less the attacks of her enemies.

AFFECTIONS.

FIRST DAY.

Sub umbrâ illius quem desideraveram sedi. (Cant. ii.)

I am set down, says the spouse, under the shadow of Him Whom I have desired. O Heavenly Spouse, quickening and mysterious Tree, who dost cover all the earth, and dost nourish with Thy excellent fruit angels and men, grant to my sinful soul a favourable refuge against the enemies which surround her, against the just terrors by which she is alarmed, and against the lightning and thunderbolts of Thine own justice, which she has such good cause to dread. Thou hast promised to hide me under the shadow of Thy wings, and to keep me as the apple of an eye (Ps. xvii. 8); grant me to rest, as the spouse, under the shadow of Thy protection, and there to taste the salutary fruits of a true confidence. No sinner can become a penitent without trusting in Thy Divine mercy. O God and Saviour, protect me from an Avenging God, put me under the shadow of Thy Cross; and since that is the tree of life which has saved me from the death which I had drawn upon myself, from henceforth it shall be the object of my joy and the source of my rest.

SECOND DAY.

Sub umbrâ illius quem desideraveram sedi.

Under whose shadow could I rest with more trust and tranquillity than that of Him Who is my God, my Creator, my Father, my Saviour, and my Spouse? Can God the Creator neglect the work of His own Hands, above all when He there finds both His own work and His own love! Can He forget, says the Prophet, to have mercy when we ask Him with all the ardour of which we are capable? Can He keep back His mercy at the height of His justice? Can a Father forsake His child who throws herself into His Arms and asks from Him an asylum? Can a Saviour allow His Blood to be lost when we ask Him to apply it to us? Can a Spouse refuse protection to the bride He has chosen, and who, with a loving trust, opens to Him her whole heart? I put my trust in the Lord; He is good, He is All-powerful. What have I to fear if I love Him? I will sit down under the shadow of Him Whom my heart desires; love shall produce my confidence, and I will support my confidence by my good works, lest it degenerate into presumption.

THIRD DAY.

Sub umbrâ illius quem desideraveram sedi.

Thy adorable Cross, O my Saviour! is the mysterious tree, under the shade of which I will put myself as the shelter from Thy justice; I will desire it, I will love it, I will carry it, I will embrace it, and it shall be all my confidence, and all my love. He who chooses always to fear Thy justice without confiding in Thy goodness, neither does Thee honour, nor loves Thee, and ever lives in the midst of troubles and alarms. Nevertheless, should not I, who am a sinner, always see Thy Almighty Hand armed with thunderbolts ready to punish me? I confess, O God of Justice, I ought to fear Thee, because I have offended Thee; but Thou desirest that I love Thee and trust in Thy mercies, because Thou art my Saviour. I will cherish these two wholesome thoughts by turns: I shall onewhile see the unfathomable depth of Thy wrath over my head; another while I shall feel the unfathomable depth of Thy goodness in my heart; at one time I shall descend, in spirit, all living into hell, there to see the eternal flames I have deserved; anon I shall put myself in the sanctuary of Thy Cross, and I shall mount up again in full trust into Thy Heart, there to taste the joys of Thy love: but my trust in Thee shall prevail over my fear, as Thy goodness prevails over Thy justice: I will be beforehand with this Thy justice by punishing myself, and I will satisfy the wish of my heart at the same time that I follow the tender inclinations of Thine.

FOURTH DAY.

Sub umbrâ illius quem desideraveram sedi.

My soul sighs only after Thee, O my God! it desires only Thee, and has no other resource after its disgraces, but to go and seek an asylum in Thy Arms, in Thy Heart and in the Bosom of Thy infinite and all-powerful Mercy. One who has offended Thee as often as I have done, has no other part to take. Thou hast an abyss of justice, which keeps me in continual alarm, and I will use every means, penance, tears, and sobs, that I may not fall therein;

but Thou hast an abyss of goodness and mercy, and it is my refuge and my resource: and happy were I, could I plunge myself there in the Blood of Jesus Christ, by which it is all filled! Thou shouldest fear, O my soul, because thou hast offended thy God; but do not lose thy trust: trust in God at the same time that thou lovest; love at once, and make amends for sin, and repose tranquilly under the shadow of Thy Beloved, and thou wilt find in a subdued trust abundant fruits of grace and glory.

FIFTH DAY.

Et fructus ejus dulcis gutturi meo. (Cant. ii.)

What fruit more bitter than distrust in the Divine Mercy, which sin, that accursed tree, produces ever in those who rest under its branches, after having given them up to grievous remorse and deadly unquietness! And what fruit more sweet, more delicious, and more wholesome than that of trust in God, which sacred love, that tree of life, fails not to produce in those who yield themselves to its enkindling flames! Alas! to live without trust and love, is not to live at all, but to languish and to die. Thy mercy, Lord, said the Prophet, is better than life; I will feed myself with it, and I shall live, because there I place all my trust: I shall die as soon as I cease to repose in Thee, and to love Thee with all my heart, because I shall then have no more of that delicious fruit which can alone sustain my feeble soul. But no! I shall not die, though I deserve a thousand deaths, because I now begin to love Thee and to hate myself, to trust in Thee and to distrust myself, and am resolved to do both one and the other until the last breath of my life.

SIXTH DAY.

Et fructus ejus dulcis gutturi meo.

How can I feed myself with the delicious fruit that the Celestial Spouse presents to my soul, I who have so often offended Him? Is it not a presumptuous boldness in me to trust in the goodness of a Sovereign Whom I have wronged a thousand times? Nay, but I have His word, I have His faith, I have His Blood: He orders me to trust in Him, and it is a sign that He will protect me; I hope all and I fear nothing, if I can but love Him and make amends to Him. These two exercises will be the basis and warrant of my confidence, and the Divine Mercy will be its moving cause; for though my sins are innumerable and my wretchedness extreme, my God has shown me that His Divine Mercy surpasses them, because it proceeds from His Love, and that is Himself. But, my soul, insult no more this Mercy, for fear thou shouldest lose thy right to confidence, or that it degenerate into presumption: implore its favours with a humble and contrite heart; lean upon it; thou wilt find it the source of the most delicious and most innocent enjoyment; return unto its heart through a loving and chastened confidence; it extends to thee its arms, run into them; it loves thee, love it; it opens to thee the whole Heart of God, open to it all thine; sustain thy confidence by love and penitence, and if thou wouldest be truly happy, never separate these two important duties.

SEVENTH DAY.

Et fructus ejus dulcis gutturi meo.

I have trusted but too much in the creature; I have too often leant upon an arm of flesh which cannot sustain me, and I have gathered from this false confidence only the bitter fruits of unfaithfulness.

The beings upon whom I have counted the most, have either forsaken me, from inconstancy and fickleness, or through weakness cannot help me, or have abandoned me through sloth, or from a bad heart have left me in sorrow. I well deserved this bitterness, O my God, because I have preferred their protection to Thine. Now I look upon their weakness and unfaithfulness as a blessing, because they teach me to trust in Thee Alone. They are inconstant, and Thou art the most faithful of all friends; they are weak, and Thou art Strength itself; they are dastardly, and Thou art the model of a perfect generosity; they have often a deceitful heart, and Thine is full of a sincere love for me. Receive me, then, under Thy Divine protection, O Celestial Spouse; from henceforth Thou shalt be all my strength and confidence, and I will hope but in Thee Alone.

Tenth Week.

LOVE IN EXACTNESS.

As the neglect of little duties is a great mark of indifference and coldness, it may also be said that exactness in fulfilling them is a great proof of the love of God. No one can love without wishing to be loved; no one can be loved by God, or love Him, without striving to please Him; he cannot please Him who is not exact in fulfilling all that He orders, and who dispenses with a multitude of little attentions and practices, which in their littleness are yet marks of a great love.

All is great in the exercise of the love of God, because the object of this love is Greatness Itself. The very least observance has its weight and its merit, because it proceeds from charity: thus the least voluntary omission, the least premeditated neglect, the least delay in executing inspirations and good impulses, are the proofs of a lax love, which will ever fall; and the Wise Man says, he that despiseth small things shall fall by little and little: Qui spernit modica paulatim decidet. (Eccl. xix. 1.) "Though the ships be so great," says the Apostle St. James (iii. 4), "yet are they turned with a very small helm," and it is to them a great help against the most furious tempests: thus also the least opening lets in there the water drop by drop; and if the sailors neglect to empty it, it is at last an enormous weight which produces a shipwreck.

The Bridegroom takes pleasure in examining all the actions of His Spouse; He wishes even that she may perceive Him near while He observes her closely, in order that His presence may render her more exact. "Behold," says she, "He standeth behind our wall, He looketh forth of the window, showing Himself through the lattice:" en ipse stat post parietem nostrum, respiciens per fenestras, prospiciens per cancellos. (Cant. ii.) These minute watchings are not unworthy of the Majesty of a God who loves and who desires to be loved, and they mark the value of our very least duties, when we perform them from love. After this most minute watching, the Bridegroom had found, apparently, some little faults to correct in His Spouse, for He says, "Take us the little foxes, that spoil the vines:" Capite nobis vulpes parvulas, quæ demoliuntur vineas. By that he designates the least faults which can spoil the flowers and the fruit of the vine, i. e. the love and good works of the soul, which is His mysterious vine.

AFFECTIONS.

FIRST DAY.

En ipse stat post parietem nostrum, respiciens per fenestras, prospiciens per cancellos. (Cant. ii.)

Behold this celestial Spouse, He standeth behind the wall and looks at me attentively. Ah! if my love was as exact as that of the spouse, I might say unceasingly, "Behold Him," En Ipse, behold my God, Who looks at me, and Who examines all my actions. I should with the eyes of faith see Him myself, I should feel Him above me by His authority, around me by His providence, and within me by His love, and I should say to myself each moment, "Behold Him;" He is standing, stat; this is to show that He is ever ready to help me, as well in the least things as in the greatest; His love is wanting in nothing, while mine is wanting in every thing. "He looks at me," says the spouse, respiciens. If He were to cease an instant to look at me, I should perish at once. I ought, then, to look at Him only in all my actions; He ought to be unceasingly present to my mind and heart; and the study of this Presence is the only means by which I can respond to the exactness of His love.

SECOND DAY.

En ipse stat post parietem nostrum, &c.

Thy Divine Wisdom, O Celestial Spouse, has put a wall between us, to hinder me from seeing and discovering Thee during this mortal life, and it is the work of Thy love. This mysterious wall is Thy holy Humanity, through which I must adore Thy Divinity; or, it is the adorable Sacrament in which Thou hast hidden Thy whole presence. Thou seest me in both of them, and Thou art attentive to procure me therein infinite blessings, while waiting till clear vision succeed to obscurity. Can it be, then, that my self-love has still raised up another wall to separate Thee from me, and to prevent me from seeing and possessing Thee! This wall is my resistance to Thy Divine inspirations: this wall is my want of exactness in fulfilling my duties in their whole compass; this wall is my neglect to acquit myself of an infinity of little duties which Thou exactest from my love. Let us break down this fatal wall, through which God does not choose to look upon us, and let sacred love destroy unceasingly that which self-love has for my misfortune built up.

THIRD DAY.

En ipse stat post parietem nostrum, &c.

Thy incomprehensible charity, O my God! has overlooked nothing which could help on my salvation and happiness; Thine eyes have been ever watching over my conduct; Thy admirable Providence has spread Itself over all my wants both corporeal and spiritual; Thy charitable and paternal care has ever made Itself felt by my soul; Thou hast observed all, and this exactness is one of the most evident proofs of Thy love. Can I flatter myself that I love Thee, I who have not yet responded to Thy care of me? Charity is not charity when it is negligent in the very least duties; it is a fire, and this fire ought always to be at work, always to burn. O sacred fire! do thou work, burn, and consume; work in me to make me exact to my very least duties, as well as to the very greatest; burn, consume, and reduce to ashes all the fruits of my self-love, and the least stains of my soul.

FOURTH DAY.

En ipse stat post parietem nostrum, &c.

My Heavenly Spouse looks at me: He observes even the most secret movements of my soul, and nothing escapes His Eyes; it is necessary then that mine turn incessantly towards Him, and that I see Him in all things. If I wish to please Him, I must be exact to correct all, to atone for all, to fear all, to hope all, and to observe all. Without exactness, it is impossible that I love Him. I ought to correct all my faults without excepting a single one. I ought to make amends for all my sins, which are innumerable; I ought to suffer all the trials which may come from Him, and all the afflictions which created things shall cause me; I ought to avoid the least imperfections which may offend His adorable Eyes; I ought to fulfil the whole law, and never dispense myself from the smallest observances. I ought to foresee all; and to be ready for any thing, to escape the surprises of the devil, and to master the sudden sallies of my self-love and sensitiveness; I ought to fear all things from my weakness, and never trust in my own heart: I ought to hope all things from the infinite goodness of my God, and never admit into my heart the least distrust. In short, I ought to observe all which gives Him pleasure, and be on my guard against all that can displease Him; it is thus that, with His Grace, I hope to prove to Him my love.

FIFTH DAY.

Capite nobis vulpes parvulas quæ demoliuntur vineas.

Let us take these little foxes that spoil the vine. It is my soul, O my Saviour! which is the mysterious vine of which Thou speakest. It is Thou Who hast planted it, when by a free love, for which I can never be thankful enough, Thou hast caused me to be born in the bosom of the Church. Thou hast watered it with Thy Blood; Thou hast cultivated it by the Sacraments and by Thy Divine Word; Thou hast consequently a right to require that it bring forth fruit; and this fruit is the precious wine of Thy love. It is pruned, because, supported by Thy grace, I have begun to cut off the useless branches which deserved only the fire. It is in flower: nam vinea nostra floruit; and these flowers are the holy desires with which Thou dost inspire me. But I fear the young foxes which make them dens, which eat up the bark of this vine, and then destroy the flowers and the fruit; these are my venial sins, which are innumerable, my vanity, my attachments, my continual dissipations, my impatience, my faint-heartedness, in following the good movements with which Thou dost inspire me, and in acquitting myself of my smallest duties with all the exactness which I ought. Let us then take, as says the Spouse, these little foxes, which hinder us from loving GOD with all our heart; let us dash them against the Stone, and may that Stone be JESUS CHRIST.

SIXTH DAY.

Capite nobis vulpes parvulas, &c.

My own thoughts, O my GOD, are those subtle and malignant foxes which desolate unceasingly the vine of my soul, and which oppose themselves to my love; they distract me, they surprise me, they trouble me, they consume me, they make me restless, and they bring me sometimes to the gates of hell when I thought to be at those of Paradise. What humiliation for me, LORD! I wish to love Thee; and at the very time that my heart strives to produce an act of love, I sometimes find it surprised by a thought which covers it with shame and confusion, and which exposes it to incur Thy hatred, if it is not careful to withstand it, and to chase it thence as soon as it is perceived. Give me, then, O Celestial Spouse, the exactness and attention which I require to extirpate from the vine of my soul those rising thoughts which, like the little foxes, cut off all the flowers, and make all its beauty to wither. Warn me, Merciful Father, when I shall be in this dangerous situation, in order that nothing hinder me from loving Thee as I ought, and as I desire.

SEVENTH DAY.

Capite nobis vulpes parvulas, &c.

It is my self-love, O my Celestial Spouse! which makes the greatest havoc in my soul. More subtle and more dangerous than the little foxes, it disguises itself in a thousand ways to devour all the fruit of my love and good works. Often I flatter myself with pleasing Thee in a holy action, which I think to have undertaken only for Thy Glory; and when I examine it closely, I perceive that I have sought Thee less than myself, and that the self-love which has crept in there, has destroyed all the merit. I have then need, O my God! of light and strength; of light, in order to discover with an exact attention all the windings of my heart, and all the ingenious turnings of my self-love; of strength, in order to uphold my soul in the midst of these shoals, and in order to renounce unrelentingly all the imperfect aims of this hurtful love. Alas! my soul is like unto a weak vine, which creeps when it has no support; suffer, Lord, that it lean itself upon Thee, that it fasten and bind itself to Thy Cross, that it strictly embrace it, for that is the centre of true strength; without that, my vine is weak, and it will soon fall to the ground.

Eleventh Week.

LOVE IN PROGRESS.

It is one of the most dangerous and most ordinary illusions of those who begin to love God, to stop in the midst of their course, and to content themselves with a common-place charity without aspiring to its perfection. True love is a sovereign whose noble ambition can bear no bounds; it is insatiable, it ever walks on with vast strides: it counts for nothing all that it has done for God, and it believes itself obliged to make successive and continual efforts, until it has attained to the Heart of God, Who is its centre and repose.

As Divine love is a fire, it must, in order to subsist, be ever at work and ever in movement; it cannot fix any point of stedfastness where it can be still; if it does not mount up, it must tend to earth; if it does not go on, it must fall back; if it does not spread into some new flames, it must lose a part of its own: and when it makes no progress, and thinks to keep quiet hold of what it has, it begins at once to languish, and at last it entirely goes out: a mere love of natural temper, which is but the ghost of love, takes its place and leaves the heart in an illusion the more deadly, because it flatters itself with loving God, while it loves but itself.

The bride is making such wondrous progress in this love, that her Spouse cannot help admiring her, and exclaims: Who is she that looketh forth as the morning, fair as the moon, clear as the sun? Quæ est ista quæ progreditur quasi aurora consurgens, pulchra ut luna, electa ut sol? (Cant. vi.) He here compares her to the morning star, which is only a light, the harbinger of the sun, and which gains a brightness more intense till it is blended with the sun. He says she is fair as the moon, elect as the sun, and that she is like both those orbs, in that she never stops in her course. This is the true symbol of a progressive love, which is marked anew to us by this cry of the friends of the bride; "How beautiful are thy feet with shoes, O prince's daughter!" Quam pulchri sunt gressus tuis in calceamentis, filia principis! (Cant. vi.) This is enough to stir us up to make each day new strides in the love of God.

AFFECTIONS.

FIRST DAY.

Quæ est ista quæ progreditur quasi aurora consurgens, pulchra ut luna, electa ut sol? (Cant. vi.)

"Who is she that looketh forth as the morning, in its rising, fair as the moon, elect as the sun?" When I gave myself to my God, and when I began to feel that I loved Him, as the dawn, a rising light was scattering little by little the darkness of my soul, and the fire of Divine love had already melted a part of the frost of my heart: then in my self-deceit I resolved to go onwards without stopping, to run and to fly till I had reached the perfection of love. What is become of these resolves, these desires, and these plans? and why has my ardour sunken? Why have I not imitated the spouse who, in a little time, has made such great advances in the love of God, that from the simple morning star she is become burning, luminous, and beautiful as the sun? I have stopped, instead of going on; I have drawn back into the darkness of night, from which I was happily come forth by the dawning and the first fruits of my penitence and my love. Alas! if I had ever gone on, if I had always loved, I should now be weaned from the things of sense. I am bound to them by more ties than ever: I should have all but given the death-blow to my self-love, and it is still all alive: my heart would be all on fire for the only object it ought to love, and it is all ice. Nevertheless, let us not be discouraged; let us begin to walk incessantly, and never let us stop.

SECOND DAY.

Quæ est ista quæ progreditur quasi, &c.

The spouse who loves her GOD it is, who never is weary of loving Him, and who makes continual advances in that love. The morning dawn has beauties of its own, it begins to bring light to our sphere; and the moon has its brightness, for she guides us during the darkness of the night: but the sun is the most beautiful of all luminaries; it gives us light and heat, and all creatures which have no sense, move ceaselessly in obedience to the voice of the Creator. It is only my slothful and idle soul which stops, although GOD commands it to be always moving, and to run unremittingly until it shall arrive at the happy end to which it ought to aspire. Nevertheless, I must needs run my course, and run it in such manner that I may gain the prize which is set before me. If I stop in my course, another will walk more quickly than I, and he will carry it away. Walk, then, O my soul; profit by all, and neglect nothing which can give a new advance to thy love. There is not a moment in thy life wherein it cannot either grow or decay: a slothful and idle love is not a true love, and it deserves no reward.

THIRD DAY.

Quæ est ista quæ progreditur quasi, &c.

The spouse walked on so fast in the path of Divine

Love, that her companions lost sight of her, and thus her course was like the swiftness of the sun, which makes every instant a new advance in light and heat, until it has climbed to its meridian; but I walk so slowly and stop so often, that I shamefully allow others, who have not started so soon as I, to get before me. It is now many years that I have entered into the Christian course of penitence and of religion; but, alas! what is my progress? Can I, without blushing, compare what I then was with what I ought to be, and with what I now am? What have I done? What have I won? Where am I? and where should I be if I had always walked on? If I am not become better than I was some years past, how ought I to blush and to weep? but, alas! am I not become worse? I dare not, O my God, give utterance to this question without abasing myself to nothing, and inferring, that if I would make my salvation sure, I must begin again to love Thee as if I had never done it.

FOURTH DAY.

Quæ est ista quæ progreditur quasi, &c.

The faithful spouse, like the dawn and twilight of the morning, goes ever on from light to light, and her love for God grows ever more intense and burning. On the contrary, the slothful and unfaithful spouse, like unto the twilight of evening, allows by little and little her light to be shorn, and her fires to slacken, the further she goes from the Sun of Righteousness, so that she enters insensibly and through her own fault into the darkness and cold of a terrible night, and she thinks not of it. Dost thou not tremble, O my Soul, to be this faithless spouse? Dost not thou fear the chastisement of this unfaithfulness, which thou shalt have to feel one day, because thou dost not feel it now, or that in spite of feeling it thou dost not quit it? If the Celestial Spouse, Who will soon be thy Judge, called thee at this moment to judge thee by the progress thou hast made in His love, shouldest thou not have reason to fear the grievous destiny of the wicked and slothful servant who was so severely punished because he had not employed his talent? (Matt. xxv.) The talent which He has entrusted to thy heart, is His love; and the profit which He exacts from this precious talent, is progress in that love: where is thy progress? Alas! fear, love, and make amends.

FIFTH DAY.

Quàm pulchri sunt gressus tui in calceamentis, filia principis! (Cant. vii.)

"How beautiful are thy feet with shoes, O prince's daughter!" says the Spouse of the Canticles. How doth it attract the Heart of God, when our souls, which are His spouses, walk unceasingly in the paths of the Divine love; and when counting as nothing the way they have already made, and all those acts of love to which they have given birth every moment of their life, they apply themselves only to multiply them and bring them to perfection, and thus without ever growing weary hasten on to become more faithful, more pure, and more ardent! Each step which we make with our bodies brings us to the end whither we must go; each act of love is a step which draws us to the Heart of God. When we cease to go forward, the world dissipates us, it makes us dull; it first stops us, and at last it fails not to make us draw back. Meanwhile I must follow the Celestial Spouse, to deserve the crown of Divine love. He always walks on, and with great strides, says the Prophet; He is a Giant Who runs; if we stop ever so little, we shall lose His traces; He will be gone away, and perhaps we shall never come up to Him.

SIXTH DAY.

Quàm pulchri sunt gressus tui, &c.

Whence comes it that all my steps have been useless and unpleasing to my God, and that up to this time I have made so little progress in love, which is the most essential of all my duties? Let us seek in the depth of our heart the deplorable source of this disgrace, and let us promptly set ourselves to mend the evil effectually. Does it not come from having overrated the bare feeling of love, whilst I neglected to bring it out into frequent acts and more toilsome practices which frightened my dainty soul? Is it not from my losing heart in weariness, in dryness, and in internal desolation, and from not having endured these trials as I ought? Is it not from having sought my consolation in the creature, instead of seeking it in God Alone? Is it not from having wanted earnestness and watchfulness to stir up the sacred fire, when I felt it begin to languish, and from not having furnished it with fresh fuel by prayer, by reading, and by faithful practice of the Presence of God? Is it not from having committed many little and deliberate faults without having taken care to make amends for and correct them; or from having indulged the affections of my heart, when they turned towards the creature or towards myself with too sensible an attachment? It must be some one of these causes, or perhaps all together, which have prevented me from advancing in love. Assist me, Lord, to know them, and give me strength to expiate them, in order that there may be in me no obstacle to the progress of Thy Divine Love.

SEVENTH DAY.

Quàm pulchri sunt gressus tui, &c.

I will endeavour, O Heavenly Spouse, with the help of Thy Grace, to make no step that is not as pleasing to Thee as those of the bride, which Thou dost praise, and that all shall tend to draw me to Thy Heart. This shall be the end of all my thoughts, of all my designs, of all my desires, of all my feelings, of all my practices, and of all my actions. I know that all the moments of my life are so many steps which conduct me, whether I will or no, to the tomb, because I am mortal: but I propose that these moments be marked and filled with so many acts of love, and that from henceforth they be so many willing steps which conduct me to the perfection of this love, because I am a Christian. Let us, then, commence from this moment to enter into the career of Divine love; let us run with even steps; let us advance without pausing; the prize is only given at the end of the course; this end is death; and if we love truly, this death will be the beginning of a happy life, which shall never end.

Twelfth Week.

LOVE SEEKING.

When a man is persuaded of the goodness, value, and beauty of an object which he loves, hath not yet won, yet would fain possess, while again he feels that the winning of it depends upon himself, he fails not to seek it with all the care and eagerness of which he is capable, and he seeks until he has found it. The continual seeking for God is, therefore, an evident proof of a real estimation and of an ardent love, and whoever does not trouble himself to seek for God in every thing, may well say to himself, he has not yet loved Him.

But how can one love God and seek Him at the same time? "He who seeks God is always with God," says St. Augustine, "although he may not yet have found Him:" Qui Deum quærit nondumque invenit, non est sine Deo. (De vitâ beatâ.) No one can seek Him without loving Him, nor love Him without possessing Him: it is through love that He is sought: it is through love that He is held, after being sought for and found: the one love is unquiet and full of innocent anxiety, the other is a happy and tranquil love. God is a hidden God in the heart of him who seeks Him, and He does not make His presence to be felt, because He wishes to prove its faith by the darkness in which He leaves it. God is a God Who manifests Himself in the heart of him who possesses Him, because that in this world He chooses to begin to crown his faithfulness. St. Augustine says, again, He takes pleasure in being sought of one man with eagerness, in order that he may enjoy Him with more delight when he shall have found Him: He shows and gives Himself abundantly to another, in order to make him seek Him yet more eagerly: Quæritur, ut inveniatur dulcius; invenitur, ut quæratur avidius. (De Trin. b. 15.)

"I will rise now," says the spouse, "and go about the city in the streets, and in the broad ways I will seek Him Whom my soul loveth:" Surgam, et circuibo civitatem: per vicos et plateas quæram quem diligit anima mea. (Cant. iii.) She rose immediately without delay, well knowing that the least idleness and the least putting off are sometimes invincible obstacles to the success of this search. She afterwards met the watchmen of the city, to whom she said: "Saw ye Him Whom my soul loveth?" Num quem diligit anima mea vidistis? (Ibid.) At last, after much search and loving solicitude she has the happiness to find Him. Behold the type of a Christian soul, who at first is buried in the sleep of idleness and listlessness, and sees clearly that she wants something essential to her happiness, because she has not God with her; she comes out from the bed of her idleness, she seeks and she finds Him.

AFFECTIONS.

FIRST DAY.

Surgam, et circuibo civitatem, &c. Quæram quem diligit anima mea. (Cant. iii.)

"I will rise, I will go about the city, I will seek Him Whom my soul loveth," says the spouse. I know, Lord, that in order to seek and find Thee, I must renounce idleness and sleep; must rise up as soon as Thou callest, go forward unceasingly, be ever in motion, not by the movements of the body, but by those of the heart, that is, by its desires and affections. Open then thine eyes, O my soul; too long hast thou shamefully slept over thy most important duties, or fulfilled them with listlessness. Come out from the bed of thy lukewarmness. Thou dost not need, as the spouse, to go into public places to seek Thy Beloved; love to be alone; discipline thyself by silence; enter often into thyself, and seek Him in thine heart; He is surely there, if thou dost love Him. If He is hidden there, it is thy fault. The self-love, which thou dost also find there, conceals Him from thine eyes, and prevents His making Himself felt. Purify unceasingly this heart from all its defilements; set it on fire with an holy love that may consume all ungodliness; then wash this heart by the abundance of thy tears: then thou wilt not find it hard to find the God Whom thou dost seek, because He will be there Alone, and He will take pleasure in showing Himself to thy spirit and in touching thine heart.

SECOND DAY.

Quæram quem diligit anima mea.

There are too many, O Divine Spouse, who never seek Thee, because they do not love Thee, and they do not know Thy value; and these are reprobates. There are scarce fewer who seek Thee and do not find Thee, because their love is defective, and they seek Thee more for themselves than for Thee; and these are blind, or hypocrites who deceive themselves in trying to deceive others. There are some who seek and find Thee, but do not keep Thee, because their love is weak, and they abandon Thee at the least trial: and these are the cowardly and inconstant. The fewest in number are those who seek Thee, find Thee, and keep Thee till death, because their love is heroic, and nothing can make them lose the rich treasure they have found. Take here thy place, O my soul! look well if thou dost seek God in all things, and how thou dost seek Him; O happy if thou art of the number of the last, since they are the nearest to the Heart of God in this life, and they will be the first in the kingdom of heaven.

THIRD DAY.

Quæram quem diligit anima mea.

Since, doubtless, we must either find God in this world, or make up our minds never to see Him in the other, I must, to insure my happiness, seek Him so well, that I may find Him and never lose Him. Let us then awake from our lethargy, let us rise with the bride, let us walk as she does; let us have the same desires, the same eagerness, and the same ardour to find Him; let us enquire of the heavens, and the earth, the sea, and all creatures; we shall find in them at least the image of their Creator, Who is the Beloved, that we seek. If these do not say enough to us, let us seek Him in ourselves: let us question our senses, our memory, our mind, and our heart. Alas! Lord, said St. Augustine (Conf.), I went very far to seek Thee, and Thou wert very near. I may find Thee in my eyes, by modesty and purity; in my mouth, by silence and by the confession of Thy greatness and of my sins; in my memory, by the remembrance of my iniquities and Thy mercies; in my mind, by holy thoughts and by meditation on Thy Divine law; but above all I shall find Thee in my heart, because, if I love Thee, it cannot be but that Thou shouldest rest there.

FOURTH DAY.

Quæram quem diligit anima mea.

The ambitious man seeks honours, and often finds nothing but shame and infamy; the voluptuary seeks pleasure, and commonly finds but vexation and causes of sorrow; the miser seeks riches, and generally, after much labour and toil, finds only poverty, and dies despoiled of the riches of both Heaven and earth. O my soul, seek God Alone, and thou shalt infallibly find Him; knock at the door of His Heart, and He will open to you, for He Himself has so promised; and thou wilt find in Him, with Him, and through Him, glory the most sublime and lasting, pleasure the most pure and delightful, and treasures the most precious and abundant. How great the blessing to be certain to find God, and to find all in God! and what blindness not to undertake a search of which the rewards are so glorious! Though it should cost much labour and fatigue, is it not enough reward to enjoy the happiness of finding God and possessing Him for time and eternity?

FIFTH DAY.

Num quem diligit anima mea vidistis? (Cant. iii.)

"Saw ye Him Whom my soul loveth?" said the

bride to the watchmen of the city of Jerusalem. What sweet restlessness! what holy boldness! what innocent curiosity! and how happy is he who has no curiosity but that which comes from the violent desire to find and possess God. If a maiden were to venture alone in the midst of soldiers without fearing their insults, to suffer them to take away her veil, to strike her unmercifully, without for all that ceasing to seek after her Beloved, what would be said of her? and would she not be thought to have the most disordered love in the world, if aught but Divine love caused these transports in her? I must, then, expose myself to all, suffer all, and risk all, if I wish to find my God. No obstacle must stop me, no outrage but must be borne in order to compass it; what I shall find will be incomparably better than what I shall have lost in seeking Him. Nothing is lost if we find God; our suffering is nothing if we possess Him. Faith teaches me that He never withdraws Himself from those who by love have sought Him; and that is enough to induce me to undertake to find Him.

SIXTH DAY.

Num quem diligit anima mea vidistis?

In order to seek God with success, there must be in my search truth, constancy, and perseverance; without these conditions I run the risk of never finding Him. There must be truth in the motive, and in the object of my search; and true love must be its motive; and there must be in it no mixture of vanity, interest, self-love, or human respect. The object must be God Alone; I ought to seek Him above all things, seek nothing but for Him, seek nothing with Him, seek nothing after Him; in a word, seek God for God Alone. Again, I ought to seek Him with all the constancy of which I am capable, and renew unceasingly and without interval my acts of love. Lastly, I ought to seek Him with a noble and unwearied perseverance, without ever giving over until I have found Him. It is thus, O Celestial Spouse, that I desire, with Thy Grace, to seek and to love Thee until death.

SEVENTH DAY.

Num quem diligit anima mea vidistis?

For a long time have I been enquiring, with the spouse, Where is my Beloved? I seek Him every where, and do not find Him. Nevertheless, LORD, Thou fillest Heaven and earth; Thou art every where, wherever I may go; Thou canst never be absent or far from me; Thou art more in me than myself; why then have I the misfortune not to find Thee? Can it be that I deceive myself? Can it be that I am mistaken? Can it be that I love Thee not? Love is the whole, the cause and end, the flower and the fruit, to which I aspire in my search. It seems to me I only seek Thee, because my heart loves Thee, and that I only wish to find Thee in order to love Thee, and to seek Thee with more perfection and ardour. Do Thou then Thyself teach me, O Heavenly Spouse! to love Thee, to seek Thee, and to find Thee; guide me to Thyself, O adorable Light, show Thyself to my mind, which desires only to think of Thee. Ineffable Love, show Thyself, and make Thyself felt in my heart, which desires only to love Thee.

Thirteenth Week.

LOVE IN ITS ATTRACTIVENESS.

THE heart of man is become so weak since the fall, that of himself he can make no step towards GOD. He needs a superior virtue to allure and drag him along, so to say; and this superior virtue is charity, which first gives sufficient strength to walk, and afterwards wings to fly. A recent penitent, who has just left the delights of a corrupt world, and who wishes to walk in the way of the evangelical counsels, would fall at each step, if he were not supported by the love which dilates his heart, which draws him on, and which ever furnishes him with fresh strength; like a sick man recovering from a long illness, availing himself of the aid of others to support his feeble and staggering body when he wishes to begin to walk, and who does not blush to allow himself to be carried wherever he wishes to go.

It is then love which is the predominant attraction to all Christians, as well to sinners as to penitents and righteous men; for this love is not without an innocent enjoyment, and it must attract the heart of man, who always loves to feel himself moved.

It is thus, on this weak side, that God was minded to attract and to lay hold of man, when He said, by the Prophet Hosea, "I drew them with the cords of a man, with bands of love:" In funiculis Adam traham eos, in vinculis charitatis. (Hosea xi. 4.) By that He promises us that He will take upon Him our flesh, and consequently a Heart with feelings like our's, in order to attract us by the most tender ties, and those most fitted to reach our hearts. However ardent the bride of the Canticles was, she quite felt that something was wanting to her love, and that she had need of a powerful attraction to complete the detachment of her heart from sensible things, and in order to approach nearer to the Spouse she loved. Thus she said to Him, "Draw me after Thee; we will run after the savour of Thy perfumes:" Trahe me post te, curremus in odorem unguentorum tuorum. (Cant. i.) Nevertheless, as it must be of necessity that the creature respond to the attractions of God, and that she make on her part every effort to follow Him, this Heavenly Spouse says to her: "Return, return, O Shulamite; return, return, that We may look upon thee:" Revertere, revertere, Sulamitis; revertere, revertere, ut intueamur te. (Cant. vi.)

AFFECTIONS.

FIRST DAY.

Trahe me post te, &c. (Cant. i.)

Draw me after Thee, said the spouse, and we will run after the savour of Thy perfumes. Without Thee, O my God! I cannot go to Thee; idleness overwhelms me, weakness weighs me down, my senses stop me, my body makes me heavy, my spirit is in darkness, and does not see its road; my will is weak, and I can make no step if Thou dost not draw me and take me by the hand. I feel sometimes, to my sorrow, a heart of flesh, which, from its unhappy susceptibility, clings strongly to sensible objects; and this sorrowful attraction hinders it from following that of Thy love, at least if thou dost not draw it more strongly to thee; sometimes I feel a heart of iron, of a hardness which cannot be softened, and a heaviness which cannot be moved by the most lively and touching thoughts. Holy Love, touch my iron heart, be my loadstone, draw it to Thee Alone, notwithstanding its hardness and heaviness; impress on it Thy nature, as the loadstone does to the iron, which suffers itself to be drawn along as soon as it is touched by it; penetrate it with Thy divine ardour, and give it strength to run after the odour of Thy perfumes.

SECOND DAY.

Trahe me post te, &c.

I hear Thy bride, Lord, pray Thee to draw her

because she desires to run after Thee, and feels truly that she can do nothing without Thee: but I also hear what Thou sayest to my soul by a prophet. "I have loved Thee with an everlasting love; therefore with loving-kindness have I drawn Thee." (Jer. xxxi. 3.) Ah! it is more Thy Heart than Thy Mouth Which here speaks to me, and these words make me expect every thing from Thy mercies. Thou dost, then, LORD, sometimes draw us to Thee without our asking Thee; and this attraction comes of Thy free grace, not from our merit, but from Thy mere kindness. How much more wilt Thou draw my soul to Thee, when she shall wish it with ardour, when she shall love Thee with all her powers, when she shall ask it of Thee, or rather when Thou shalt inspire her to ask it of Thee with fervour! Draw me then, LORD, with the Spouse; hear at this moment the ardent prayer that Thou Thyself formest in my heart, and which Thou dost articulate upon my lips; draw me, tear me with a holy violence from the mire where I am sunk, and add strength to the attraction of Thy love, that it be ever victorious in my heart.

THIRD DAY.

Trahe me post te, &c.

To be drawn to GOD, in order to be united to Him, and to fix her abode in His Heart, was the ardent desire of the spouse, and it ought to be that of all true Christians; but to draw GOD Himself to abide with me and in my heart, to induce Him, to force Him with a loving violence to descend to fill it with His adorable Presence, is a privilege to which I should not have the boldness to aspire, if this same GOD had not said, in express terms, "We will come unto him, and make Our abode with him." (St. John xiv. 23.) To be drawn to GOD, and to draw GOD to us, behold two very glorious and sublime attractions: nevertheless, this double attraction is the work of one love alone. I cannot love God if I be not loved by Him; I cannot love Him and be loved by Him if He draw me not into His Heart, and if I do not at the same time draw Him into mine. Draw me, then, O Celestial Spouse, or suffer Thyself to be drawn; raise me unto Thee, or bow down Thyself to me, notwithstanding my lowliness and Thy greatness, or rather inflame me with Thy love, since I am sure to obtain both these attractions, if I only love Thee.

FOURTH DAY.

Trahe me post te, &c.

Can I doubt that I really am drawn by the Divine Love, when God has made such visible steps to draw me to Himself? He humbles Himself, and is not ashamed to ask of us our heart; nevertheless, we rebel against this attraction, and are not ashamed to refuse it Him, and to prefer the deceitful attractions of the world, which we know to be His most irreconcileable enemy. What can be more astonishing than God entreating the creature rebelling against his Creator, who asks only of him his love; God attracting a creature flying from His attraction, instead of praying for it, and following Him! What tenderness is there on one side, and what hardness on the other! At one time He draws us, and solicits us tenderly, as a father and a friend, and we do not listen; anon, as a Sovereign who asks authoritatively that which is His right, and we disobey Him. How blind we are to our own interest! In following the attraction of the world, we possess neither God nor the world; but in loving God, and in following His attraction, we possess Him, and all things in Him, and we become the masters of the world.

FIFTH DAY.

Revertere, revertere, Sulamitis; revertere, revertere, ut intueamur te. (Cant. vi.)

"Return, return, O Shulamite: return, return, that We may look upon thee," says the Spouse. It is for thee, also, sinful soul, to return to Me; it is for thee to respond to the attraction of My Love; hitherto I have made steps enough to draw thy heart; it is for thee to put all in force to follow Me, and to attract Mine; it is for thee to aid My voice by a prompt return. I have made thee hear it long enough, and thou hast neglected it; set out then to come to Me, since My Grace draws thee, and in drawing thee gives thee all the strength thou dost need to follow that which draws thee: if thou do not this, I will not call thee, and will never draw thee. Two things will prove to Me the steadfastness of thy return and thy faithfulness to the attraction which draws thee, and these are hatred and love: the hatred of the sin thou hast committed, and love to the God Who draws thee to Himself. What more hideous than sin! Canst thou not hate it? What more worthy of all the tenderness of thine heart than God! Canst thou not love Him?

SIXTH DAY.

Revertere, revertere, Sulamitis, &c.

What an excess of goodness is here! What eagerness! Dost thou call Thy spouse four times to induce her to turn to Thee! How doth this sweet repeated call render it undoubted that Thou dost draw me to Thee, and evidently prove the favourable dispositions of Thy Heart towards me, since I cannot doubt that Thou art ready to do for me what Thou hast done for her, if only I love Thee as she has loved Thee! But why, Lord, dost Thou draw me with so much earnestness? It is, Thou sayest, to look upon me. But, alas! what wilt Thou see in me? My soul is defiled with an infinity of strange affections; how will she be able to sustain Thy Divine looks, Thou Who art Purity Itself? Thou wilt see in me Thy work, Thy gifts, and Thine image: but Thy adorable Eyes will also discover the sins by which I have defiled Thy work, the thoughtlessness with which I have received Thy gifts, and the shameful lines which I have added to Thy image to disfigure it. Yet, O my God, look upon me such as I am, and have compassion on my miseries, which I humbly uncover and make bare to Thine eyes. Draw me by Thy Divine looks, they are all-powerful to reform me, to make me perfect, and to make me go to Thee. By a single look Thou didst win and convert Peter; I ask from Thee the same grace, I hope for the same favour.

SEVENTH DAY.

Revertere, revertere, Sulamitis, &c.

I cannot turn to Thee, Lord, if Thou dost not draw me; I cannot reply to the attraction with which Thou drawest me, if I do not know and love Thee. Open then my eyes and heart: my eyes to discern Thee; my heart to make me full of love. If Thou wouldest draw me on to mortify myself, make me but know it, I will then make it my chief point, and all my practices shall tend to mortify my spirit, my will, my flesh, and my whole being. If Thine attraction tend to draw me to humility and lowliness, I will seek to reply to it with all possible faithfulness; I will ever have my nothingness and Thy Greatness before my eyes, and I will look upon contempt and humiliations as so many favours. Meanwhile, till I realize this, I will labour to love Thee with all my heart. Love is the dominant attraction which draws all Christians to Thee: and I am sure not to be deceiving myself, as long as I follow it with ardour. Whatever else Thou mayest demand of me, whatever other attraction there may be, with which Thou wilt favour me, love is the light which will discover to me this secret, and a Heavenly fire which will carry me through it with alacrity.

Fourteenth Week.

SINCERE LOVE.

Divine love without sincerity is not a true love, but its shadow; it is rather a fine imposture and a criminal hypocrisy. As God is essentially Truth and Simplicity, He wishes neither for lying duplicity nor made up devotion in the worship He exacts from His creature, and He demands truth and simplicity in the most essential act of religion, which is love.

This sincerity of love consists in a perfect agreement and harmony between the understanding and the heart, the tongue and the hands; that is to say, between thoughts and feelings, the expressions and the works. It is an unswerving uprightness, a simplicity of heart, a purity of intention and action, which all together seek and love God for the sake of God Alone, and which has Him Alone for the beginning, the centre, and end of all its aims, desires, steps, and practices, as well externally as internally; which seeks truth only by straight and simple paths, without ever straying away.

" The upright love Thee," says the spouse: Recti diligunt te. (Cant. i.) As though she would say, It is not by winding ways and out-of-the-way paths that we can come unto Thee, and prove that we love

Thee, but by sincerity of heart. Men may be deceived by a feigned love, to which may be lent the specious outside of a sincere love; but no one, LORD, can impose on Thee, since Thou knowest the most secret movements of the heart.

This spouse herself practised this sincerity of love which she praised, for her Spouse tells her she has doves' eyes: Oculi tui columbarum. (Cant. iv.) The dove is the emblem of simplicity and purity; and there is neither falsehood nor division in her love. The eyes mark the sincerity of the intention; they are speaking mirrors where the feelings of the heart are often represented; there joy can be seen and sorrow, hatred and love. When the eye looks at an object, it draws it to itself; it receives its form and image, and transforms it to itself; and when this object is agreeable, it also makes the eye sweet to look upon. When a Christian loves GOD with all his heart, his eye, i. e. his love, looks on Him Alone; he receives the impression and resemblance of this Adorable Object, and his love becomes like to that of GOD's, which is Sincerity Itself.

AFFECTIONS.

FIRST DAY.

Recti diligunt te. (Cant. i.)

Those who have an upright heart love Thee, and none can love Thee without it. Praises, protestations, and outward shows, will ever be but doubtful signs of the sincerity of love. Men judge of the heart only by the words, and GOD judges the words by the heart. Its most secret movements are known to Him; nothing that passes there escapes Him; He has formed it to be the seat, the throne, and the sanctuary of love; it is by this heart that He wishes to be loved, and He desires that there might be uprightness and sincerity in this love. Ah! LORD, I have given Thee outward marks of love, that were not sincere, because they did not come from the heart, and it disowned them in secret while my mouth proffered them! I said, I love Thee, and I believed it was enough to say it in order to love Thee, while all my actions gave the lie to my mouth. I said, I am all Thine, and I was all vanity, all for the world, all for self-love, all for my own feelings, obstinacy, sloth, and idleness. Now I know I have not had an upright heart, and that my love wanted sincerity; but I will now put all in practice to acquire it.

SECOND DAY.

Recti diligunt te.

Let us diligently search our own hearts: it is there we shall learn, if we have all the uprightness and sincerity requisite to love GOD. Let us try if we can find in the heart, the tongue, the mind, and the hands, that unity, harmony, and agreement which form the sincerity of love; after having examined it, we shall perceive, perhaps, that there is more outward appearance than reality. To remedy this evil, let us quit our own heart to enter into That of GOD; we shall there see an excellent model of that sincerity we want. He has said a thousand times that He loved us; but He has added to these protestations proofs which convince me of the sincerity of His Love. These proofs are the sufferings and the effusion of all His Blood. Behold an authentic act which guarantees to me the sincerity of the Heart of GOD. His Adorable Blood is the ink with which He has signed it; the Scourge, the Thorns, and the Nails, are the pen with which He has written, and the graver with which He has engraven it in indelible characters. Let us remember these precious characters, and read them every day; let us form those of our love upon this matchless original: and to show Him the sincerity of our love, let us be ever ready to do for Him what He has first done for us.

THIRD DAY.

Recti diligunt te.

I should do injustice, and a cruel outrage to Thy Heart, O My God! if I doubted of the sincerity of Thy love. Thou hast given proofs of it so signal, so strong, and so manifest, that I cannot but be convinced: I have then only to love Thee sincerely, and I am sure that Thou wilt love me in the same way. The love of my heart answers to Thine; mine cannot be Thine if Thine be not mine. How urgent is this motive to engage me to love but Thee Alone. Couldest Thou fail to answer to my love, Thou Who hast loved me first, and Who hast loved me in order that I may love Thee? Thou Who hast asked for my heart, sinner as I am? Thou Who, not content with having sealed with Thy Blood the witness of Thy love, hast furthermore given me a thousand assurances of it every moment of my life? Ah! Lord, from henceforth, when my mouth shall say, I love Thee, it is my will that my heart may first say it; this heart shall be its voice, and this mouth the echo; the one shall be the motive cause, the other the organ. They shall always harmonize together; the abundance and fulness of one shall be the outpouring and sincerity of the other.

FOURTH DAY.

Recti diligunt te.

What more delightful to a heart which feels that it is created only to love, and which, moreover, feels itself carried on by its nature to fulfil this function, than to protest loudly to God that it loves Him, and to apply itself a thousand times a day to this Adorable

Object? Is this the sincere love which God exacts from me? No, it is only its prelude; only an equivocal sign, which may well accompany true love, but which may also subsist with a false love. These are the means, O my soul, to discern the truth in so delicate a matter, and in which you may so easily be a dupe. This God Whom thou, as thou thinkest, dost love so tenderly, dost thou in like manner serve Him? Dost thou renounce, without a moment's hesitation, all which is opposed to the truth of thy love? Love may exist without feeling, as may feeling without love; mere feeling is not a proof of the sincerity of love. It always satisfies the heart, but often deceives it: acts must needs surpass feelings; and these successive and generous acts are the undoubted proofs of a sincere love, when they have a supernatural motive to animate and support them; feelings are often the production and effect of a love purely natural, which lacks uprightness and elevation.

FIFTH DAY.

Oculi tui columbarum.

"Thou hast doves' eyes," says the Spouse to His beloved. The dove is pure, simple, and sincere; she loves with constancy Him Whom she has chosen, she loves Him Alone, and all others are indifferent to her. Her eye, that is to say, her love, inclines ever to Him, and there escapes from it no demonstration of tenderness which comes not from the heart, and which the heart does not own; and that is true sincerity. My love for God will never be sincere, if it does not resemble hers; it is the blameless model which the Celestial Spouse proposes to me. "If thine eye be single," He says in another place, "thy whole body shall be full of light" (Matt. vi. 22); if my love is upright and sincere, all I think, wish, and do, will be right; all my designs, projects, steps, and feelings will refer to this love, as the copy to the original; they will proceed from it, as effects from a cause: and they will tend to it as lines to a centre. Such from henceforth shall be the rule of my love.

SIXTH DAY.

Oculi tui columbarum.

To have eyes like those of a dove, as had the bride of the Canticles, is ever to look on God Alone in all things. The eye inclines naturally to what the heart loves; one is the organ, the mirror, and the interpreter of the other; the eye never turns to an object without carrying away and bearing its image during all the time that it looks upon it. God, in forming us, looked upon us with an eye of love, and He has imprinted on us His image. Ever since our creation He has still looked at us tenderly, and He has taken our likeness and espoused our miseries. He desires also that I look upon Him until the eye of my heart has taken in all the features of His Image, and until it has taken them in such a manner that they should never be effaced: but as, in order to form a perfect vision, there must be nothing between the eye and the object that the eye looks upon, I must see if I have not, through my fault, put any thing between God and me, which may hinder me from looking upon His Face as I ought, and interpose some obstacle to the image and gracious impression I ought to receive from it. Is there not between us some creature, and that some little sensible attachment, which fills with darkness the space I have put between God and me? Let me carefully remove it, that I may see the Face of God Alone, and induce Him to favour me more readily with His Divine looks.

SEVENTH DAY.

Oculi tui columbarum.

In what way does God draw to Him my eyes and my heart? What is the innocent charm, what is the cause, the attraction, which draws my love. It is the uprightness and sincerity of His Heart, it is His goodness, of which I have such very sensible proofs. It is that which persuades me; it is that which draws me, and raises me up; and it is because I am sure that His love is sincere and affectionate. But who is there then, says a holy doctor, who loves God with a true sincerity of heart? (D. Chrysost.) It is he who knows, who owns, and is convinced that all goodness and happiness is in God, that He Himself is all goodness and happiness, and that there is neither happiness or true goodness but in God Alone. Herein is the reason, the basis and principle of the sincere love we owe Him. Join, O my soul, feeling to this knowledge, and careful practice of good works to this feeling; thou wilt thus have all the truth and sincerity of love.

Fifteenth Week.

TENDER LOVE.

The tender love which we bear to God is, says a holy man, an exquisite and delicious taste for Divine things (D. Bon. de 7. itin. tit. 4); it is an intimate and sensible delight; it is a sweet reflection of the chaste joys, and of the heavenly suavity with which God from time to time favours those whom He loves, either to detach them more completely from earthly pleasures, or to attach them to Himself by chains more sweet and strong; and the more the soul loves with a burning love, the more also it is plunged in this ocean of delights, where it "tastes" with the Prophet, "how gracious the LORD is." (Ps. xxxiv.)

This tender love has its source, its stream, and its effects. The Heart of GOD is the source of it; it is the principle, the centre, and end of the most pure joys; because the essential love which He beareth to Himself makes all His happiness, and He tastes this happiness with infinite joy. From this copious source there flows a torrent of delights, which runs with a ceaseless and gushing stream upon all the blessed, whose happiness consists in loving and feeling that they love; but it has also its little overflowings upon the heart of the faithful; and it is this, which we call tender love, and it produces in them wondrous effects. Whence comes that distaste for the false joys of the world and all the pleasures of sense; whence those pure and burning feelings; whence that happy pliability of the heart, which turns itself to GOD at the least inspiration.

Sinners and penitents have need of this tender love in the first fruits of their conversion. As their heart is still carnal, and pleasure has made upon their senses an impression hard to efface, it must needs be that GOD of His infinite goodness should present to them a pleasure more pure and agreeable, and chase away, says a holy writer, the sweetness of crime by the sweetness of innocence, that the second may take its place, and be victorious over the first; vincat dulcedo dulcedinem. (D. Bern. de amore Dei.)

When the Spouse says, "Let me hear thy voice, for sweet is thy voice:" Sonet vox tua in auribus meis, vox enim tua dulcis (Cant. ii.): what is here meant is the voice and the language of the heart, which is love, which even sweetens the tones of the voice when it is blended with a true tenderness. He afterwards uses a stronger mode of speech, which contains a declaration more exact and tender when He exclaims, "How fair and how full of grace art thou, O My dearest, the delight of My Heart!" Quàm pulchra es, et quàm decora, charissima, in deliciis! (Cant. vii.)

AFFECTIONS.

FIRST DAY.

Sonet vox tua in auribus meis, vox enim tua dulcis. (Cant. ii.)

"Let me hear thy voice, for sweet is thy voice," says the Spouse. Alas, Lord! the world has been able to say to me, and I have said a thousand times to the world, what Thou dost say to Thy bride; and this is my misery. It has enchanted my ears and heart by the seducing sweetness of its deadly language, and I have answered it in a like strain. It has called me, and I have answered; it has melted me, and I have loved it. Now I wish to have with it only a stern intercourse; I will hate it, I will flee so far from it, that it shall never hear my voice, and that I shall never hear its voice, lest it be infectious to my heart, and draw from it some feeling of profane tenderness, which would hinder me from feeling that of Thy Divine Love. Make me hear Thy Voice, O Celestial Spouse, that mine may reach Thee. Speak to my heart, in order that I may speak to Thine. I am so weak, that I have need sometimes to feel that Thou dost love me tenderly, to support me against the false sweetness of the world, and against the dread and fear of Thy justice, which sometimes seizes me in such a manner, that I only walk by the lurid light of Thy lightnings and thunderbolts. Put in the place of this voice of thunder the

Voice of the Spouse in all its mildness, which may draw from my eyes at the same time tears of tenderness and penitence.

SECOND DAY.

Sonet vox tua in auribus meis, &c.

The voice of my love can make no sweet sound to Thy ears, LORD, till Thine has made the delight of my heart. Thy Voice, however sweet it may be, cannot make the delight of my heart; it cannot even hear it, till all worldly delights be banished from it for ever. I cannot taste how sweet it is to listen to, to love, and to feel Thee, till I regard all the pleasures of the earth as a deadly poison, diluted in a sweet and deadly liquor, which leaves a disgusting bitterness, and causes certain death. Speak, then, to me, to make me worthy to speak to Thee: speak to my mind, my soul, and my heart, in order that all that is within me may speak to Thee, and that Thou mayest take pleasure in hearing my voice as that of the spouse. Favour me with this Divine language, which is sweetness itself, and which can only express itself by tenderness, feelings, and transports towards Thee. Impose an eternal silence on the voice of the world and its pleasures. Now I listen, LORD; speak to my soul. It is attentive, I wish to hearken only to Thee, and to speak but to Thee for the rest of my life, in order to hear Thee, to love Thee, and to enjoy Thee for ever in the other.

THIRD DAY.

Sonet vox tua in auribus meis.

Hardened must be the man who does not open his heart as soon as GOD knocks at its door, and that He makes it hear His voice. He must be very insensible who does not rejoice in His Divine language, which is sweetness itself. Whence comes it then,

Lord, that I am so long without loving Thee, and without feeling that I love Thee? It is the hardness of my heart which is the cause of it. But why have I the misery to bear about a heart so hard for Thee to soften and to melt? It is that it is too tender and too easily moved by creatures. It is, then, its tenderness which produces its hardness; its fires are the cause of its coldness; it is void of feelings and love for Thee, because it is full of tenderness for what it ought not to love; it is deprived of Thy sweets, because it seeks for them with too much eagerness amid created objects, and things of sense. "Heal, then, Lord," exclaims St. Augustine, "the inward palace of my heart; drive away, fling down, and put out all its irreligious emotions; empty it, to fill it with Thyself Alone; purify it, and make it worthy never to enjoy any other sweet, and to feel no other tenderness than that of Thy Divine Love."

FOURTH DAY.

Sonet vox tua in auribus meis.

What is to be done, O my God, when this miserable heart, which I have, is insensible to Thy voice, and incapable of speaking to Thee with feelings of tenderness and love, as it is too often through its fault? What am I to do to make it more attentive to Thy Divine language, and to give it a taste for it? What am I to do to draw upon this ungrateful soil the dews and showers of benediction, which may render it fruitful in desires and feelings for what it ought alone to love? At first I will try what fear can do, which, when it is chaste and filial, cannot fail to lead to true love; I shall fear Thee at first as my King and Judge; I shall fear and love Thee afterwards as my Father, Whom I shall dread to displease; at length I shall come by these steps to love Thee purely and tenderly as my Saviour and my

Spouse: but I can neither fear nor love Thee tenderly without Thy help. I ask it, LORD, and I hope it from Thy infinite goodness.

FIFTH DAY.

Quàm pulchra es, et quàm decora, charissima, in deliciis! (Cant. vii.)

"How fair and how pleasant art thou, O love," thou makest the "delights" of my heart! What glory is it for a creature to be the delight of the Heart of its GOD! and how ungrateful, how cruel to myself should I be, if this GOD of goodness were not the delight of my heart! What is there which might put an obstacle to this Divine favour, that makes all my glory and happiness? Nothing but an unworthy tenderness for some perishable creature: but what a hateful comparison would that be between GOD and His creature; between the joy of being loved by the Almighty, and of loving Him tenderly, and the pleasure of clinging to this creature! If I have a heart greedy of pleasures and feelings, I ought to seek the most exquisite, the most pure, and the most lasting, and I shall find them only in GOD Alone. The tenderness and sweetness which are tasted with Him reward the heart, abundantly and with interest, for all those that it sacrifices to Him, and which it freely denies itself for His love.

SIXTH DAY.

Charissima in deliciis.

All was mutual between the Spouse and the bride; each made the pleasure and the delight of the other. If the Spouse says that she is His dearest in His joy, the bride says also that she has felt her soul melt as soon as she has heard His voice. To taste His love as I ought, He orders me, by His Prophet, to pour out my heart before Him. (Psalm lxii.) But how,

O my God, can I pour out my heart? Only what is melting and liquid can properly be poured out, and my heart is harder than the stone of the desert. There is nothing in it fit to pour out, since it is dry as an unfruitful ground which has not been watered. I understand by these words, O celestial Spouse, that Thou wouldest have me love Thee with so much tenderness, that my heart may gush forth and melt itself, and that my eyes may pour it forth and be dissolved in tears of love for Thee Alone. I yield, Lord; but do Thou Thyself soften this heart which till now has been but too insensible to Thee, and too sensitive to creatures, and give me grace to pour it forth a thousand times a day in tears of penitence and tenderness.

SEVENTH DAY.

Charissima in deliciis.

Compare, O my soul, the chaste joys that are tasted with God to the deceitful and seducing delights that are tasted away from God. Judge them without prejudice: call hither to thine assistance all thy reason, and hearken to it. What does it say to thee? What is the love of God? What the love of the creature? That is eternal, this is perishable: the love of God purifies and fills the whole heart with an ineffable sweetness; that of the creature seduces it: it palls upon it, and it leaves there a void which weighs it down. If thou wilt not submit to this reason, call hither thine own experience; it will suffice to induce thee henceforth to take delight in God Alone, and to disgust thee of the creatures. Thy weak and inconstant heart has, perhaps, loved each by turns; recal to memory those happy and those miserable moments. Charmed at first with an irreligious tenderness, thou hast but too much given thyself up to it: but was this pleasure without a mixture of bitterness? and with how many disgusts, regrets, and remorse of conscience hast thou purchased the tasteless delights that thou didst enjoy in it! Thou hast at length happily turned thine heart towards God: what delights and what innocent pleasures hast thou felt in it! Give thyself up, then, wholly to this tenderness; make thyself worthy to feel it, and put no obstacle to it; it is accompanied by a chaste enjoyment, which charms, elevates, sanctifies, and hallows, and no one is ever weary of it but through his own fault.

Sixteenth Week.

STRONG LOVE.

The same definition applies to strength and love; all that is suitable for the one is suitable for the other also. They proceed from the same cause, they have the same properties, they go by the same road and arrive together at the same end; they have the same advantages, and they produce the same effects. St. Augustine defines strength to be a real love, fortitudo est amor (De Mor. Eccl. v.), which undertakes all, suffers all, resists all for God's sake, which supports for Him Alone the most severe assaults of grief without being cast down or complaining; and the most lively solicitations of sensuality without allowing itself to be corrupted by it.

The truly strong man draws motives of consolation from no place but his own heart in the most severe troubles, because that his love dwells there; or from the Heart of God, because he is there himself, yea, there by his love; he only resists the pleasures of sense because he loves something else more noble, more great, more pure, and more lovely than those pleasures, which are unworthy to occupy a noble heart which is made for GOD Alone. "Thou art beautiful, O my love, and full of sweetness," says the Spouse, "comely as Jerusalem, terrible as an army ('in battle array') with banners:" Pulchra es, amica mea, suavis et decora sicut Jerusalem, terribilis ut castrorum acies ordinata. (Cant. vi.) But how are this beauty and sweetness to harmonize with terror? Does sweetness strike with fear? Does beauty make a person formidable? It is not carnal beauty which produces these effects, but it is of spiritual beauty alone that the Spouse here speaks, and this beauty proceeds only from love and charity. The bride by this love was perfectly united to her Beloved; it is this which rendered her strong and terrible to all her enemies, who would have dared to attack her purity. Strength comes from unity, unity from love, and love forms all the beauty of the soul. When an army, ranged in order of battle, is arrayed in serried ranks, when it holds a close union with its chief, it is terrible, it cannot be broken; and when a soul is perfectly united to JESUS CHRIST by love, she is always victorious.

To confirm this truth, the Spouse says, at the end of His Canticle, that "Love is strong as death:" Fortis est ut mors dilectio (Cant. viii.); that is to say, according to the opinion of St. Gregory, that as death quenches the virtue of the senses of the body (Greg. hîc), so love has strength to render our soul insensible to the attractions of false pleasures, and to carry it up to GOD notwithstanding the obstacles which are set against it.

AFFECTIONS.

FIRST DAY.

Pulchra es, amica mea, suavis et decora sicut Jerusalem, terribilis ut castrorum acies ordinata. (Cant. vi.)

"Thou art beautiful, O my love, and full of sweetness; thou art comely as Jerusalem, terrible as an army in battle array." I learn by this word that a man is strong with God, for God, and even against God, when he loves Him with a strong love, and above every thing. Great, Almighty, and Invincible as He is, love makes Him stoop, it bows Him down, overcomes Him, disarms, and triumphs over His Heart. It is very strange, O Lord of Hosts, that love can have strength to disarm Thine arm, uplifted to blast the sinner, and to make Thee, so to say, withdraw Thy judgment, and transfer the criminal from the dreadful tribunal of Thy Justice to that of Thy Mercy. What shall I add, O my God, to form in my heart powerful motives for love, but this, that I now know that by love Thy Supreme Greatness has stooped down, Thy infinite plenitude is diffused, that Thy Divine Nature has joined to itself another which is mine, that Thy dreadful Majesty is to us as a Friend, and that it is by the strength of this same love that the creature can ascend unto Thee, and has the inestimable privilege of entering even into Thy Heart without fear of being repulsed?

SECOND DAY.

Terribilis ut castrorum acies ordinata.

A Christian who loves God with all his strength, is by himself as strong as a whole army in battle array. He counts not on human assistance, but on God Alone, Who is the controller of the greatest events. Strengthened by His sole assistance, he never wants when he loves, he accomplishes all things, he conquers in all, and nothing can resist him; there is no affliction which can overthrow him, no want of success which can discourage him, no enemy whom he cannot overcome, and no enterprise that does not prosper in his hands. Now show, O my soul, the proofs of the strength of thy love. What hast thou done for God? where are thy victories over the least of thy passions? where are the enemies that thou hast thrown down? where are the labours that thou hast gone through, and the sufferings which thou hast endured for His Glory? Notwithstanding all thy protestations of courage, strength, and love, the least difficulties have scared thee, the least labour has disheartened thee, the least adversity has overthrown thee, and thy pretended strength has lasted only until that which was to be its special trial came on. Thou hast then never loved, or thou hast loved very weakly.

THIRD DAY.

Terribilis ut castrorum acies ordinata.

There is no man who has not his weak side, by which the devil beats out for himself a road into his heart, by which he may bring in corruption; and this weak side is a ruling imperfection, which is most commonly the ground which he has to contest, and which he ought to make the subject of his fears and precautions. But it is wonderful, O God of strength, that Thou hast Thy weakness as well as mortals. But Thy Apostles teach us that this weakness is stronger than the strength of all men together. (1 Cor. i. 25.) Thou hast vouchsafed to reveal it to me, to give me an advantage over Thee, by making known to me that this Divine and Almighty weakness is nothing but the love which Thou hast for me. This is the weakness which conquers the strong man and even strength itself. Love is, then, stronger than an army in battle array, since by it I can take my God on His weak side, and by it He suffers me to wrest from His Hand the thunderbolt which was ready to crush the sinner. It is, then, by the strength of my love that I shall have a hold upon the Heart of my Creator and my Judge, that I can incline Him towards me, and make Him propitious to me. Since I know this I should be very miserable if I did not avail myself of it.

FOURTH DAY.

Terribilis ut castrorum acies ordinata.

With nothing but the love of God in the heart, we are stronger than a whole assembled army; without this love we are weakness itself. It is then a great blindness of mind and heart to love the creature whom we cannot love strongly without an extreme weakness, and not to love the Creator Whom we cannot love strongly without being delivered from all our weaknesses. The love of the creature is insipid, wearisome, and ruinous; it reduces, beats down, weakens; it yields to all, and it spreads corruption everywhere. The love of God is strong, and it strengthens; without it I fall even to the dust of the ground and unto the deepest abysses of hell; with it I raise myself, and I take my flight even to Heaven. Choose, my soul! thou feelest thy weaknesses, of which thou hast but too grievous an experience; hasten to the Source of true strength; thou wilt surely find it in the love of thy God.

FIFTH DAY.

Fortis est ut mors dilectio. (Cant. viii.)

Love is strong as death, says the spouse. Its empire is even more wide, because death only carries on its victories upon the earth, and love triumphs over the earth and the Heavens. Shut up in the narrow limits of the heart of man, it spreads everywhere its conquests, even to the Heart of God, of Which it makes itself the master; it overthrows the cedars of Lebanon by humbling the proud; it breaks the hardest rocks by converting the greatest sinners; it divides the flames of fire, it quenches those of concupiscence, and it puts out those of hell. There is no sin that it does not blot out, no sinner that it does not reconcile, no penitent that it does not support, no just man that it does not consecrate, no combatant that it does not crown. It is so strong, that there is no darkness it does not chase away, no vengeance it does not turn aside, no graces it does not draw from Heaven. It is able to shut up hell and to open paradise, for itself and for others: it holds even the key of the Heart of God; it enters There, and it helps others to enter. When shall I love strongly enough, O my God, to obtain all these great and good things?

SIXTH DAY.

Fortis est ut mors dilectio.

I should not fear death now, O my God; nay, it would be the object of all my desires, if I had but always loved Thee as strongly as I am able, and as I ought, because love is stronger than death. But, alas! this miserable world has a thousand times come between to weaken my love, and to carry away a part of my heart; strengthening its array with that which I stole from the most essential of my duties: happy still, if after having been so long without loving Thee, I was courageous enough to replace, by a strong and constant love, the frightful void of my early life! It is my purpose, it is my desire, O my God, and I am resolved to execute it, whatever it may cost my slothfulness and self-love. Yes, Lord,

I wish to love Thee strongly, and without weakness; solely and without division, continually and without loosening my grasp. See, Celestial Spouse, the resolutions I here take in Thy presence; receive them, be their guardian and depository; strengthen me to make them efficacious; engrave them in my heart, lest I forget them; deposit them in Thine, lest they be lost by my weakness, like those which my heart has formed so often, and which have only served to render me more criminal in Thine eyes.

SEVENTH DAY.

Fortis est ut mors dilectio.

In what consists true strength? It is to suffer and to love, without fearing the impressions and consequences of suffering, though it were to extend even to death. To love without suffering or being willing to suffer, is a real weakness which merits nothing: to suffer without loving, is to suffer uselessly, and like a reprobate: but to love and suffer together, is the quality of the strong, and of the lovers of Jesus Christ. I am much deceived, O my God, when from the issue of some passing movements of tenderness (perhaps all from natural temperament), I have said to myself that I loved Thee with all my heart! Alas! I own that I was then in a delusion; and my listlessness in fighting and suffering for Thy love, when the occasion has presented itself, has but too truly charged my love with weakness: I know it, Thou hast opened my eyes; but I must now see how to make amends for it.

Seventeenth Week.

HIGH-SPIRITED LOVE.

Strong love and spirited love are very nearly the same thing, and resemble each other in most of their features: it seems, notwithstanding, that by "strength" we mean the turn of mind of a man ready to undertake and to endure all for God, and that "spirit" designates the courageous Christian as actually engaged with his enemies, or who has just obtained over them a complete victory. The one marks the virtue in its substance, the other in its exercise. Strength is used indifferently of the soul and the body; noble spirit is the portion and attribute of the soul alone, and consequently love alone can set it in motion. I mean the love of God, which is the soul of true generosity.

A noble-spirited Christian encounters all dangers, because he loves: his courage increases in the same measure as his difficulties increase and his enemies multiply. Far from fleeing them, he provokes them when it is necessary; he pursues them, he engages them, he overcomes them, and he attributes his victory to God Alone. He does not allow himself either to be elated by ambition, or overcome by grief, or cajoled by caresses, or frightened by threats; he counts for nothing his goods, his body, his blood, his life, and he seeks death with pleasure, when the God Whom he loves so commands. Such is the idea of noble-spirited love. The matchless bride of the Canticles had, with a generous spirit, sacrificed to His love all the outward marks of her beauty, which she had exposed to the burning rays of the sun: nevertheless, the children of her mother must needs still provide new trials of her love by fighting against her: filii matris meæ pugnaverunt contra me. (Cant. i.) And because she had the spirit to bear up under all their insults, they afterwards did her justice by confiding to her the keeping of their vineyard. It is thus, says a Saint, that she knew how to draw glory and profit from what her courageous love had made her endure: in tantum se profecisse ex eis quæ passa est, gloriatur. (D. Bern. hic.) Thus the Spouse, who calls her to receive her crown, induces her to pass over the highest mountains of Amana, Shenir, and Hermon, and to disengage herself by a generous spirit from the dens of the lions and the leopards: Veni de Libano, veni, coronaberis de capite Amana, de vertice Sanir et Hermon, de cubilibus leonum, de montibus pardorum. (Cant. iv.) These mountains mark the great actions she ought to undertake for God; and these lions and leopards are the types of the temptations of the devil, who, like unto a roaring lion, seeketh whom he may devour (1 Peter i. 8), and the bride must, with a high spirit, overcome all, if she wishes to merit the crown.

AFFECTIONS.

FIRST DAY.

Filii matris meæ pugnaverunt contra me. (Cant. i.) My mother's children were angry with me. It is Thy bride, Lord, who holds this language; and I could well hold it with her, since I have had enemies at home as well as strangers, who have attacked me as she was attacked: but she has been generous, and I have been slothful, though I had the same helps, and the same rewards were held out to me. The divine love which burnt in her heart, has given her courage to vanquish her enemies; and my listlessness has a thousand times shamefully cast me down under their feet. Her enemies have praised her, after having seen her strength and high spirit, and have entrusted to her what they held most precious; and mine have despised my weakness, and have stripped me of what I had most costly. They have not trusted me as a keeper, since I have not kept my vineyard, which is my own heart. The devil, the world, pleasure, ambition, idleness, self-love, my flesh, and all my passions, are the enemies which have fought against me. Alas! where are my victories? Lord, if I had loved Thee with a generous spirit, it had been enough to enable me to fight, to conquer, and be crowned. If I had opposed love alone to all the enemies who conspired against my innocence, I should have kept it, and they would have been cast to the ground. Inflame me with this love, O my God, and I shall be victorious.

SECOND DAY.

Filii matris meæ pugnaverunt contra me.

Thou hast loved me, Lord, and Thy generous love has omitted nothing to give me proof of it. Thy brothers, Thy own children, have fought against, and have persecuted Thee even to take away Thy life, and Thou hast extended the largeness of Thy love, even to die for those who caused Thee to die. I could not be ignorant of it; nevertheless I have joined myself with Thy rebellious children to do Thee fresh outrages. What wilt Thou that I do, O my Saviour, to repair so many disorders? Shall I live in the midst of the attacks of my enemies? So be it; but give me courage enough not to yield. Shall I give Thee all the blood in my veins? I owe it Thee, and it but ill repays Thee that which Thou hast given me. Shall I give Thee all the blood of my heart by the tears of my eyes? Fain would I do so, but it is for Thee to make them flow and roll down my cheeks, and I cannot shed them abundantly enough to make amends for all my slothfulnesses; happy still in this, that Thou dost content Thyself with the little I can give Thee, and that Thou dost ask nothing from my heart, but that I love Thee with a generous spirit unto death.

THIRD DAY.

Filii matris meæ pugnaverunt contra me.

If I love my God, and I love Him with a noble-spirited love, all my enemies will fight against me in vain; I shall never fear them, and the whole world cannot harm me. Charity cannot be offended, because she takes offence at nothing. Enemies, enviers, slanderers, persecutors, I defy you; if I love, I shall triumph over your attacks. Ye can take away my goods; but if my love has a generous spirit I shall be always rich enough, and ye cannot take away my love, which alone makes all my riches and treasures. Ye may blacken my reputation; but as I hold you cheaply quit of all homage of praise and applause, I, with all my heart, give you a free leave to blame and to defame. Happily for me, ye cannot blacken me before my God, and His esteem alone makes amends to me, and rewards me, for all your contempt. Ye can persecute my body, but there I will even help you on by my penances; the sooner it shall perish, the sooner shall I be delivered from this domestic enemy, which is a burden to me. What harm, then, can ye do me? If I am resolved to suffer all, and if I think I deserve all the outrages ye can do me, ye will only give more loftiness of spirit to my love, more brilliancy to my crown.

FOURTH DAY.

Filii matris meæ pugnaverunt contra me.

A noble spirit is the true character of the love of

God; a slothful love, which warreth not, is no love at all. Some people think they have done all, and have won a noble-spirited love, when they begin to feel some movements of tenderness which carries them towards God; but if they advance ever so little, and meet with enemies in their road, they soon perceive their error. The hidden paths of Divine love are not unfolded, and do not disclose themselves except by the light of the arrows of the Lord. In proportion as a man walks therein without allowing himself in any sloth, love gains new strength and new loftiness of spirit: frequent combats support it instead of weakening it. It is thus, my God, that I believed I loved Thee, whilst I was all sloth. Now I perceive but too well the difference between my love and a generous love. I see that the path lengthens before me in proportion as I come nearer, and that I must begin to love as if I had never done it: but I am resolved, whatever happens to me, never to be discouraged.

FIFTH DAY.

Veni de Libano, veni; coronaberis de capite Amana . . . de cubilibus leonum, de montibus pardorum. (Cant. iv.)

Come from Lebanon, my spouse, and thou shalt be crowned; pass the highest mountains, get fairly away from the dens of the lions and the leopards, says the Spouse. Not to have the will to do any thing great for God, to refuse to fight unto death, is not to love Him. To be cast down at the least disappointment, is a temptation which overthrows only the slothful. He does not love who feels disposed to renounce all the honour of the victory, if he can be released from the fatigue of the combat. Softness is a monster in a soldier of Jesus Christ. The height of the mountains ought not to frighten him; the fury of the lions and leopards ought not to make him quake, for he has the help of the Grace and Strength of Jesus Christ, Who fights in him, and he has before his eyes the crown which is promised him. Fight with a noble spirit, O my soul! if thou wouldest be crowned; keep hold of thine arms until death: without stoutly making and keeping to this resolution, do not flatter thyself that thou lovest God, or art beloved of Him.

SIXTH DAY.

De cubilibus leonum, &c.

God calls me to be crowned, my vocation is then plain, and I cannot doubt of it. The free love of God is then nothing else but the free choice of God; God has gratuitously chosen me, and I have voluntarily chosen Him; this twofold choice is the proof of His goodness, and forms all my happiness and glory. To follow out this twofold choice as I ought, I should make another, which proceeds from the generous spirit of my love: it is to ascend the highest mountains, as He commands me; that is to say, to undertake generously for His love all that He will put into my heart, however great and difficult; this is to beat down lions and leopards: in other words, to combat and to vanquish all temptations, without ever submitting to the Evil one: in a word, I ought to choose, without hesitation, rather to die a thousand times for love of Him than live to offend Him. The choice is made, Lord; give me courage to keep it unto death.

SEVENTH DAY.

De cubilibus leonum, &c.

To love God as long as we feel the delights of this love, does not cost much to the heart, because it is borne along with pleasure: but to love Him in conflicts, in dryness, in abandonments, in afflictions, and in sufferings, as well as in peace and in sensible delights; to love Him when pleasure tempts us, when the world persecutes us, when our body is in pain, when our mind is overpowered, and our very heart is mute to us; there is the true character of a noble-spirited love. I look forward, O my God, to many combats and sacrifices, which it will cost me to acquire this noble spirit: but alas! how much has it been to my cost to love the world against my duty! What violence have I done to my freedom, to my body, to my mind, and my heart! what cowardly compliance, what constraint, what slaveries, and what criminal victories have I not obtained over myself in order to offend Thee! Fatal and ruinous spiritedness, which now costs me so many tears! Ah! is it not right that it should cost me at least as much to love Thee? Make amends, O my soul! repair this criminal high spirit by an innocent loftiness of spirit; fight, suffer, undertake all for the love of thy God; He deserves it of thee, and the world did not deserve it.

Recapitulation of the Seventeen preceding Weeks.

PRAYER TO OBTAIN THE LOVE OF GOD IN THE PURIFICATIVE LIFE.

Holy love, adorable source of all purity, fire celestial that dwellest in the Heart of my God, take entire possession of mine, and make Thyself its absolute master. Kindle there the flames which are wholly heavenly, to smother those which are opposed to true charity; burn there all the bonds and unholy ties which have rendered it unworthy of loving Thee;

consume there by Thy Divine heat, the least impurities and the least filth which displeases Thine eyes; purify it from the most secret defilements that self-love conceals from its knowledge; and re-establish there all the features of Thy image, which I have obscured by my sins. Efface from it even the least traces of earthly pleasures and feelings, which have so often rendered it criminal, and put Thou in their place feelings of love which are worthy of Thee.

Give to this unfeeling heart the sighs of a true penitence, where grief and love are equally expressed (First Week). Make it bring forth sighs and lamentations, which may efface the sins of which it is guilty, and which may draw upon it Thy Graces and Thy Mercies (Second Week). Give it an ardent desire for the sufferings which it has but too much deserved (Third Week). Make it docile to Thy voice, that it may obey Thee in all things, whatever it may cost to its daintiness and self-love (Fourth Week). Make it relish humiliations, contempt, and lowliness, to punish its pride and rebellions (Fifth Week). Penetrate it with a lively gratitude for the infinite favours which it has received from Thy charitable hand, and give it grace never to forget them (Sixth Week). Deny it all consolations which would oppose themselves to its love, and make it love this denial (Seventh Week). Support it against its languor; make it act by Thyself, or act in it, in order that all its actions answer to the feelings of its love (Eighth Week). It has presumed too much on itself, from henceforth it wishes to trust in Thee Alone (Ninth Week). It has but too much neglected its most essential duties, it wishes to fulfil them with all the exactness of which it is capable (Tenth Week). It would have made an infinite progress in this love, if it had always loved (Eleventh Week); if it had sought Thee Alone in all things (Twelfth Week); if it had been faithful to follow the attraction with which Thou dost favour it (Thirteenth Week); and if it had always loved sincerely, without a mixture of vanity, of complaisance, and hypocrisy (Fourteenth Week). Creatures have demanded its tenderness, Thou hast demanded it also: it has granted it to them, and it has refused it to Thee (Fifteenth Week). Uphold my weakness, O my God! Give me that strong love which endures all, resists all, and never yields (Sixteenth Week). Inflame my heart with that noble-spirited love which is alarmed at nothing, and which undertakes all for Thy glory and for my salvation (Seventeenth Week).

AFFECTIONS

FOR THE

ILLUMINATIVE LIFE.

Eighteenth Week.

LOVE OF THE INTELLECT.

ALTHOUGH Divine love is ordinarily not so much a function of the intellect as of the heart, the former must, nevertheless, concur in it, and love GOD after its own manner. The love of the intellect is comprehended in the precept by which we are commanded to love GOD with all our soul, because the intellect is a faculty of the soul, and it can concur in it in two ways: by meditating and by humbling itself. It meditates upon the greatness of GOD, it enters into the detail of all His acts of goodness, and it presents them to the heart to make it feel them; it communicates to the heart all the illuminations it receives from GOD, and the heart returns them more pure and more ardent, because they have passed through the fire of love: there is between these two powers a mutual exchange of illuminations and of affections, when they act in concert, from which results a perfect knowledge and love of GOD. It is the mind which weighs merit; by it and by its lights are things justly appreciated, and affections formed in the heart:

and this love of appreciation, esteem, and preference, is of no less value than that of tenderness, and is much less subject to the illusions of self-love.

In the second place, it acquiesces humbly in the orders of God; it submits to Him all its aims, its illuminations, and its knowledge: in concert with the heart, it makes of them a noble sacrifice, and this sacrifice is true love.

Scarcely has the spouse begun to speak the language of Divine Love, when she asks for light to know Him well Whom Alone she ought to love; and it is thus that she enters into the illuminative life. "Tell me," she says, "O Thou Whom my soul loveth, where Thou feedest, where Thou makest Thy flock to rest at noon?" Indica mihi quem diligit anima mea, ubi pascas, ubi cubes in meridie. (Cant. i.) She asks to be enlightened, and conducted to the noonday rest, when the rays of the sun are both brightest and most ardent, lest, she adds, "I turn aside by the flocks of Thy companions:" Ne vagari incipiam post greges sodalium tuorum. (Ibid.) Without this she would have wandered, and fallen into the snare of false love: for love cannot be ardent if it is not enlightened; and the heart cannot love God unless the mind serves it for a guiding-light.

AFFECTIONS.

FIRST DAY.

Indica mihi quem diligit anima mea, ubi pascas, ubi cubes in meridie. (Cant. i.)

Tell me, O Thou Whom my soul loveth, where Thou feedest, where Thou makest Thy flock to rest at noon? My heart cannot follow Thee, if Thou dost not enlighten my mind to teach it where Thou art. All is wanting to the one when Thou art not present to the other; the one is in dryness and insensibility when the other is in ignorance, darkness, and dissipation, as it often is. I cannot love Thee unless my mind approaches Thee as well as my heart. Enlighten the one, O Divine Sun, that the other may be inflamed; dispel the darkness of my mind; fix its lightness; instruct its ignorance; give it light, which shall impart at once unction and fire; guide it safely towards those happy and fertile pastures that Thou providest for Thy most beloved sheep: then dart Thou upon my heart the bright and burning rays of the mid-day sun; that walking amid light and fire, I may at length find the place of Thy rest and of mine, and may never cease to know and to love Thee.

SECOND DAY.

Indica mihi quem diligit anima mea, &c.

Everlasting pastures, heavenly repose, burning and brilliant Sun! my mind and my heart sigh after Thee: my mind is ambitious of knowing Thee only, that my heart may love and possess Thee. Thou hast taught me, O celestial Spouse, that eternal life consists in knowing Thee (John xvii.), and that in Thy light shall we see light. (Psalm xxxvi.) How great, then, is that happiness which Thou designest for my mind, and what ought it not to do to become worthy of it! It shall love Thee in its own manner, by sacrificing to Thee its lights, its headstrong fancies, its pride, its false prejudices, and its vain curiosity. It shall have but one chief occupation, to meditate day and night upon Thy eternal Truths; it shall have but one study, to know and to please Thee; it shall aspire to one science alone, that of the Saints; it shall have but one Object present to it, That Which it is designed to know and to love in time and in eternity.

THIRD DAY.

Indica mihi quem diligit anima mea, &c.

How full is my mind of darkness and ignorance, and how barren is it, when it is called upon to provide my heart with pasture and with fuel to nourish its affections and to maintain its fires! Speak to it then Thyself, O Divine Shepherd, feed it with Thy eternal Truths, lest it seek strange pastors, who would give it no nourishment but falsehood and error. Do Thou bring it into the abundant pastures of Thy Divine Word. This Word is light itself. This Word, "is it not like as a fire?" said the Prophet. (Jer. xxiii. 29.) Give my mind docility to obey it, and my heart fervency to love it. Adorable Sun, cried St. Bernard, I cannot walk without Thee; enlighten my steps, and furnish this barren and ignorant mind with thoughts worthy of Thee. Adorable fulness of light and heat, be Thou the true Noon-day of my soul; exterminate its darkness, disperse its clouds; burn, dry up, and consume all its filth and impurities. Divine Sun, rise upon my mind, and never set.

FOURTH DAY.

Indica mihi quem diligit anima mea, &c.

I cannot find Thee, O my God, without seeking Thee; and I cannot seek Thee if Thou dost not help me, and show my mind where Thou art. (D. Aug. Conf.) Thou hast done it already, Lord, and hast given me light enough to know and to love Thee. I have only, then, to consult my mind; for that will tell me, if it reasons in a Christian manner, that there is nothing more perfect and more amiable than Thee; and that I ought to love Thee, because Thou hast first loved me. (1 John iv. 19.) If my mind allows itself to be convinced of this truth, my love will soon enlighten my reason, and will discover to it in Thee fresh beauties and new charms, worthy of all the tenderness of my heart. My natural reason, enlightened and elevated by this superior and supernatural love, will take a new flight. All that is gross and earthly in it shall perish, says St. Augustine; then shall it be transformed into affection: my mind will be happily blended with my heart, my knowledge with my love; they will be lighted by the same light, and burn with the same fire; I shall love that I may know, and know that I may love better. (Aug. Conf.) Enlighten me, then, O Heavenly Spouse! maintain between my mind and heart a holy exchange of light and love, that I may know and love Thee perfectly.

FIFTH DAY.

Ne vagari incipiam post greges sodalium tuorum. (Cant. i.)

Show me the place of Thy rest, lest I turn aside, says the bride. Alas! how far have I already gone astray in seeking Thee, O Divine Shepherd! But how should my mind have done otherwise than stray, for it does itself no violence in order to fix its attention on That Which should be ever present with it? and how should it not wander when it follows the footsteps of the strange flocks of the world and of its vanities, and neglects to learn where the true Pastor of the soul rests with His faithful sheep? How should it find pleasure in the pastures of prayer, of Thy Divine Word, and of Thy Adorable Presence, when it does not strive against its wanderings? How could it, with the bride, rest at noon near its Shepherd, that is, know and love Him truly, and never depart from Him, when it seeks its rest in creatures, and thus runs after false shepherds, who lead it to destruction? This day, O my God, it acknowledges Thee Alone for its true Shepherd. It is lost when it departs from Thee, it strays when it loses sight of Thee. Thou art its Sun; it is in darkness when it sees Thee no more. Thou art its Nourishment; it sinks with weakness when it is no longer with Thee. Thou art its Fire, and its Heat; it becomes all ice when Thou art absent. Thou art its Life; it languishes and dies as soon as it withdraws itself from Thy Light and Thy Love.

SIXTH DAY.

Ne vagari incipiam post greges, &c.

It is impossible, O Divine Shepherd, that I should do otherwise than stray in seeking Thee, unless I make the knowledge and love of Thee my great object. I cannot go to Thee or love Thee without a heart, neither can I do so without a mind, and a docile, submissive, and earnest mind. My heart shall impart to my mind its tenderness, its affections, and its fervour, and it shall give unction to its light, which, without this unction, would produce only dryness, pride, and vanity: but the heart also will need the mind to direct its love. As it is liable to be deluded, and to fall into the snares of self-love, my mind shall correct the dangerous declensions to which it is subject, shall purify this very self-love, shall exalt it, and give it, by its light, a fitting object, even melting and blending it with the love of God. If my heart asks of my mind, enlightened by grace, what it is truly to love ourselves, it will answer, that it is to love our good, and fear our ill; to seek our true happiness, pleasure, exaltation, and profit. Let my mind give a right object to all its movements; then, without ceasing to love myself, I shall love God with my whole heart.

SEVENTH DAY.

Ne vagari incipiam post greges, &c.

How long, Lord, will my wandering and unsettled

mind be occupied with an endless number of strange objects, which hinder me from loving Thee, if my mind does not bend itself to put an end to these continual strayings and wanderings? If some man made me frequent protestations of friendship, service, and affection, and yet acknowledged, when questioned, that neither did his mind dwell on me, nor did he seek my presence when it might easily be obtained, I should justly treat him as a false friend: for neither to think of those we love, nor to be present with them, is a monstrous and strange sort of affection, or is, in truth, indifference. How then, O Divine Spouse, can I protest to Thee that I love Thee, when I think less of Thee, and have Thee less before me than the creature and the world? I must have loved them better than Thee. What blindness and what injustice! Help me, LORD, to amend this; fix for ever the lightness of my mind, check the ever-craving versatility, which is its unhappy characteristic; but cure also my faint-heartedness, which assists in the evil; give me a love for calm meditation, that it may lead me to the love of Thee.

Nineteenth Week.

LOVE OF THE HEART.

THERE is nothing upon the earth more vast, more noble, more sublime, more worthy of GOD, or more resembling GOD, than the heart of man, says a devout writer. (Medit. ap. S. Aug. c. vii.) It is the marriage-bed of the Bridegroom of souls, the object of the tenderness of the GOD of Love, the most magnificent throne of the Incomparable Sovereign, and the most august sanctuary of the Holy of Holies. Neither is there any thing greater, more precious, and more noble than Divine love; it is above the whole law, and contains it all; it surpasses all virtues, and is itself alone all virtues; it converts sinners, supports penitents, perfects saints, consecrates virgins; it makes martyrs, crowns the blessed, and is the delight of just men, of angels, and of God Himself.

The admirable affinity that is found between the heart and love, teaches us plainly that they are destined one for the other, and that as love is made only for the heart, so the heart is made only for love, and for the love of God. Therefore, when its love begins to fail, it languishes, desponds, and dies, because love is its nourishment, its strength, and its life: vita cordis amor est. (De subst. dilect. ap. S. Aug. c. vi.)

It is not surprising that God should demand the love of our heart, for He has first given us His. This is admirably expressed in the holy Canticles, when He says Himself: "Thou hast wounded My Heart, My sister, My spouse, Thou hast wounded My Heart:" vulnerasti cor meum, soror mea, sponsa, vulnerasti cor meum. (Cant. iv.) Can an invulnerable God be wounded, wounded to the heart, wounded by His own creature? How astonishing is the power of love? The Hebrew word denotes abstulisti, Thou hast ravished My Heart, Thou hast taken it: as if the faithful had power, after wounding the Heart of God, to remove it into their own bosom. They can do so, and this privilege is given by God Himself: but they must consider that it is impossible either to wound the heart of God, or to draw it to themselves, unless their own be wounded by the chosen arrow of Divine love.

The bride's heart was so filled with this love that sleep was not able to interrupt the feeling. "I sleep," she says, "but my heart waketh:" ego dormio, et cor meum vigilat. (Cant. v.) But how can the sleep of the body accord with the vigilance of the heart? Sleep is an image of death; all the organs are suspended, the mind cannot think, the heart can neither love nor feel; she must have spoken, say the holy Fathers, either of the delightful and sublime sleep of contemplation, during which the heart alone wakes, speaks, and feels, whilst the rest is inactive and motionless; or the feelings of love with which the bride was imbued had made so strong an impression upon her heart and imagination, that, from habit and inclination, during all the sleep of the night she dreamt only of that charming and Divine Object which occupied her heart every moment of the day.

AFFECTIONS.

FIRST DAY.

Vulnerasti cor meum, soror mea, sponsa, vulnerasti cor meum. (Cant. iv.)

"Thou hast wounded My Heart, My sister, My spouse, thou hast wounded My Heart," says the Bridegroom. It is so, my God, I have wounded Thy Heart, for Thou hast taken my likeness after giving me Thine; but the wound must have been very deep, for it caused Thee to shed all Thy Blood, and the same love which wounded Thee led Thee also to die for me. This wound is glorious to Thee, for it shows how far the wondrous love of the Heart of God can go; it is profitable to me, for it is the source of my happiness. Good were it for me, if, like the bride, I might make another and a sinless wound in Thy Heart by my love, and if my heart, penetrated with true tenderness, might also pierce and penetrate Thine in my favour! But, alas! this guilty heart of mine has made innumerable other grievous wounds in Thine by its ingratitude and faithlessness. I have pierced Thy Heart, not by my love, but by my hardness; I wounded it in a far more cruel and painful manner when mine criminally suffered itself to be wounded by the love of the creature. O Heavenly Spouse, tear from my heart this shameful and degrading arrow; and pierce it instead with that of Thy Divine love.

SECOND DAY.

Vulnerasti cor meum, &c.

How is it possible, O God of Majesty! that Thy Love has brought Thee down so far as to take a Heart like mine, in order to feel more vividly a tenderness of which I was unworthy, and which Thou wouldest not have felt in all its extent without this Heart of flesh? But how incomprehensible is this miracle of Thy Divine love, for Thou hast taken this Heart only to suffer it to be pierced for the sake of a heart so ungrateful as mine! The wound is but too evident; for, far from being ashamed and keeping it secret, Thou sufferedst it to be pierced upon the Cross, in the sight of the whole world, that none might be ignorant of the excess of Thy tenderness, and that Thou mightest be enabled to say to each of our souls, in the natural as well as in the mystic sense, "Thou hast wounded My Heart, My sister, My spouse," the spear pierced Thy Heart; and from thence came forth water to wash me, and Blood to complete my redemption. Even in Heaven Thou bearest yet this most glorious Wound. The scar of Thy Heart will never close; through a whole Eternity Thou wilt glory in this loving Wound, the triumphant proof of Thy tenderness. Adorable Heart of my God, wound mine to render it conformable to Thine; wound it so deeply by Thy love, that it may be wholly laid open, and never healed. Wound it with the same steel which pierced Thine, that blood may flow if Thou requirest it of my love; or wound it with a burning wound, that salutary water may flow forth, and tears of love and tenderness from my eyes.

THIRD DAY.

Vulnerasti cor meum, &c.

Were I blind enough to allow my heart to be wounded by the love of a creature, I might be repaid by indifference: but if I love my God, He will infallibly reply to my love; and if I give Him my heart, He will assuredly give me His. An enemy may wound me without being himself wounded: but my heart cannot be wounded by Divine love without its wound being shared by the Heart of my God. It must be then much better to love Him than the creature. What gain for me that my heart cannot be wounded without wounding His invulnerable Heart, and that this most glorious wound may be the work of my love! But before my heart can feel this wound which gives strength, health, and life, I must purify it from all that opposes my love. Let us enter into this heart, we shall find more to do there than we think; let us remove all the self-love which prevents us from knowing it and turning it to God; then shall we see all the duplicity which disguises, the attachments which corrupt it. We shall see it now overcome by sloth, now puffed up with pride, now distracted by visible objects. These things hinder it from feeling the health-giving and quickening wound of Divine love. Help me, Lord, to purify it; purify it Thyself, or give me another heart worthy of Thine. It cannot be worthy, if it be not the heart of a child to Thee, to my neighbour the heart of a mother, to the devil that of an enemy, and to myself that of an inexorable judge.

FOURTH DAY.

Vulnerasti cor meum, &c.

The Divine Spouse suffers His Heart to be wounded only that that of His bride may be pierced and wounded by the same arrow, which is love. He is, indeed, far more jealous of the heart than of the mind; He sometimes permits the mind to be employed upon the knowledge of His creatures; but He forbids the heart to love them, lest this love be an injury to Himself. Why has God put such narrow limits to our heart, whilst He gives a greater liberty to our mind? The heart is vast and limited at once. God has given it so vast an extent, that the whole world is not sufficient for it, and it cannot be filled but by an infinite object: yet He restrains it to the single Object which it ought to love. I perceive, Lord, that Thou dealest thus because knowledge does not always poison the mind, but, on the contrary, a moderate consideration of visible things often leads it to a better knowledge of Thee. But I have but too grievous experience, that the love of the creature often brings corruption into the heart; it distracts it, unsettles it, makes it earthly, divides it, softens it, wounds it, and it should never be wounded but by Thy Divine love.

FIFTH DAY.

Ego dormio, et cor meum vigilat. (Cant. v.)

"I sleep," says the bride, "but my heart waketh." In a soul that aspires to perfection, the mind must yield to the heart, curiosity to love, light to flame, speculation to feeling. This last is far more exquisite, more sublime, more lively and more sweet. It is, then, humiliating for me, O my God, that my heart has been so long buried in the sleep of indifference, and that I have in truth not yielded enough to my reason because I desired to yield too much. This heart demanded all of me, and I might have given it all by loving Thee. My reason was too desirous of knowing Thee, and failed in its attempt: my heart was not wakeful enough to Thy love. Blind heart! thou dost not understand thy true interests. It is no longer time to slumber over thy most essential duty, which is love; on the contrary, it is time to awaken from thy drowsiness. Love thy God, direct towards Him all the tenderness of which thou art capable; so shalt thou procure the greatest of all goods, shalt feel the purest of all pleasures, shalt labour with less difficulty, and prosper with greater success. My heart shall love Thee, then, O my God! it shall watch over all my steps to make them obedient to Thy love.

SIXTH DAY.

Ego dormio, et cor meum vigilat.

Why does my mind, which is but blindness, endeavour, with vain curiosity, to know more than is permitted? and why does it not call the heart to the aid of its weakness? The more efforts it makes alone, the less will it succeed. It is vain for it to watch and to labour, it will only reap from its wrongful toils ignorance, error, dryness, and vanity. Thy love, O my God, said St. Augustine, has taught me a far surer means, and a far shorter path to go to Thee. I will arouse my heart from its heavy sleep, I will make it act; its feelings of love shall bring forth fire and light at once; I will no longer listen to my intellect, except when it follows the attraction, the impression, and the feeling of my love. I am sure that it will have light, when my heart loves Thee as much as it can and as it ought. It will, moreover, possess Thee, if it loves Thee. To love and to possess Thee is far better than simply to know Thee, and for that shall my heart henceforward watch.

SEVENTH DAY.

Ego dormio, et cor meum vigilat.

When the heart has once given itself unreservedly to God, when it has acquired true love, and become habituated to it, it can no longer sleep to any of its duties, because love is a fire which arouses it unceasingly. It then acts easily, and by inclination; and this happy inclination leads it only toward the Heart of God, the Centre of its desires, the only Object of its love. It is a propitious descent, which assists its progress unmarked; a pleasing torrent, which carries it away unobserved. It is never surprised, because it is always vigilant. Thus all that it thinks, desires, and does, bears the character and impression of its love. Like the bride, the sleep of night hardly causes any interruption. The imagination, impressed with the same feelings that occupied the heart during the day, often represents pleasing images of them; so that it may be said, I sleep, but my heart waketh. Ah! if my heart had acquired this habit of love, it would be occupied only with God, and this occupation would be its delight. It would be on its guard against the sudden assaults of the devil. My mind would be calm; my imagination ever chaste and tranquil; I should be delivered from innumerable extravagant thoughts, injurious illusions, and dangerous phantoms which humble me, and every moment of my life would be devoted to God.

Twentieth Week.

ATTENTIVE LOVE.

As God is extremely attentive to hear us, to observe us, and to do us good, because He loves us, He requires also extreme attention from those who profess to love Him. Far more progress may indeed be made in the love of God by the ears than by the eyes, and it is much easier to hear than to know Him. When the risen Saviour appeared to Magdalene, the eyes of her who loved Him knew Him not. But when He had opened His Lips to call her by her name, "Mary," that single word had so much power, that it passed instantly from the ears of her body to those of her heart. Her eyes, assisted by the heart, knew Him, and she worshipped Him. Thou desirest to see God, says St. Bernard; thou art presumptuous; His brightness is immense; He dwells in inaccessible light; He has put His tabernacle in the sun, and thine eye is too small and too weak. (D. Bern. in Cant.) Wait to see Him openly, till this eye be strengthened by the light of glory; be contented to see Him now through the dimness of Faith; but thou mayest hear Him if thou art attentive, and thou wilt be attentive to His Voice if thou lovest Him.

As this Voice is spiritual, secret, and delicate, it requires also a loving and collected attention: Secretum consilium, says St. Augustine, secretum quærit auditum. (Epist. cvii.) At the least alien movement, at the smallest sound that created objects make in the heart, this Heavenly voice is silent. To hear it perfectly, we must retire from the tumult of the world. As solitude opens the ears of the heart, so company closes them to God to open them to the creature; and we cannot be attentive to both at the same time.

At the very time when the Spouse charged the daughters of Jerusalem not to awaken His bride, this voice beloved of her heart, though gentle and addressed to others, awoke her, and opened immediately her ears, her eyes, and her heart. "I hear," says she, "the Voice of my Beloved:" Vox dilecti. (Cant. ii.) Her attention must have been extraordinary, since sleep could not divert it.

But this attentive love was immediately rewarded by a visit from her Beloved, in which He gave Himself the trouble to instruct her with admirable care and tenderness, which induced her to say: "My Beloved spake unto me:" En dilectus meus loquitur mihi (Cant. ii.); to teach us that the Celestial Spouse takes pleasure in speaking and in making secret visits to composed and attentive souls alone.

AFFECTIONS.

FIRST DAY.

Vox dilecti. (Cant. ii.)

I hear the Voice of my Beloved! says the bride. The soul that professes to love the Lord is not permitted to be heedless, or to sleep when He speaks, and to be inattentive to the sacred impulses of this love, which are the Voice of the Heavenly Bridegroom. As heedlessness is a proof of indifference and coldness, continual attention is an evident proof of esteem and of love. If I had been attentive to the first inspirations with which God favoured me, He would have spoken much more frequently to my heart: but the continual carelessness in which I have lived, has rendered me unworthy of hearing His Divine language, and has prevented me from speaking to Him; to-day God shows me what He desires of me; how do I know that to-morrow He will have the same goodness? how do I know that a moment's delay will not draw down upon me the utmost evils? how do I know that this sacred fire, which He begins to light in my heart, will not be extinguished, to be rekindled no more? how do I know that this Voice of tenderness will not be turned into a Voice of thunder, if I am not attentive to it? Henceforth, LORD, I will hearken to Thee; speak to my heart, and give it all the docility which it requires to hear Thee with all the attention that Thou deservest.

SECOND DAY.

Vox dilecti.

Sacred Love calls thee, O my soul! the Voice of the Bridegroom is heard by the ears of thy heart. He seeks thee, solicits, urges thee; answer and say like the bride: "Ah! I hear the Voice of my Beloved;" He speaks to my heart, He comes to me. Speak, Celestial Spouse; make me hear this sweet Voice, the Voice of Love Itself, which speaks to me only to instruct me, and to inflame me with a holy fire. Let me be attentive to this Divine language; let me not lose one word of it, for that would be to lose an inestimable treasure, which, perhaps, I might never recover. If I am attentive, this Divine Voice will be repeated, and will become more intelligible and more frequent. Every time that my GOD speaks to me, He humbles Himself to take the first steps to demand my heart: I should be most ungrateful if I did not reply, and at least make the second.

THIRD DAY.

Vox dilecti.

An attentive heart, and a heart imbued with love, are the same. True love is not easily compatible with forgetfulness of the words of the beloved object, especially when sincere esteem is joined to love; on the contrary, they are most carefully collected, examined, delighted in, and kept unforgotten for ever. When shall I love Thee perfectly, O Divine Spouse? When my mind thinks more of Thee than of all other things; when it strives to the utmost never to lose Thy adorable Presence; when all creatures together are unable to divert its attention; when I act always as under Thy Eyes, and seek them ardently; when I love Thy Divine Word, whether written, spoken, or inspired, more than all the treasures of the earth; when I impose eternal silence on all creatures, that Thou Alone mayest speak to my heart. When will this be, O my God? Grant me this Grace from this moment.

FOURTH DAY.

Vox dilecti.

We willingly lend the ear of our heart, and have pleasure in listening, when that which we love, and love sincerely, is spoken of. The soul which truly loves God, says St. Bernard, withdraws and enters into itself without unwillingness and constraint. When it hears God speak, or when any speak of God, it banishes all other thoughts, to give its whole attention to this Divine language, because it finds it most pleasing of all things. The Divine Word suspends all the operations of the soul, transports it, carries it away pleasurably. At the Voice of God alone, at His first Word, the whole heart is opened to make room for Him. Nothing is heard with more joy, read with more pleasure, sought for more earnestly, studied with more application, kept more faithfully, entertained with more satisfaction, enjoyed with greater delight; nothing, in short, brings forth more abundant fruits. After this can I dare flatter myself that I love God? If I examine my mind and my heart with regard to their attention to His Voice, alas! my continual weaknesses and wanderings tell me but too plainly that I have not yet loved Him.

FIFTH DAY.

En dilectus meus loquitur mihi. (Cant. ii.)

My Beloved speaks unto me, says the bride, behold Him. She saw Him, then, at the same time that she heard Him. Indeed, she had listened with so much attention, that she well deserved that He should show Himself to her soul. To speak to God, to hear God, to see God, as far as a creature is capable of doing so in this life, are the fruits and the rewards of attentive love. How often wouldest Thou have spoken to my soul, O Heavenly Spouse! how much darkness wouldest Thou have dispelled in me, by the light of Thy Divine Inspirations, if I had not opposed almost invincible obstacles, by my negligence, the wanderings of my heart, and my wilful deafness. I have been but too attentive to the tumultuous language of my passions and of my self-love; but too much have I listened to the seducing voice of the corrupt world, and I have not heard Thine. This has made me lose innumerable affections proceeding from grace and good impulses, and has made me commit numberless faults. Deceitful world! I will hearken no more to thee. Unquiet and turbulent passions, it is vain for you to speak; I will answer you no more. I reserve all the attention of my mind and heart to listen to God Alone; He alone deserves it.

SIXTH DAY.

En dilectus meus loquitur mihi.

The Mind and Heart of God are unceasingly watching over me, as if He had me alone to guide and to love. There is not a single moment of those which compose my life, in which His adorable Mind does not guide me if I am willing to follow Its light and Its impulse, and in which His merciful Heart is not tenderly interested in all that concerns me, and this continual attention proceeds only from His Love. He is always ready to speak when I am willing to hear, and to hear me favourably when I desire to speak to Him. I should be most ungrateful if I did not reply, by my attention, to the attention of the Mind and of the Heart of God. Henceforth, Lord, I will apply myself only to hear Thee; my mind shall think of none but Thee; my heart shall love no other save for Thy sake. I aspire, even without presumption, to think and to love as Thou dost: my mind and heart shall so walk in Thy paths, that I shall form my judgment of each of my actions upon Thine. I will ask myself, or I will ask Thee what Thou thinkest of it, and I will endeavour to think in like manner. I will hate in myself all that Thou hatest, and I will love only what Thou lovest.

SEVENTH DAY.

En dilectus meus loquitur mihi.

The bride was occupied only with her Beloved; He was the Object of all her desires and disquiet; she sought Him alone day and night; her mind was closely applied to Him; her heart fainted when He was absent; her imagination, filled with Him alone, furnished her in sleep with none but pure and pleasant dreams, and she saw every where the image of this Beloved. It is not surprising, then, that at the first word of this Spouse, Whom she loved so ardently, she started from her sleep, and exclaimed: Behold, my Beloved speaks to me. When we think of none but God, and sigh for Him Alone, when we speak to no other, and hunger only for His Divine Word, His Voice strikes the heart as soon as He speaks: if a tender emotion arises in the heart, the affection is immediately formed, and a holy fire is lighted at the first whisper of this Divine Voice; as we have much pleasure in hearing it, we are careful that our attention shall not wander. Why, then, Lord, hast Thou so often spoken to my heart without success, and without its having been attentive to Thy Voice?

Whence proceeds this sinful deafness? From my indifference and my slothfulness. Heal me, LORD; put far from my heart those strange voices which prevent me from hearing Thine; speak Thou Alone, for Thou only deservest to be heard.

Twenty-first Week.

DISINTERESTED LOVE.

SELF-INTEREST is so fair a delusion, and so subtle a poison, that it insinuates itself insensibly into the generality of the friendships which men contract with one another; so that if this interest were separated from those ties which seem indissoluble, they would immediately fall, because they would then have neither support nor motive. It may even be said, that what is called disinterestedness in most men, is in truth most frequently a traffic or a deep game of self-love, which consents to risk something of little value, in order to arrive more surely and skilfully at a more certain benefit.

Self-interest insinuates itself also sometimes into the love of GOD, and destroys it wherever it is found: for it is not to love Him as He deserves, and as He desires to be loved, to do it with views so gross, so base, and so unworthy of Him. As Divine love is unquestionably the greatest of all treasures, and as there is no good thing which it does not contain and procure, it should consequently absorb and destroy in the heart all interested views, and all desire of temporal advantage, of what nature soever.

I know that the disinterestedness of the purest charity is not a loss, and that it may aspire to the eternal blessings promised to it: but the most perfect and sublime motive for its hope should be love; and the assurance of loving God and of being loved by Him throughout eternity, should be the soul and main-spring of all its desires.

The Spouse who regards the heart of His bride as a delicious garden which produces innumerable flowers and fruits, and suffers itself to be stripped of them, because it produces them only for those who gather them, says these remarkable words: Withdraw, O north wind, and come, thou south; blow upon my garden, that the spices thereof may flow out: Surge, aquilo; veni, auster; perfla hortum meum, et fluant aromata ejus. (Cant. iv.) The north wind is dry, it checks every thing by its coldness, it produces and gives nothing: the warm south wind, on the contrary, gives fertility to the earth, and is the symbol of an ardent and disinterested love. It is, properly speaking, the Breath of the Holy Spirit, which produces in the mystic garden of the bride the most exquisite perfumes, that is, the chaste thoughts, the pure feelings, detached from self, which compose disinterested love.

The companions of the bride, who from hearing the language of Divine love, began to speak it, said, that if a man would give all the substance of his house for love, he would utterly contemn it as nothing: Si dederit homo omnem substantiam domûs suæ pro dilectione, quasi nihil despiciet eam. (Cant. viii.) Indeed, the man who has stripped himself of all for the love of God, says St. Gregory, from that time looks on God Alone. This look enlightens him; and when he compares the infinite treasure of love with what it cost him to acquire it, he looks upon what he has left as mire: Postquàm Deum conspexit, in illius visione quidquid possederat nihili pendit. (Greg. hic.)

AFFECTIONS.

FIRST DAY.

Surge, aquilo ; veni, auster ; perfla hortum meum, et fluant aromata ejus. (Cant. iv.)

Withdraw, O north wind, and come, thou south ; blow from every side in my garden, that perfumes may flow out abundantly, says the Spouse. Withdraw, sordid interests, which have but too much dried up and chilled my heart. Withdraw, interests of temporal goods ; love alone is more precious than all the treasures of the earth. Withdraw, interests of false greatness ; we are truly great only when we love Him Who is Greatness itself. Withdraw, interests of pleasure ; that which is solid, pure, and lasting, can be procured by Divine love alone. Withdraw, interests of health ; I think only of that of my soul, and it will be well if my heart loves what it ought to love. Withdraw, interests of reputation ; love alone will make me esteemed by God, and if I have His esteem, I count that of men for nothing. No, Lord, interested views shall never enter into the business of my love. Thou deservest well that I should love Thee for Thyself Alone, and sacrifice to Thee all that I possess; and since I have nothing but by Thee, I should hope for nothing but from Thee.

SECOND DAY.

Surge, aquilo ; veni, auster ; perfla, &c.

Come, O south wind, come alone, O Divine charity, come into the garden of my soul ; kindle in it by Thy breath a holy fire which may inflame me, which may drive away and consume all interested views unworthy of Thee. Melt all the ice of my heart, warm it by that pure and celestial ardour which carries fruitfulness everywhere, that I may produce flowers and fruits at once, that is, works, desires, affections, and virtues. Come Thyself, O Celestial Spouse, into Thy garden, my soul, to gather the lilies that Thy love has planted and cultivated there. May the perfumes flow out unceasingly, and the pleasing odour ascend to Thee, since it comes from Thee. The flowers and fruits belong to Thee, LORD. If I have good feelings, Thou hast formed them; if I breathe sighs, Thou hast originated them, and it is only by the breath of Thy grace that they ascend from my heart to Thine. If I have holy desires, Thou inspirest them; if I have practised any virtues, I owe them to Thy Love. Receive all then, LORD, for all good things that I have come from Thee; henceforth I will have nothing of my own, not even my virtues, since they exist only by Thee; it is enough that I love Thee.

THIRD DAY.

Surge, aquilo; veni, auster; perfla, &c.

Let those mercenary souls depart, who love the consolations of God far more than the God of consolations; who love the gifts better than the Giver; who consent to consecrate their heart to Him, only when they feel pleasure in doing it; who abridge their practices of piety in proportion as God abridges their delights and sensible pleasures. But I perceive, O my God, that I here condemn myself, and that I have almost always loved Thee from interested views, which my self-love hid from my eyes. I am resolved to love Thee henceforth for Thyself Alone, without any mixture of temporal interest. Though the north wind should dry my soul, and should deprive it of all the joys it has loved too well, my heart will not fail to raise up unceasingly to Thy Throne the perfume of its love. I am resolved to be as faithful to Thee in barrenness as in abundance, in affliction as in prosperity, in grief as in joy. If I acquiesce humbly in this state, Thou wilt be gracious enough to cause the fertilizing south wind to breathe upon my dry and parched soul, and inflame it with feelings of tenderness. Yet, O God of love, I renounce this, provided that I may love Thee, and accomplish in all things Thy adorable Will.

FOURTH DAY.

Surge, aquilo; veni, auster; perfla, &c.

Let the north wind desolate me by its dryness, and excite around me a tempest of tribulations, I will not, therefore, cease to send forth from my heart the perfume of Divine love, and the only reward that I will ask for this love, shall be Love Itself. If I claimed, in virtue of my love, any thing less than God, Who is Love Itself, this would be rather the traffic of a mercenary than the love of a true Christian, who ought to love only for the sake of loving. Deprive me then, O Lord, strip me of all; I consent to it, provided that I love Thee. What good thing could I possess, if I did not love Thee, since Thy love alone is truly good? What evil, what poverty can I fear? Is it possible to suffer, to be in want of any thing when I love Thee? What pleasure could I enjoy, if my heart were destitute of charity? Is not that the centre of the most delightful enjoyment? What desires can the heart form? It would be very blind to desire any thing but to love Thee in this world and in the next.

FIFTH DAY.

Si dederit homo omnem substantiam domûs suæ pro dilectione, quasi nihil despiciet eam. (Cant. viii.)

If a man would give all the substance of his house for love, say the companions of the bride, he would afterwards contemn them. What, then, can I offer to my God to purchase His esteem and His love? Can all that I possess be compared with this inestimable treasure? Can charity be too dearly purchased, since it is God Himself, and since God is all that is good? Shall I now hesitate to part with all that I enjoy with too much affection, in order to love Him Alone? I must be very blind to do so! At what price then, LORD, wilt Thou that I purchase the privilege of loving Thee? What are the goods which Thou dost demand of me in exchange for this love? I have already sacrificed to Thee all outward things, but are all those of the earth comparable to Thy love? I feel assuredly that Thou demandest of me more spiritual and more precious things; the substance of the inward house of my soul, my thoughts, my aims, my desires, my affections, and my too sensible attachments; Thou wilt have me sacrifice to Thy Love my daintiness, my vanity, my prejudices, my self-love, and all my passions. Be it so, but give me strength to do it, since Thou inspirest me with the desire.

SIXTH DAY.

Si dederit homo omnem substantiam, &c.

My GOD has loved me freely, I ought to love Him disinterestedly; He has given me all His substance, in order to have my love, I ought to return Him all mine, and even then I shall make but a feeble acknowledgment of His Love. He could do without me, but I cannot do without Him, or live without Him. He has taken to Himself a feeling Heart only to love me feelingly. He has given me a heart of flesh only that I may love Him in like manner. What interest, O my GOD, hast Thou to love me, Thou Whose whole happiness consists in loving Thyself, and Who, by the blissful necessity of Thy sublime and independent Being, findest infinite satisfaction in dwelling in Thine own Greatness? What goodness, what disinterestness, to descend even to our low estate, and to our nothingness, to fix Thy Heart there! Can we, having a heart formed by Thy hand, and in the image of Thine, do otherwise than love Thee for Thyself Alone? Can we not love Love Itself? says St. Bernard. Quidni ametur amor?

SEVENTH DAY.

Si dederit homo omnem substantiam, &c.

Can I ask any thing of my God, but that I may love Him with all my heart? Does not this love contain all the greatest and most precious things that I can desire? It is all, it supplies the place of every thing to me; I need nothing when I love Him, because He is All to me as I am all to Him. But can I desire any thing else with Him without despising Him, and making an odious comparison between Him and that which I should desire, which would not be Him? Ought He not to suffice my heart? He desires, then, that I give myself wholly and disinterestedly to Him, and it is for my good to do so. In whose hands can I better be than in His? I belong to Him, because I am His creature, and because He has bought me with the Price of all His Blood (1 Cor. vi. 20); yet He asks me to give myself to Him, as if He had no right over me; He desires that my offering of myself be free, although it be absolutely necessary for me. Therefore He gives me to myself, that, giving myself voluntarily to Him, He may reckon it to me as if He were indebted to me for it. What goodness! and what noble disinterestedness!

Twenty-second Week.

LOVE OF ESTEEM.

When the mind, disengaged from every passion, has weighed the true value, and is persuaded of the real merit, of an object presented to it, it cannot refuse its esteem to it. And when it has given it, the heart does not hesitate to give its love; and from these different operations of the mind and heart there results but one, the love of esteem, otherwise called love of appreciation. This love is far more noble, more lofty, more durable, and obtains greater favours, than the simple love of tenderness. The one is properly only in the heart, the other in the soul and all its powers. The one often consists in feeling only, and sometimes it loves God only when it finds pleasure in loving Him; the other turns towards Him by reflection, and because its reason is convinced that He Alone deserves to be supremely loved. Love of tenderness is formed by a sensible impression which pleases and touches, and this love almost always ceases as soon as the feeling passes away. Love of esteem is formed by impression and conviction together; so that even if the feeling diminishes, the conviction remains, the impression of the infinite merit of God abides in the mind and the heart, and we act even in dryness as if we felt.

It was, then, after being very strongly convinced of the infinite merit of the Heavenly Bridegroom, that the bride exclaimed, Behold, Thou art fair, my Beloved, yea, pleasant! Ecce tu pulcher es, dilecte mi, et decorus! (Cant. i.) She had been praised by her Spouse in very nearly the same terms: but, equally sensible of her own nothingness, and filled with the love of esteem which her Spouse had produced in her by His matchless Perfections, she returned Him all the praises which she received from Him.

She says again, that her Beloved is the chiefest among ten thousand. Electus ex millibus. (Cant. v.) She shows by this expression that she is not contented with simply esteeming Him, but that she gives Him an absolute preference in her esteem ; and that He undoubtedly holds the first place in her mind and in her heart. She declares and protests assuredly, that in Beauty and Perfection He surpasses all beautiful and perfect things, that consequently He is lovelier than all that is lovely, and that when compared with other objects, most worthy of love and esteem, nothing can be worthy to be esteemed in comparison with Him. This is the true character of love of esteem.

AFFECTIONS.

FIRST DAY.

Ecce tu pulcher es, dilecte mi, et decorus ! (Cant. i.) Behold, Thou art fair, my Beloved, yea, pleasant, exclaimed the bride. It is so, Lord ; Thy Beauty only is supremely lovely, for Thou Alone art supremely Perfect. The beauty of created things strikes the senses only, often corrupts them, and by their means carries corruption into the heart. Thine strikes at once the mind and the heart ; the mind finds a subject for esteem, the heart for love, and by it both of these faculties are consecrated. Can my mind consider that Thou art the most perfect Being, the purest Spirit, the most sublime Greatness, the most plenteous Fulness, the most lovely Beauty, the most generous, faithful, and tender Friend, and in consequence most complete in all loveliness, without giving

Thee its whole esteem? Can it be persuaded of these truths, and my heart not give Thee all its love? Beauties of things created, consisting only in false brilliancy, ye are but hideous deformity when compared with that of my Heavenly Spouse. I cannot esteem you, for ye are nothing; consequently I cannot love you blindly without sin: I reserve my love of esteem for God Alone.

SECOND DAY.

Ecce tu pulcher es, dilecte mi, et decorus!

Is it possible to be blind enough to love those we cannot reasonably esteem? What unnatural love is that inspired by merely outward beauty, which deserves no esteem, because it passes away "as a flower," and because it may often cover an interior full of faults, weakness, and pitiable deformity! The only true beauty is that which proceeds from the soul; and that alone may innocently be loved, because it may rightfully be esteemed. But as it exists only as an outpouring of the Beauty of God, its Source and Origin, let us forsake the stream to seek this Source; let us leave the copy to ascend to the Original. Spotless and eternal Beauty, That never fadest, I can have no eyes but for Thee; I desire to esteem and love none but Thee, or but for Thy sake. But alas! O ancient and ever new Beauty, exclaimed a holy penitent, I have loved Thee too late, I have compared Thee to created beauties, I have preferred them; they have carried away my love and my esteem, which they did not deserve; now I restore both to Thee, I return to Thee for ever all the esteem of my mind and all the love of my heart.

THIRD DAY.

Ecce tu pulcher es, dilecte mi, &c.

The more I know the creature, the more I know

also its deformity, and the more my reason persuades me to hate it. I cannot be long intimately associated with it, without discovering its weakness, nothingness, and falseness. When my heart has been so unhappy as to suffer itself to be imposed upon by it, it soon grows weary, because it discovers nothing worthy of esteem, and the faults that it perceives greatly surpass the brilliant qualities which dazzled it at first: it withdraws its esteem, which often degenerates into contempt. It is not thus with Thee, O my God! Thy beauty wearies not. The more my mind is applied to Thy knowledge, the more is my heart led to Thy love. When I compare Thee with created beings, this comparison, though odious in one sense, produces in me an appreciative love of esteem and preference. Henceforth, Lord, I will esteem the Object of my love, and my love itself, a thousand times more than all the creatures and treasures of the earth.

FOURTH DAY.

Ecce tu pulcher es, dilecte mi, &c.

Why does the love of the creature, enchanting and charming at first, afterwards weary us? and why do we, in the end, neglect that which we loved most ardently in the beginning? Why do the righteous and the perfect never weary of loving God? and why, the more they love Him, do they desire more to love Him? Because God has put in the depth of man's heart a feeling for true merit; and when it acts without being dazzled, surprised, or infatuated, it seeks this merit; it does it justice, esteems it, cleaves to it, and finds it only in God. But when the heart suffers itself to be overcome by passion, it loses this discernment, this feeling, and this equity which God has given it; the creature despoils it of it, and puts in its place an evil propensity to turn all to poison; the heart becomes almost incapable of giving its esteem to God, because it has given itself up to another. Restore to me, Lord, this feeling for true merit, if I have lost it: strengthen it, if it is weak; purify it, if it is corrupted; make known to me more and more Thy priceless Worth, that I may esteem and love none but Thee.

FIFTH DAY.

Electus ex millibus. (Cant. v.)

My Beloved is chosen among ten thousand, says the bride. He would be most unhappy, O my God! who was not persuaded that Thy Worth is infinitely greater than that of all things. But to be convinced of it, and not to choose Thee, and not to esteem Thee more than all things, is a much greater misfortune, and far more crying injustice. Blind heart, open thine eyes to the light of faith, thou wilt know that one moment of the love of God is better than an age of pleasure, since it procures eternal joy; that one look from Him is better than the caresses of all created things; that a single Drop of His Blood is better than all the treasures of the world; that one day of joy in His Tabernacles is better than an everlasting abode in king's palaces. Thou hast chosen Him among ten thousand; maintain thy choice, it is thy duty and thy advantage; and above all, make no more comparisons between Him and any creature, for they do not deserve to be compared with Him.

SIXTH DAY.

Electus ex millibus.

It is a great disgrace to man to have a heart capable of love, and a mind capable of esteem, and not to know how to choose the best part, and not to attach himself to the only fitting objects. A prophet long since reproached him with not knowing how to value things according to their true worth. "Woe unto them that call evil good, and good evil." (Isa. v. 20.) Let us understand, indeed, and love, for God wills it; but let us well discern the qualities of the object before giving it a preference in our esteem and love, because our eternal happiness or misery depend upon this important choice. Let us love only that which is supremely amiable; let us love that only which we may love without sin; that only which we may love eternally; that only which has power to make us perfectly happy; that only, in short, which we shall never regret having loved perfectly. That is only Thou, O my God! I have chosen Thee among ten thousand; all the rest deserve neither the attention of my mind, nor the tenderness of my heart; I renounce all, but Thee Alone, for Thou art All to me.

SEVENTH DAY.

Electus ex millibus.

It is a bad choice to turn our esteem and love towards ourselves; there is but one Object that we ought to choose among a thousand, and that is God; any other choice must proceed only from a blind intellect, and from a heart spoiled by self-love. To love ourselves, and to have no other aim than self, is an unworthy love which excludes the love of God. Let us study what we are, and we shall feel only contempt and horror for ourselves. If we well examine ourselves, as well as all other creatures, we must acknowledge that we, like them, have nothing but principles of death. What pleasure is there in loving death, and that which bears death within it? Thou Alone, O my God! art within me the principle of life; and Thou art so only when I love Thee; there is, then, nothing in me that I esteem and love but Thee, since I cannot live but by loving Thee:

Thee in consequence do I choose, Thee only will I esteem and love in this life and in the next.

Twenty-third Week.

WISE LOVE.

As God is Supreme Wisdom, says St. Bernard, He desires to be loved not only tenderly, but also wisely. The love of God is the most sublime and the most eminent wisdom of Christianity; it knows no other, and there is none beside; this love contains within itself all the rules, the lessons, and the practices of wisdom; it contains all its light, and communicates all the docility that is required to learn it well. Thus, as wisdom suffices to make us love God, so the love of God suffices to make us wise; and a strong love will make us possessed of perfect wisdom; so that the degree of our love will always be the degree of our wisdom both of mind and heart.

The great reason of this truth is, that Divine love is not a fire only, but also a light; it illumines and inflames at the same time; it teaches to love, and teaches how to love. Besides, it is unquestionably by love that we draw near to God, the only Source of true Wisdom; and we cannot draw near to Him without receiving its precious out-pourings.

The upright love Thee, says the bride: recti diligunt te (Cant. i.); as if she would say, Thou art not to be approached by crooked paths, but by the ways of uprightness; and love, which is true wisdom, must teach me them; or, according to some holy interpreters, none but the upright and wise of heart love Thee wisely. The hearts of fools either refuse to love Thee, in order to abandon themselves to the love of the creature, which is the most shameful of all follies; or make an insulting mixture of this love with Thine; or, lastly, they love Thee without order, without light, without discretion, and without wisdom.

This same bride gives thanks to her Heavenly Bridegroom, for having been careful to regulate her love, after graciously bringing her into His banqueting-house.

Introduxit me in cellam vinariam, ordinavit in me charitatem. (Cant. ii.) Her love was ardent, but perhaps too precipitate; perhaps she had at first followed natural temperament more than Grace; she needed this true wisdom to regulate the transports of her love without diminishing its ardour. In this mystic banqueting-house, in the wise intoxication produced by the delicious wine of charity, she learnt not only What to love, but also how to love rightly. It is thus that charity should be regulated by wisdom, lest precipitation, impetuosity, and indiscretion bring disorder and confusion into love, and make it bear too much resemblance to carnal love, which knows not how to moderate its heat and transports, because it is always accompanied by folly.

AFFECTIONS.

FIRST DAY.

Recti diligunt te. (Cant. i.)

The upright love Thee, says the bride. True wisdom, which is true love, knows nothing of crooked ways, but goes to God by one path, and that path is always the shortest and the straightest; it has no other artifice than innocence, no other cunning than Christian simplicity. An upright heart such as that of the bride, seeks and loves God for God Alone, as St. Augustine says. (Psal. lxxvii.) As the light of Divine love always illumines its steps, it commits no errors; as the fire of this love inflames it wholly, it never admits any strange fires; love enables it to perceive them, and makes it abhor them; and as it is the love of GOD which causes it to love, and which loves within it, it cannot love but wisely. When, O Heavenly Bridegroom! shall I have this upright heart equally filled with wisdom and with ardour? Upright to go to Thee with simplicity, without crooked ways, without respect to man, and without artifice; wise to discern, and to avoid the snares which the devil, the world, and the flesh are ever laying for my love; and ardent to execute, without delay, all that the wisdom of Divine love inspires me to do. Thou, LORD, must give it me.

SECOND DAY.

Recti diligunt te.

Divine love is a fire full of light and wisdom. It ought to be quick without precipitation, ardent without imprudence, zealous without indiscretion. It should be animated by tender confidence lest it fall into indifference; but true wisdom should regulate this confidence, and keep it in a just mean, lest it degenerate into presumption. Henceforth I will impose this rule of wisdom on my love, in order to acquire true uprightness of heart, without which it is impossible to love GOD rightly. I will avoid alike a fearful and a presumptuous love, which are but phantoms of true love. I desire, O my Saviour! that the ardour of my love may lead me to undertake all, to hope all, and never to distrust Thy Goodness, whilst the uprightness and wisdom of my love shall guide me safely. I will fear because I am a sinner; I will love because Thou art lovely. I will love Thee as my Spouse, I will fear Thee as my Judge, I will open my whole heart to Thee as to a faithful Friend, and I will reverence Thee as my GOD and Sovereign LORD.

THIRD DAY.

Recti diligunt te.

I have need of an upright heart and of a wise and prudent love, to avoid the two fearful precipices which encompass me. The way which leads me to the Heart of God is straight, but it is narrow; it has on either side the terrible abysses of presumption and despair. Rashness digs the pit of presumption, mistrust and servile fear that of despair. I must walk wisely between these two abysses, and the torch of Divine love must ever light my steps. I am a sinner; but, as the Goodness of my God is infinite, I will put my whole trust in Him and will never despair; the wisdom of my love shall bring me back to this, when I have an extravagant and mistaken fear. God is Just, He is Wisdom Itself; He admits to the Throne of His Love, which is His Heart, none but pure and penitent souls. I will never presume upon His Goodness; and whatever tenderness I feel, I will never forget that I am a sinner, and that I have deserved hell. The wisdom of my love shall bring me back to this, when there is too much boldness and rashness in my confidence.

FOURTH DAY.

Recti diligunt te.

He who has acquired true uprightness of heart, has acquired true love, and he who feels this love must possess the most eminent wisdom; so that none but the upright in heart can attain to these two things, love and wisdom. Thy Love alone, then, O my God, shall henceforth be all my study, my reason, my aim. If I am asked why I love Thee, I will answer with a holy Doctor, That I love Thee in order to learn how to love Thee truly; this is all my study: that I love Thee only because I love Thee, and desire to love

Thee; this is all my reason, and I am content never to have any other: lastly, that I love Thee only in order to love Thee more perfectly; this is all my aim and desire in this world and in the next. If I am enabled to possess this advantage, and if I am faithful in preserving it, I shall possess the loftiest wisdom that ever existed; grant me this grace, LORD, that I may never have any other study, reason, aim, or wisdom.

FIFTH DAY.

Ordinavit in me charitatem. (Cant. ii.)

My Spouse has regulated my love, says the bride. All that comes from GOD is disposed in order, because He is Wisdom Itself; thus charity, which St. Augustine calls the eldest daughter of the Heart of GOD, must be regulated. Deceive not thyself, then, in this, O my soul, for thy eternity depends on it; labour to acquire order, rule, and wisdom in love, that thou mayest discern plainly what thou must love, and how. Make not an unworthy present of thy love to objects which would seduce and ruin thee; love not that which it is forbidden to love, it would be a folly deserving no less than eternal punishment, Not to love GOD first, or to love any creature more than GOD, or as much as GOD, or not to love it simply for GOD's sake, is a confusion and disorder that destroys true charity. Remember that thou hast but one heart, because thou hast but One GOD to love, and this heart is extremely narrow. There is not room enough in it for GOD and the world together; there is only space for one of the two: choose wisely which thou wilt admit, and shut the door upon the other.

SIXTH DAY.

Ordinavit in me charitatem.

The heart of man is the source and cause of all his

good and all his evil, of all his virtues and all his vices, of all his happiness and all his misery; and he can be truly happy only when his love is wise and well-regulated, that is, when he loves God Alone supremely, and the creature for God's sake. But when he perverts this necessary order, his love is but confusion and folly. There is a love which is a passion, because it turns indifferently to the first object which flatters and seduces it: there is a love which turns only with order and wisdom to the objects which present themselves, and this love is the virtue of charity, which the Heavenly Bridegroom regulates in our heart as well as in that of the bride, if we listen to Him with the same docility. I shall then be happy, O my God, not merely when my heart loves, but when it has wisdom enough to love entirely That only which is entirely lovely, which is Thyself Alone. This is the only happiness that I desire, the only wisdom to which I aspire; and I cannot possess it unless Thou sendest it from Heaven into my heart.

SEVENTH DAY.

Ordinavit in me charitatem.

What disorder and confusion, O my God, do I sometimes feel in my heart! How do I need that true wisdom which should order and regulate my love, to discern what it ought to love, and to stop the blind precipitation of my heart, when it desires to love that which it ought to hate! Alas! it goes but too often into one of two extremes, equally vicious. At one time it has too much tenderness that it ought not to have; at another time too much indifference and hardness to that which it should love tenderly. Sometimes I am all fire for what should freeze me, sometimes all ice for that which should inflame me. Melt this ice, Lord, extinguish this fire, kindle another by the breath of Thy Divine Spirit, which is charity itself; harden this false and pernicious tenderness, soften this cruel and ruinous hardness, regulate my love, teach me what to love and what to hate, and how to hate or love; be Thou to me the rule of both.

Twenty-fourth Week.

CHASTE LOVE.

CHASTE Love is here understood in two ways; first, as an absolute and general abandonment of the smallest sensual pleasures, which may cause some little defilement to the mind and heart. We speak not here of gross pleasures, which are supposed to have been expiated in the purificative life, and which are the subject of penitent and lamenting love; but of the slightest blemishes, which are contrary to the perfection of chastity. We understand, secondly, by chaste love, a delicacy of love which can suffer no division or reserve in the heart, and which gives its whole tenderness to GOD without suffering any rival or competitor. The first does homage to the Infinite Purity of GOD, the other to His Zeal, and to His Divine Jealousy.

It is impossible to love GOD truly without supreme love for purity. CHRIST JESUS, a Virgin, the Son of a Virgin Mother, the Spouse of virgins, cannot rest but in a chaste heart. There, and not elsewhere, is His delight. Thus the degree of purity is that of Divine love, whose joys are more deeply felt by the heart, says St. Leo (Serm. de jejunio), in proportion as it is emptied of all others, and resolved to know no other: Castus animus ita gaudet Deum amare, ut in nullo extra illum cupiat delectari.

But this is only the first degree of chaste love; the

second consists in emptying the heart of all affections foreign to this Divine love, and banishing from it every thing that might cause the smallest sensible attachment, and all that might stain and hinder it from loving God supremely, such as love of praise, care for self, and for the esteem of men, attachment to our own opinions; in short, all propensity and inclination to any thing which is not God, or is not sought for God's sake.

The bride was deeply imbued with these feelings when she said, that "the Eyes of her Spouse were as the eyes of doves by the rivers of waters, washed with milk:" Oculi ejus sicut columbæ super rivulos aquarum, quæ lacte sunt lotæ. (Cant. v.)

Here are many emblems of chaste love united in one oracle. The dove is a very natural emblem, for her love is undivided. Water is another, for it serves to wash away stains. The milk with which these doves are washed is so also by its whiteness. Such is the Heavenly Bridegroom, and such should be the bride who desires to love Him, and to be loved by Him.

She says in the following verse, that "the Lips of her Spouse are like lilies, dropping the purest myrrh:" Labia ejus lilia distillantia myrrham primam. (Ibid.) The lips assist in forming speech, and speech is the instrument of the heart: they ought to resemble the lily, which is the type of purity, and they should distil only the first myrrh, which is always the purest. The love of God should be always pure and unmixed in the heart, which should love nothing but for the sake of God.

AFFECTIONS.

FIRST DAY.

Oculi ejus sicut columbæ super rivulos aquarum quæ lacte sunt lotæ. (Cant. v.)

The Eyes of the Bridegroom are as the eyes of doves by the rivers of waters washed with milk. The bride here draws a portrait of Thy incomparable Purity, LORD, and Thou settest this Portrait before my eyes, that I may copy it, and may strive by chaste love to resemble every feature of this excellent Original. Give my heart, then, the wings of the dove, that it may no more touch the earth, which is full only of corruption, and where I find none but objects which seek to draw to themselves the love that I owe to Thee, and thus to tarnish the brightness of my chastity. Give me those wings of the dove which the Prophet asked (Psalm lv.), to flee from the world, to fly into the wild solitude, or rather to take my flight towards Thee, there to find the rest that I seek, and which I shall not fully enjoy, save in another life. Till that happy time I will be like this chosen dove; my dwelling shall be near the healing waters of Thy Grace and of Thy Sacraments, that I may wash there, whenever I am so unhappy as to contract the slightest stain. As long as I live, give me the grace ever to find those pure and life-giving waters to purify me from the least defilements. Add to these waters the precious Milk with which Thou washest Thy most chaste doves, Thy brides, that I may preserve a whiteness and purity like theirs to my death.

SECOND DAY.

Oculi ejus sicut columbæ super rivulos, &c.

Who can boast of having the eyes of the dove? Who can flatter himself that his heart is pure and free from the least defilements? Who can glory in perfect chastity, says St. Augustine, or promise himself that he will preserve it unspotted to death? Alas! the purest souls have reason to lament, to fear, and to be continually upon their guard, assured that, whilst they have a heart and a body of flesh, they have the precious treasure of chastity in extremely frail vessels. Yet, O Heavenly Bridegroom! I cannot love Thee unless my eyes and heart are pure, like those of the dove: give me both, that I may love Thee with a chaste love; place me, as this dove, in the desert, to remove me from all objects which might tarnish the brightness of this incomparable virtue, that my eyes, like hers, may ever look on Thee Alone. Place me near the rivers and torrents which flow from Thy Heart, that I may wash myself every day of my life. Wash me Thyself yet more with the milk of Thy Grace and with Thy Blood, which is Purity itself, that I may love Thee purely to the last breath of my life.

THIRD DAY.

Oculi ejus sicut columbæ super rivulos, &c.

Chastity and charity are two inestimable treasures: God gives them, the heart contains them, humility keeps them. They are so inseparable, that it is difficult to lose or possess one without the other. In proportion as my heart increases in purity, it will also increase in love. To preserve them carefully, I must have eyes like the dove, and like her fly to the fountains of water in the wilderness, to wash myself continually, because continually I may fall. A careless thought, a natural propensity not instantly restrained, a little inclination deliberately followed, a sensible attachment, a sudden look, a surprise, a word, an imperfect feeling: these things, O my God, make me fear all from my own heart; these may obscure the lustre of the angelic virtue that I ask of Thee; these may deprive me of my love and my innocence. Produce, increase, and preserve both in me, Lord.

FOURTH DAY.

Oculi ejus sicut columbæ super rivulos, &c.

Moisten this dry and barren heart, LORD, with the sanctifying waters of Thy Grace; wash it, purify it in that most pure Blood which Thou hast shed for me; restore to it the whiteness of milk which Thou gavest it in Baptism, or rather tear and divide this sensual heart, which does not love Thee with sufficient chastity. Annihilate it, substitute for it a chaste and pure heart, which shall love Thee Alone; grant me the prayer of the penitent Prophet; make me a clean heart: Cor mundum crea in me, Deus. (Ps. li.) I will be careful to preserve it in that purity that Thou givest it, and never to admit anything which may sully it anew; I will wash it so often by my tears, that there shall not remain the least spot to offend the incomparable purity of Thy Divine Eyes.

FIFTH DAY.

Labia ejus distillantia myrrham, &c. (Cant. v.)

His Lips distil the purest myrrh, says the bride. Our GOD is a Jealous GOD; He requires us to give Him the first myrrh, which is always the most pure. This mysterious myrrh is our love. He requires that it be chaste and unmixed, without division and without reserve; for to seek to admit into our heart the love of the creature with that of the Creator, is an impure mixture. He is, in truth, so Jealous of our hearts, that He will either possess them without reserve, or abandon them entirely. When He sees any hidden idol, He is wroth, He leaves all to His unworthy rival till the terrible day, when He will break both idol and idolater. Let me die, O my GOD, rather than make any injurious reserve in my heart for the creature; let me die, rather than make there any impure mixture. I desire that my whole heart shall love Thee, that it shall love Thee with a chaste love, that is, that it shall love Thee Alone.

SIXTH DAY.

Labia ejus distillantia myrrham, &c.

It is necessary to make a choice in life; but the important thing is to choose rightly, because eternity depends upon it. To choose to love God and the creature at once is impossible, because the one excludes the other, and this would be offering God a mixed and impure myrrh, which He will not accept. To choose to love them one after the other, is to run a strange risk; for if we love the creature first, and give to that the first myrrh, which is due to God Alone, the heart is worn out, the affections exhausted; and when we afterwards desire to turn to God, we are wearied, and often give Him only the sad remains of a languid love, of which the creature has gathered all the flowers, and taken all the first fruits. If we love the creature last, death will not fail to surprise us, and the consequence is no less than inevitable hell. Choose, then, my soul, but choose to love God Alone, to love Him first and last; give Him without reserve all the myrrh of thy heart. Thou hast no other choice to make. Give room in thy heart to nothing less than Him, to nothing which is not in perfect agreement with Him, lest He withdraw from it, and never return.

SEVENTH DAY.

Labia distillantia myrrham, &c.

How many secret and scarcely discernible impurities within my heart, adulterate that purest myrrh which it ought to distil, and oppose themselves to the chaste love that I owe to Thee, my God! What hidden monsters do I unceasingly caress! What self-love! How many sensible attachments to my own thoughts, to my judgment, to my interest! How many but too natural and too strong inclinations for created things! What propensity towards the earth and its good things! What consideration, what daintiness, what superfluous cares for this perishable body! What base and unworthy thoughts of this supremely pure Being, Whom Alone I ought to love! How often has the love of the world overcome that of my God! How often with base compliance have I compared and even preferred the creature to the Creator. Purify this heart, then, Thyself, O my God! Purify the myrrh that Thou requirest me to offer Thee, and give me that chaste love, without which I can neither please nor possess Thee.

Twenty-fifth Week.

FAITHFUL LOVE.

Reciprocal fidelity is the bond and tie of brotherly love, and faithlessness destroys it, and declares its weakness and falseness. It is also the nourishment and support of the holy intercourse of love, which exists between the Heart of God and our heart; and this intercourse ceases as soon as fidelity fails. It is always the creature who is unfaithful to the Divine love; God never has been, and never will be, faithless. The Immutability of His Being, the Truth of His Words, and the Goodness of His Heart, are the pledges and guarantee of the faithfulness of His Love.

Fidelity is, therefore, one of the most essential proofs of love; and an exact and noble fidelity, constant amidst the perils to which it is exposed, is a mark of great love. Thus we cannot merit the reward and the crown of love, says the Beloved Disciple to the Bishop of Smyrna, unless we are faithful unto death. (Apoc. ii. 10.)

The bride laments, in the beginning of her Canticle, that she has not been faithful in keeping the vineyard entrusted to her: Vineam meam non custodivi. (Cant. i.) This vineyard, according to some holy interpreters, is a type of her own heart, over which she had not watched sufficiently: so true is it, that when we have not yet entered the spiritual life, we give no regard to slight acts of faithlessness. But when we begin to love truly, Divine love, which enlightens and inflames, makes them appear terrible; we complain of ourselves, and amend. The bride will soon become faithful, since she begins to blame herself for her faithlessness, and her fidelity will augment in proportion as her love gains fresh increase.

She has so well profited by this first feeling, and kept her vineyard so faithfully, that she invites her Beloved to come in the morning to visit it with her, because she is sure that He will find flowers there. "Let us get up early to the vineyards," she says; "lèt us see if the vine flourish:" Manè surgamus ad vineas, videamus si floruit vinea. (Cant. vii.) The faithfulness of this love also does not content itself with flowers alone; fruit succeeds to them in such abundance, that "every one to whom this vineyard was let, for the fruit thereof, was to bring a thousand pieces of silver:" Vir affert pro fructu ejus mille argenteos. (Cant. viii.) Could this mysterious vineyard, which is her own heart, yield less, since the faithful bride protests that it is always before her? Vinea mea coram me est. (Ibid.) If we desire to acquire faithful love, our eyes will be always on our heart, lest the smallest imperfect desire or affection escape it.

AFFECTIONS.

FIRST DAY.

Vineam meam non custodivi. (Cant. i.)

"I have not faithfully kept my vineyard," says the bride. Alas! if I had faithfully kept the mysterious vineyard that God confided to me, my own heart, I should have made far different progress in His Divine Love. If I had surrounded it with a good hedge, the little foxes would not have spoiled it so sorely. If I had guarded my senses, both external and internal, my heart would be God's Alone, and nothing would be able to shake the faithfulness of my love. If I had carefully plucked up the weeds of this uncultivated vineyard by the roots, that is, if I had destroyed the foreign affections which have dried it up and deprived it of all its moisture and nourishment; if I had dug it well, to permit the rain of heaven to penetrate it thoroughly; if I had pruned it at the proper season, had cut off at one time vanity, at another sensible attachment to creatures, at another self-love; if I had carefully tied up my vine to hinder it from trailing on the earth; if I had been careful to bind my heart by faithful love to Jesus Christ Alone: this vineyard, chosen of God, would have wept in its season, and its tears would have augmented its love; it would be fair with leaves, and beautiful in the Eyes of the Heavenly Spouse; it would have borne the sweet-scented flowers of good desires and affections; it would have produced also abundant fruits, and I should have obtained from it the delicious wine of perfect charity. But, alas! I have not kept my vineyard well: I must, then, be more faithful to Divine love, and for that will I labour.

SECOND DAY.

Vineam meam non custodivi.

Who can boast of having well kept the vineyard of his heart? Alas! if we carefully examine the faithfulness of most men who pride themselves upon it, and who make it a subject of vaunting and self-praise, it is easy to perceive that it is but the vain phantom of true faithfulness, which is to be found only amid the really devout. A thousand times have I spoken loudly against unfaithfulness; I have blamed it in others as an odious quality; but, my soul, examine what was the principle of thy words and actions. How hast thou acted towards God? This examination must cover thee with confusion, for it throws upon thee that blame which thou hast laid on others. Thyself hast badly kept the vineyard. A thousand times hast thou failed in faithfulness to God; how canst thou be always true to men? Confess that this false virtue, which thou hast practised towards them, proceeded only from vanity and self-love. But with regard to God, how often hast thou failed towards Him! how many resolutions vanished! how many protestations of love forgotten! how many promises at the foot of His Altar, at the feet of His Ministers, retracted the very next day! how many projects, how many magnificent plans for a pure and more perfect life effaced almost as soon as they were sketched! Ah, Lord! what cause have I for confusion!

THIRD DAY.

Manè surgamus ad vineas, videamus si floruit vinea. (Cant. vii.)

Let us get up early to the vineyards; let us see if the vine flourish, says the bride. I dare not speak to Thee, my God, with like confidence. It would be presumption for me to speak thus, and to invite Thee to come and examine the vineyard of my heart, for I have neither cultivated it carefully nor kept it faithfully. For, alas! what wouldst Thou see in this heart worthy of Thy Divine notice? Wouldst Thou find there those pleasing flowers, those holy desires, that ardour, and those transports which always precede the fruits of perfect Love? Thou wouldst see at most some faint desires which have as yet had no efficacy; Thou wouldst find some changeable feelings which, like worthless flowers, have yet produced no fruit. Yet descend into my vineyard, not to examine rigorously if it has any flowers, but Thyself to place there the flowers and fruit of faithful love. Give them to me, LORD; after that I will invite Thee to come thither to rest and take Thy pleasure.

FOURTH DAY.

Manè surgamus ad vineas, videamus, &c.

Come, Heavenly Bridegroom, descend into my vineyard, graciously visit my heart, and give it that faithful love which it wants; discover Thyself to me, in order that I may regulate my fidelity by Thine. How does Thy wondrous faithfulness at once charm and confound me! It charms me because it is sublime, and because I have sensibly experienced it. Thou hast never failed in Thy Word to me; nay, the effects have rather surpassed than equalled Thy Divine Promises, and I have ever found Thee ready to open Thy Heart to me, when by Thy Grace I had become worthy to enter. It confounds me, because I have not replied to it by mine, and because my breaches of faith are innumerable. My vineyard has ever borne only barren flowers, and of an ill scent; they have fallen or faded in the very bud. O Faithful GOD, Who art Faithfulness Itself, give me a heart that can resist all temptations to discouragement and unfaithfulness; strengthen me whenever the fidelity of my love is endangered; aid me, support me, and give me grace to be faithful to Thee till death.

FIFTH DAY.

Vir affert pro fructu ejus mille argenteos. (Cant. viii.)

My vineyard is become so fruitful, that every one for the fruit thereof, must bring a thousand pieces of silver, says the bride. We speak, then, no more of flowers; the Heavenly Bridegroom requires from the vineyard of my heart abundant fruit; and it will never produce any unless it has kept itself well, and acquired faithful love: the very name which I bear should engage me to do so. I am a Christian, it is the same name as that of Faithful, and I cannot be one if I am not the other. Far from bearing fruits meet to be offered upon the table of the Heavenly Bridegroom, I shall fall into the greatest unfaithfulnesses, if I begin with the very least. Neglect then nothing, my soul! a drop of water, often repeated, will at length wear away the hardest stone; a little spark causes the most dreadful fires. If one day thou art wanting in faithfulness to thy very smallest duties, if thou pourest thyself out in vain joys, if thou give loose to thine inclination, if thou failest, or even deferrest, to obey an inspiration, these small acts of faithlessness will lead thy heart further than thou believest; to-day thou wilt neglect one practice, to-morrow two; then they will become burdensome, thou wilt do them no more, and wilt become altogether unfaithful; no fruit will be found more in thy vineyard, and thou wilt love thy God no longer.

SIXTH DAY.

Vir affert pro fructu ejus mille argenteos.

My soul, remember that happy time when thou

wert all fire for thy Divine Spouse, when thou broughtest to Him daily a thousand pieces of silver for thy vineyard, when thou wert careful to multiply thy desires, thy affections, thy acts of love, and pious practices. Wherefore, then, art thou become unfaithful? Why does the ungrateful soil of thy heart scarcely produce anything? Why is there hardly any fruit in thy vineyard? Why hast thou now so many barren intervals devoid of love? If thou hadst foreseen it, what precautions wouldst thou not have taken to avoid thy present state of feebleness! Why has a cold and slack charity succeeded thy former ardour? Faithless soul, seek the source of the grievous sterility of thy heart, put it in order, produce unceasingly flowers and fruits, lest the Master of the House pluck up thy vine and cast it into the fire.

SEVENTH DAY.

Vinea mea coram me est. (Cant. viii.)

My vineyard, says the Bridegroom, is ever before me. It is to my soul, to my heart, Lord, that Thou speakest! I am Thy vine, Thou plantedst me in Thy Church by Baptism, Thou hast rained upon me the fertilising and life-giving waters of Thy Mercy, Thy Grace, and Thy Sacraments; Thou hast moreover watered me with Thy Blood. Not content with having appointed pastors to watch over me, Thou watchest unceasingly Thyself, and Thou art so faithful a Keeper, that Thy adorable Eyes are never turned from me, because Thou lovest me, and desirest that I may bring forth fruit worthy of eternity. To this loving and exact fidelity mine shall be answerable; I will turn my eyes upon my ways and upon my own heart, which is Thy vine and my own; I will never lose sight of it; I will guard it in such a manner that the passers-by shall never trample it under foot, and shall never carry away the mysterious Wine of my love. I reserve it for Thee Alone, Heavenly Bridegroom. I will preserve it so faithfully, and in so pure a vessel, that it shall never be diminished, adulterated, or corrupted, and that it shall at length be found fit to be all admitted into Thy Divine Cellars.

Twenty-sixth Week.

DESIRING LOVE.

An ardent desire of loving God, and a hearty love for Him, are the same thing. As love cannot exist without desire, when the object is away, so desire can proceed only from love. Vainly then do we flatter ourselves that we love God, if we are not enabled to desire Him more than all the pleasures of the senses, all the honours of the world, all the good things of this life, and life itself.

Desire in general is the thirst, the hunger, the restlessness, and the goad of profane, as well as of Divine love; but with this difference, that earthly desires, as long as they are desires, cause a wearisome thirst that is never quenched, a hunger that is never satisfied, a restlessness that knows no repose, and a goad which wounds and never heals; while Holy desires are at once the thirst and the refreshment of Divine love: hunger and food, restlessness and calm, the wound and the cure, they are at once the origin and the consequence of love, the cause and the effect, the breath which kindles it in the heart when it is weak and languid, and the flame which proceeds from it when it is ardent: like natural fire, says St. Gregory (26 Mor. c. 10), whose rising flame, if depressed and beaten down by the breath which, far from extinguishing it, gives it new increase and new ardour.

He who desires God, says St. Bernard, loves always to desire; and he who loves, desires always to love: qui desiderat, semper amat desiderare; et qui amat, semper desiderat amare. (De Am. Dei.) His desires increase and multiply in proportion as his love augments; they enlarge his heart, give it greater capacity, and make it more fitted for the Divine love which requires great hearts. Thus, as he desires only that he may love better, he loves only that he may desire better.

Almost the whole of the Holy Canticle is composed of desires; it begins and ends with them, to give us to understand that we ought to desire all our life. The bride begins to desire as soon as she begins to speak (Cant. i.); Let Him kiss me with the Kisses of His Mouth. At one time she says to her Spouse, Draw me after Thee (ibid.); at another, Let me see Thy Countenance; let me hear Thy Voice (Cant. ii.): again, Come, my Beloved (Cant. vii.); I charge you, O daughters of Jerusalem, if ye find my Beloved, that ye tell Him that I am sick of love (Cant. v.); and she finishes her canticle by saying (Cant. viii.), O that Thou wert as my brother, that sucked the breasts of my mother. These are very pure and ardent desires, and the bride is also careful to justify them by making a solemn protest that her Divine Spouse is most sweet, and altogether to be desired: totus desiderabilis. (Cant. v.) Therefore it is not surprising that she desires Him Alone, and says to Him, in the violence of her transports, Come, my Beloved, come to me; I desire none but Thee; I love none but Thee: Veni, dilecte mi. (Cant. vii.)

AFFECTIONS.

FIRST DAY.

Totus desiderabilis. (Cant. v.)

My Beloved is altogether lovely and desirable; every thing in Him should excite my most violent desires: His Divine Eyes are brighter than the sun; they are the refuge of the unhappy and the interpreters of His Love; all the words of His adorable Lips are oracles; they utter only the language of tenderness to those who love Him, and the sound of His Voice is sweetness itself; His Majestic Face is radiant with light; and if the happiness of the blessed consists in looking upon It, that of the righteous consists in desiring It: His Hands are full of treasures, of Graces, and of Blessings, and they seek only to pour them out abundantly on those who desire them: His Heart is the centre of the purest, the most ardent, and the most delightful love. Very blind should I be not to desire this Beloved, since I cannot desire Him without loving Him, nor love Him without possessing. The desire of earthly good things is very unprofitable, for it leaves the heart restless, and deprived of that which it would have. I will then desire nothing but Thee, my God, and I will desire Thee every moment of my life, for I feel that I possess Thee and that Thou comest to me as soon as I desire Thee.

SECOND DAY.

Totus desiderabilis.

Now, O my God, that I begin to know Thy Worth and Thy Loveliness, now that I strive to love Thee with all my heart, I have but one desire, which contains all others that my heart could form, and I have but one fear to which all my old terrors yield. My sole desire is to be loved by Thee, and to love Thee Alone in time and in eternity. I seek nothing but this, for this comprehends all. For, alas! said the prophet, "Whom have I in heaven but Thee? and there is none upon earth that I desire in comparison of Thee." (Ps. lxxii.) Is it not enough that "Thou art the God of my heart, and my portion for ever?" But my only fear is, that I may lose, not my health, not the esteem of men, not the good things of the earth, not my own life, but Thy Love. This is the greatest evil that can befall me, the only loss that I fear; I count all besides as nothing.

THIRD DAY.

Totus desiderabilis.

My God is altogether Lovely, because He is infinitely Good and infinitely Perfect; He is altogether Desirable, because He is the Source of all good. Why then have I hitherto loved and desired Him so little? I cannot know God without loving Him; I cannot love without desiring Him; and I cannot desire Him without unceasingly sighing to possess Him. My soul, says St. Augustine, is a Sigh of God. The sigh has two principles: the heart which conceives it, and the mouth which forms it and by which it is breathed out to go towards the object that it desires. Bear then, my soul, the likeness of the Heart and of the Mouth of God, Who has graciously sighed for thee. If thou art a sigh proceeding from both, sigh unceasingly for Him Who made thee what thou art by one of those sighs; love Him Alone, desire Him only, and return as often as possible, by sighs full of tenderness, to the adorable Principle whence thou proceedest, since that is also the happy End which thou must seek to attain.

FOURTH DAY.

Totus desiderabilis.

It is strange blindness and insensibility to be persuaded that God possesses all imaginable Perfections, to know that He is infinitely Desirable, that desires may procure thee blissful possession of Him, and yet not to desire Him with all our heart! But, you say, my desires grow weak, and my love languishes at times. Strengthen and sustain the one by the other; desire, and you will love more ardently; renew unceasingly your acts of love, and your desires will be revived, and will soar anew towards God. Divine love is the father of holy desires. Holy desires calm the heart, while they inflame it, and render it more susceptible of the impressions of Divine love. An ardent desire, breathed at a fitting time, is a favourable wind which rekindles the nearly-extinguished fire. It is the Breath of the Holy Spirit, Who thus gives new ardour to our fainting love. If there is pleasure in loving God, there is also pleasure in desiring Him: these two functions blend harmoniously in the heart; they unite to seek together the same end, which is the Heart of God. When shall I unceasingly desire to possess that which I love, and when shall I always love to desire that which is altogether desirable, and which alone I ought to love?

FIFTH DAY.

Veni, dilecte mi. (Cant. vii.)

Come, my Beloved, I desire none but Thee. I would love Thee with all my soul, with all my strength, and with all my heart, as Thou commandest, and I love Thee but feebly. I would have the entire possession of that which I love, and I cannot in this life! When shall I be delivered from this body of death (Rom. vii.), which hinders me from the full enjoyment of my God? My heart is impatient, agitated, inflamed with desire to draw nearer to Thee, and it makes but powerless efforts. It says to Thee, like the bride, Come to me, my Beloved; draw me to Thee. But, alas! how can I unite myself to Thee? My heart is in darkness, and Thou dwellest in inaccessible light; it is upon the earth, and Thou in Heaven; it is carnal, and Thou art a pure Spirit. Yet I will go to Thee, O my God, and Thou wilt come to me: I will go to Thee rather by the desires and emotions of my heart than by the movements of my body: my ardent longings shall lessen the infinite distance between Thee and me; the desires of my heart shall raise me to Thee, and Thy Love shall bring Thee down to me.

SIXTH DAY.

Veni, dilecte mi.

A heart truly imbued with the love of God always desires; it ceases not to breathe sighs towards this supremely lovely Object, and to say, Come, my Beloved. It forms its most violent desires without trouble or disquiet; and it finds as much pleasure in desiring as in loving. As its love cannot be satiated, it always hungers after God. The more it drinks of this sacred stream, the more it thirsts, because the God Whom it loves is Love itself. For to love Love itself, says a Father, is to move in a mysterious and endless circle. It returns always to its Adorable Origin, and is ever recommencing to love and to desire; this sacred Fountain, springing up unto eternal life, is unceasingly in motion; between it and the Heart of God there is a constant flow and refluence; there are always new charms which produce new flames and new desires, which inflame, nourish, and never satiate. Happy hunger, happy thirst, happy desires, happy love, when will you occupy all my soul? and when will you be all the delight of my heart?

SEVENTH DAY.

Veni, dilecte mi.

One deep calleth another, says the Prophet-King. (Psalm xlii.) There is a Deep in Heaven, it is the Heart of God: there is a deep on earth, it is the heart of man. These two deeps desire one another, call one another, and say, Veni, dilecte mi, Come, my Beloved. The heart of man, which feels its weakness, its emptiness, and its extreme poverty, feels also its need of the Heart of God, without which it cannot exist, and it strives to unite itself to It in order never to part. The Heart of God desires the heart of man; It calls and solicits it tenderly, as if It had need of it. The One is an infinite fulness of purity, wisdom, and light; the other a frightful void of all good things, and a lamentable fulness of darkness, sin, and misery. Go then, my soul, where thou art called, hasten thither by thy love, fly by thy desires; invoke the unfathomable deep of the Heart of God; lose thyself blissfully in that abyss of Grace and Goodness; it is thy Beginning, thy End; it should be thy Centre; abide there, it is thy place; thou canst form no other desires without renouncing thy temporal and eternal happiness.

Twenty-seventh Week.

EAGER LOVE.

As Divine love is a Heavenly fire, it is always marked by a certain eagerness which shows its ardour, which proves it, and gives it its value. He who truly loves God, hastens to labour for Him, and is earnestly desirous of fulfilling all the duties of charity, however severe they may seem. The ardent precipitation of love takes the place of all precaution. However eager he may be, he makes no false steps. This eagerness, far from being opposed to wisdom, is on the contrary its effect and fruit, because charity, from which it proceeds, and which sets in motion the mind, the heart, and the hands, is wisdom itself, and enlightens while it transports. He runs, therefore, with a blessed and happy swiftness, and never falls, because this charity ever upholds those whom it causes to move, and can perfectly unite prudence with promptness in action.

The bride, who was perfectly aware of her weakness, felt truly, also, that she could not go fast enough to follow her Beloved Who proceeded with gigantic strides, unless by the help and assistance of Himself Who called her. Draw me after Thee, she says, and we will run after the odour of Thy ointments; trahe me post te, curremus in odorem unguentorum tuorum. Hardly could she walk, yet she desired to run swiftly in the ways of Divine love, and she needed to be drawn by Love Itself, Whose gentle violence and ever-victorious strength draws to Itself the most rebellious and the hardest hearts, and gives them wings to fly rather than to run, until they arrive at the happy end to which they aspire, the possession of God.

In this she desired to imitate her Beloved Who came to her with infinite eagerness. Behold, she says, "He cometh leaping upon the mountains, skipping upon the hills; like a roe, or a young hart:" ecce iste venit saliens in montibus, transiliens colles: similis est capreæ, hinnuloque cervorum. (Cant. ii.)

But lest the bride should insensibly relax in her loving eagerness, and indifference succeed to her first ardour, the Bridegroom commands and ordains to her this eager love. "Behold," says she, "my Beloved spake, and said unto me, Rise up, My love, My fair one, and hasten;" en dilectus meus loquitur mihi: Surge, propera, amica mea, (Ibid.) to give her to understand that we must always be eager to execute that which Divine Love commands.

AFFECTIONS.

FIRST DAY.

Trahe me post te, curremus in odorem unguentorum tuorum. (Cant. i.)

Draw me after Thee, says the bride, we will run to the odour of Thy Perfumes. When an extremely active principle is applied to an unresisting object, it makes what impression it pleases. When the strength of a superior power infinitely surpasses the weight of the subject that it desires to set in motion, it draws and raises it up rapidly, because it can do it without difficulty. Draw me then, Heavenly Spouse, Thou Who hast promised me, that when Thou wert lifted up upon the Cross, Thou wouldest draw all men unto Thee (St. John xii. 32); Thou canst do it without effort. My heart is docile, it will make no resistance, and Thou art Strength Itself; say but one word, and Thou curest the heaviness of my soul which hinders it from going to Thee as eagerly as it ought and desires to do. Enlarge my heart, that I may run swiftly in the way of the most essential of all Thy commandments, which is love. Set it on fire to consume all sensible attachments, which are an enormous weight, and which render it incapable of running after the odour of Thy Divine Ointments. It has been rebellious, draw it; it is fleshly, raise it; it holds to the earth, tear it away, and give it wings to fly to Thee.

SECOND DAY.

Curremus in odorem unguentorum tuorum.

I feel but too much, O my God! that I am of the number of those children of men whom Thou reproachest by Thy prophet with having the heart gross. (Isa. vi.) It is this body of corruption and death that I carry about which weighs me down and hinders me from running eagerly to Thee. Draw me, then, LORD, with that gentle violence with which Thy love is always accompanied. Thy Divine Attraction will render me stronger, more ardent, and more prompt. I dare not say that I will run, because I cannot even walk when I am not with Thee: but we will run together, for I shall be united with Thee. My heart will find no obstacles when Thou shalt have drawn and supported me by Thy Love. I shall fear neither to fall, to lose my way, or to stop in the midst of my career, however hasty my steps, because the way of Thy charity is all light, and it will discover to me the stones of stumbling (1 St. Peter ii. 8), which might stop my steps, and the precipices where I might perish.

THIRD DAY.

Curremus in odorem unguentorum tuorum.

Run, O my soul, to the odour of the Perfumes of the Heavenly Bridegroom. These Perfumes are delicious enough to draw all hearts, for they are no other thing than Divine love. Run quickly, fear not fatigue: he runs easily and rapidly who runs freely: he runs freely who runs by Love: and to obtain more quickly the desire of his heart, he who is drawn, elevated, and transported by the fire of charity, loses all consciousness of his own weight. Quickly follow this Divine attraction; suffer thyself to be borne away by this sweet torrent; yield to this pleasing violence. If charity puts thee in motion, consent to it, answer to it. It is delightful, it is strong, it detaches from the earth, it conducts to God, and thou canst not go to Him too soon. It separates thee from pleasure only to substitute another more pure, more charming, and more durable; by its means thou wilt be released from the weight of thy sins, thy earthly affections, and thy slothfulness; defer not a moment, lest thou lose all and acquire nothing. Weak delays are a symptom of an indifferent heart; and thou canst not better show the ardour of thy love to God, than by promptness and eagerness.

FOURTH DAY.

Ecce iste venit saliens in montibus, transiliens colles. (Cant. ii.)

"Behold, my Beloved, He cometh leaping upon the mountains, skipping upon the hills," says the bride. Happy should I be, Heavenly Bridegroom, if I could regulate my eagerness by Thine, and run to Thee as promptly as Thou comest to me when I call Thee to my assistance! He rode upon the cherubim, says the Prophet, and did fly: He came flying to me upon the wings of the wind (Ps. xviii.); and rejoiceth, says he, as a giant, to run in the ways of love. (Ps. xix.) Again, He bowed the heavens also and came down (Ps. xviii.) instantly to me, though the space be infinite, to show me the eagerness of His Charity. When I love Thee, I possess Thee; when I desire Thee, Thou art at my side; when I think of Thee, Thou art present with me; when I wish to go to Thee, Thou comest immediately to me; when I pray to Thee, my prayer is animated by charity: I may say, with the spouse, "Behold, my Beloved speaks in me;" and by an inward feeling I perceive Thee. I feel in my heart, says St. Ambrose, the odour of Thy Divinity, which fills me, and embalms me with its perfumes: En adest, et intimo sensu odorem divinitatis agnosco. Be not, then, weary, LORD, of coming to me; haste Thee to help me, and make me ever eager to go to Thee.

FIFTH DAY.

Ecce iste venit saliens in montibus, &c.

Remember, my soul, that if thou art in the ways of Divine love, thou art not without a companion. CHRIST walks with thee; He walks swiftly and without stopping: if thou hastenest not, He will go onward; thou wilt lose sight of Him, and wilt never find His Footsteps again; thou will go astray, wilt lose thyself, and be in danger of never rejoining Him. The way is long, the time short; the more quickly thou goest, the more nearly wilt thou approach to GOD; the more nearly thou approachest, the greater wilt thou find the distance, because thou wilt know better the infinite distance between the creature and the Creator. Yet be not discouraged, thou wilt be assisted; the Heavenly Bridegroom will draw thee, He will take thee by the hand, and thou wilt find pleasure in ever walking with new eagerness, until thou arrive at the happy moment which He has fixed from all eternity, to crown thy perseverance.

SIXTH DAY.

En dilectus mens loquitur mihi: Surge, propera, amica mea. (Cant. ii.)

My Beloved spake, says the bride, and said unto me, Rise up, hasten, My love, My fair one. How often, LORD, have I heard the pressing and tender solicitations of this Voice without making fit return? Alas! I feel but too often that indolence dejects me, that sleep overcomes me, that indifference weighs me down, that labour disheartens me, and that it is with difficulty that I rise, move, and hasten, though Thou callest and invitest me to go quickly to Thee. Ah! I have listened to indolence too long; from this moment, LORD, I will obey; I run to Thee as a thirsty hart to the Water-brooks, as a desolate soul to Comfort, as a sick man to a Physician, as the blind to the Light, as the hungry to Bread, as the thirsty to Water, as a child to its Mother, as the miserable to Mercy. Arouse my indifference, give me strength to run, and never stop. Give wings to my love, like those of the dove, to fly to Thee, and to rest in Thee.

SEVENTH DAY.

Surge, propera, amica mea.

Pay attention, my soul, to the Voice of GOD, which calls thee, and listen no more to that of thine indolence and listlessness. Rise immediately when thou hearest thy Bridegroom speaking to the ears of thy heart; run immediately on, receiving inspiration; prove thy love by thy eagerness; fly directly thou feelest the Divine flame of charity. Thou knowest not how soon it may go out; nothing more is necessary than a little delay, a little weakness, a little neglect of thy pious practices. As long as Divine love burns in thy heart, it will extinguish that which the passions would kindle there; thou wilt not have so lively a feeling of them, or at least the feeling will in no degree injure thy innocence. If thou desist for a moment, they will rekindle to punish thy want of zeal; and it will cost thy heart many weaknesses, or terrible combats and great labour, to return to the path from which thou hast strayed, because thou hast followed it with too little energy.

Twenty-eighth Week.

LIBERAL LOVE.

The hand is never niggardly when the heart is full of good will, says St. Gregory. (Mor. xix.) It will be in vain for a rich man to tell me that he has a poor friend whom he loves perfectly: I will never believe him, till their fortunes be equal, and till he has raised his so-called friend from wretchedness; for love, without liberality, if liberality is in our power, is only a delusion and an imposture.

It is by liberality also that God has proved to us the excess of His Love. He gave us all the good things that we possess; and not content with this profusion, He has also given Himself wholly and unreservedly, that is, according to the expression of Tertullian, all that He is and all that He has: Totum quod ipse est et habet, in summo dedit. (De Resur. cap. ix.)

God Alone, in truth, can give everlasting, immense, and infinite gifts; because His Love, which is Himself, is Everlasting, Immense, and Infinite. Amongst men liberality perishes by liberality itself, because their riches are limited as well as their love: but God can always give, for He is inexhaustible.

The Bridegroom is compared to those doves who are always by the great rivers of water: Resident juxta fiuenta plenissima (Cant. v.); a figure of the liberality of God, Who pours into our souls the abundant waters of His Grace, until by their love they become worthy of those eternal torrents of delight with which they will be inundated in Heaven.

The bride afterwards adds, that the Hands of her

Spouse are as gold rings full of jacinths: Manus illius tornatiles, aureæ, plenæ hyacinthis. (Ibid.) The roundness marks the perfection of the gifts of God: gold is the richest of all metal: the Jacinths, of which His Hands are full, and which are of a purple colour, may figure the Blood of Jesus Christ, the most precious of all His Gifts.

Lastly, she strives to respond to the Love and Liberality of her Spouse, by offering Him all that she possesses. Now she offers Him a delicious wine, mixed with spices, and the juice of the pomegranate; and now she says, At our gates are all manner of pleasant fruits, new and old, which I have laid up for Thee, O my Beloved: In portis nostris omnia poma; nova et vetera, dilecte mi, servavi tibi. (Cant. vii.) She desires to possess nothing which she does not present to the Spouse, and the God Whom she loves.

AFFECTIONS.

FIRST DAY.

Resident juxta fluenta plenissima. (Cant. v.)

The Eyes of my Spouse are like the doves by the rivers of waters. The Heart of my God is the abundant source from whence flow the precious torrents of His Graces and of His Mercies; He loads me with favours only because He loves me; I have, then, only to open my heart to Him, and it will be immediately filled. Never had a miser more pleasure in receiving than this Liberal God feels in giving. As His Fulness is infinite, He demands only to pour it out; as His Riches are inexhaustible, and the more He gives the richer He is, He seeks only to give to those who are worthy to receive. But, my soul, remember that thou must restore somewhat to God, in order to be fit to receive from God; and that this flood of liberality and of treasures will cease to flow when there is no reflux and return from thee. Grace descends from Heaven, but it must ascend again by acts of grace, otherwise it will descend no more. Thou hast but too often choked up the channel, through which this torrent passes, by thy ingratitude; thou hast built up a dike, which has stopped it; thou hast received all from God; give Him all that thou art, and all that thou hast, if thou desirest that He should continue to thee a Loving God and a Liberal God.

SECOND DAY.

Resident juxta fluenta plenissima.

I owe all to my God, Who has given me all; His Liberality towards me is a torrent which never ceases to flow, and mine can be but limited; yet He is content with the little that I can give Him. In order to maintain liberal love in my heart, He is so gracious as to give me somewhat to return to Him; and when I give Him that which comes from Him, He fails not to receive it as a gift, to count it as a debt, and to return it me a hundredfold. He has loved me as if there were none but me; all that He has given to others has diminished nothing from that which He desired to give me, for I may possess Him wholly. If He has given Himself wholly to me, I ought to give myself wholly to Him. Liberal love is, then, a debt which I must pay with all that I have, and with all that I am. Thus the least portion of my heart that I give to any creature, is a robbery of His love. I have been guilty of this robbery; let me hasten to restore Him all; otherwise, far from giving Him any thing, I cannot acquit myself of the debt which I owe Him.

THIRD DAY.

Resident juxta fluenta plenissima.

Thy Gifts, O my God, are pleasant streams, which never cease to flow but when we oppose some obstacle to them. Thou hast given me innumerable Gifts, and my only return has been ingratitude. Prepossessed by too much tenderness for the creature, I have given to it a part of that which I owe to my Creator. I owe to Thee, O Heavenly Spouse, all my mind, my heart, my love, my labours, and I have not given them to Thee. How rich should I now be in spiritual goods, if I had faithfully restored myself to my Divine Benefactor, with all the good things that I have received from His Liberal Hands! My graces would be far more abundant, my love much more ardent. These are incomparable blessings and treasures, of which I have deprived myself, because I have given nothing to my God, and have not paid Him that which I owe.

FOURTH DAY.

Manus illius tornatiles, aureæ, plenæ hyacinthis. (Cant. v.)

The Hands of my Heavenly Spouse are as rings of gold, and full of Jacinths, says the bride. Thus, Lord, Thy bride praises Thy liberal Hands. I repeat her praise with deep gratitude, because I have received from Thee as many favours as she did. They are encircled like a ring. This figure, which is the symbol of the perfection of Love, denotes also that they move quickly, to pour out for me the infinite Treasures that they contain. They are of gold, and full of Jacinths. This rich metal, this fulness, and these precious stones, are the symbols of Thy liberal Love, and sure tokens that Thou art ready to pour out in my heart the mystic Gold of Thy Love, the

Fulness of Thy Charity, and the Precious Stone of Thy Grace. Thou hast offered me these great treasures, and I have been blind enough to make myself unworthy of them, by giving Thee nothing in their stead. Thou wouldest be satisfied with my heart, and I refused it Thee. I give it Thee now, O Heavenly Spouse; receive it, and be its Master for ever.

FIFTH DAY.

Manus illius tornatiles, aureæ, plenæ hyacinthis.

God Alone gives liberally and unreservedly the most precious treasures. There are defects in the liberality of men which prove that their love is not perfect. Some of them indiscreetly heap favours on those for whom they have a blind predilection, whilst they refuse them to those who merit them better. Others let them want long before giving, and thus diminish the value of the gift by selling it too dearly. Others give for a time, and then cease to give; their benefits are subject to withdrawal and repentance. Thy liberal Love, O my God, acts not thus towards me: Thou givest to all, because Thou lovest all; and one who desires Thee is sure to be very soon enriched. Thou givest as soon as Thou art entreated, and Thy promptness in giving is a second gift. Thou givest also for ever, and never ceasest to load us with favours so long as we render ourselves worthy of them. By Thy Love, Lord, I desire to regulate mine. I give Thee all that I have, from this instant, without delay. I give myself for ever, and to the last breath of my life, that I may be more surely Thine throughout eternity.

SIXTH DAY.

In portis nostris omnia poma; nova et vetera, dilecte mi, servavi tibi. (Cant. vii.)

At our gates, says the bride, are all manner of

pleasant fruits, new and old, which I have laid up for Thee, O my Beloved. How happy are they, and how faithful must they have been to their God, who, like the bride, have under their roof all sorts of fruits to present to Him, who have kept the old for Him, and have also new to give Him; that is, who have loved Him from the time they first knew Him, are full of the good works of their youth, and offer unreservedly to Him a new heart filled with love! Where are the old fruits? What have I given to God in my youth? or, rather, what have I not given to the world, God's open enemy? It has had the first fruits of my heart; and I have given myself over but too much to its spirit, its prejudices, its fashions, and its customs; and I have given hardly any thing to my God. But where are the new fruits which I ought to present to Him as a daily tribute, in acknowledgment of the favours He gives me every day? What have I given Him yesterday? What have I given Him to-day? What can I offer Him at this moment? Alas! my heart is devoid of love, and my hands of good works. I am poor, O Heavenly Spouse, and by my own fault; give me, then, somewhat to offer to Thee; give me Thyself, in order that I may give myself to Thee.

SEVENTH DAY.

In portis nostris, omnia poma; nova et vetera, &c.

It is a very palpable delusion to pretend to love God without offering Him the new and old fruits that He requires of our charity. Divine Love will never subsist in those interested and mercenary hearts which are always asking and never giving. The favours of Heaven cease to flow when they meet with no return. To maintain a holy exchange of love between the Heart of God and ours, we must render to

Him according as we receive. CHRIST'S Love for us cost Him all His Blood; ours must also cost us something. I consent to it, LORD; but I am poor, and Thou art an inexhaustible Source of treasures. Hast Thou need of my goods? (Ps. xvi. 2.) And in my indigence can I give Thee anything? Yes, LORD, I shall find in my poverty itself a provision for liberal love. I have desires like all the poor, and Thou art their only Object; I offer them to Thee with all my heart; but I will make them efficacious, and accompany them with good works, that I may never appear empty in Thy Presence.

Twenty-ninth Week.

CONTINUAL LOVE.

THE most sublime of all sciences incontestably is that of Love. Its principles are all divine, its speculations very exalted, its duties infinitely extended and multiplied, its study in consequence the study of a whole life, which indeed hardly suffices to acquire it in perfection. The further we go, the greater distance we perceive remaining; the more discoveries we make, the more are we aware of our ignorance; the more we feel, the more we perceive that we might feel more.

It is impossible, therefore, to advance in this elevated science, without persevering and continual application. If we rest, we fail not to grow slack and cold; the mind loses what it had thought, the heart what it had felt. If we allow the love of self, or of other creatures, to succeed at intervals to the love of GOD, the one has time to efface the blessed impressions of the other; these frequent interruptions hinder us from profiting by our first acts of love; these cannot have any influence upon those that follow, they are at too great a distance; and the consequence of this alternation is, that we must begin anew; that at the end of our life we know how to love God no better than at the commencement.

The soul that truly loves never stops; it ever ascends, says St. Augustine; it is more perfect to-day than yesterday, because it loves constantly; its tenderness augments as it continues to love, the second act of love that it produces is always more perfect than the first, and the third more ardent than the second, because these acts meet, and are joined together.

The love of the bride is compared to a fountain of gardens, a well of living waters, and streams from Lebanon: fons hortorum, puteus aquarum viventium, quæ fluunt impetu de Libano. (Cant. iv.) These waters are always in movement; they descend from Lebanon with unvarying rapidity; it is a precious stream from that mysterious River of which the prophet speaks (Psa. xlvi.), which rejoices the Saints in Heaven continually and without interruption.

The Bridegroom says again, that the stature of His bride is like unto the palms: statura tua assimilata est palmæ. (Cant. vii.) The palm ascends ever towards Heaven until it has acquired its full perfection; it produces fruits of admirable sweetness; its leaf never falls, and it preserves its verdure notwithstanding the snow and the frost. We must never cease to love God; and whatever disappointments and trials befall us, we must unceasingly bear the delicious fruit of charity.

AFFECTIONS.

FIRST DAY.

Fons hortorum, puteus aquarum viventium, quæ fluunt impetu de Libano. (Cant. iv.)

The love of my bride is like a fountain of gardens, a well of living waters, and streams flowing impetuously from Lebanon, says the Bridegroom. The Heart of my God is the abundant Source from whence run unceasingly the pure and life-giving waters of Divine Love; and the heart of the bride is the fountain which receives them, and the mysterious well which contains them, in order to water continually the spiritual garden of my soul, above all when it is in dryness, and can with difficulty produce flowers and fruits. Thus she can always love, because God always provides the means. It is a flow and refluence of love which never ceases if the soul is attentive and faithful. I may at all times ascend by my love to the Heart of God, because He has given these mystic waters life and strength enough to re-ascend to their Source. Each time that I ascend there, I draw and bear away with me more abundant and more living waters, to flow for ever, and ever new ardour to love for ever. Why, then, unfaithful soul, dost thou not continually love Thy God?

SECOND DAY.

Fons hortorum, puteus aquarum, &c.

When we try to induce a sinner to do penitence, he consents to it for some days, but refuses to do it during his whole life, though it is his duty, because he complains that his eyes cannot always weep. His tears are dead waters, which soon dry up, because they flow from no spring, and because his penitence is false. When we try to induce a weak Christian to love God, he consents to do so at times and at intervals; his heart even turns to Him with pleasure; he is quite willing to love the world at one time, and God at another; when he is wearied of one of these loves, he refreshes himself with the other: but he will not consent to love continually and uninterruptedly, because he complains that his heart cannot always love the same thing. False love, false tenderness! Weak and blind soul, open the eyes of faith, and thou wilt see in God a Beauty ever new, and worthy of unceasing love. Pray to Him, and He will enable thy inconstant heart to love Him always.

THIRD DAY.

Fons hortorum, puteus aquarum, &c.

If we have once truly enjoyed God, and drunk deep draughts of the waters of this living spring of the Divine love; if our soul, the mystic garden of the Spouse, has been well watered by it, we no longer regard continual love as a prodigy; we are always thirsty, and ever find the means of quenching thirst; and this thirst gives us as much pleasure even as the water which quenches it: we have not to make long journeys in search of this spring, we find it in our own heart, and may draw from it continually. The living water which it contains is always in motion, ever seeking to ascend. As I draw water from this mysterious well, God continually provides me with more. With His Grace I may prove my love to Him as often as I breathe; I may give Him my heart a thousand times a day by new acts of love. This heart ceases not to be mine, though I give it to God. He restores it to me to enable me to give it to Him continually. Thus, O my God, do I aspire to love Thee always.

FOURTH DAY.

Fons hortorum, puteus aquarum, &c.

Holy and inexhaustible Fountain of Divine Love, flow unceasingly into my heart, and never cease to water it with Thy quickening waters, which spring up into eternal life. Enable me always to love Thee, and to make Thee some return; enlarge this heart and make it capable of containing more; water it, drown it, plunge it in this River of delights; open it entirely to receive unresistingly the torrents of pleasure which flow from the Heart of my God, and give these waters power to ascend unceasingly to that Adorable Heart which is their Source; empty mine of those dead and stagnant waters which have flowed, unhappily for me, from the love of the creature, and let them never return; enter it like an impetuous torrent to carry away with Thee all the defilements which my self-love has introduced into it. O Sacred Love, said St. Augustine, Who burnest unceasingly, and art never extinguished! inflame my heart with Thy Divine Ardour? O amor qui semper ardes, et nunquam extingueris, accende me.

FIFTH DAY.

Statura tua assimilata est palmæ. (Cant. vii.)

Thy Stature, says the Spouse, is like to a palm tree. This tree is always green, notwithstanding the frost; and the bride is always fervent, notwithstanding disappointments. It ascends unceasingly towards Heaven; and the bride never ceases to raise herself towards God by her love. You may strive to bend down the palm tree; it either resists, or rises again immediately: the faithful bride never falls, because she always loves, and because love is her strength. The palm tree is upright, so is the bride in all things. It is the badge of victory; the bride always combats until she has obtained it, and she is victorious only because her love is continual, and because she is unceasingly upon her guard. If my heart had been to God like that of the bride; if it had had the uprightness, the elevation, and the continual life of the palm tree: if my love had been permanent, instead of transitory, I should always have obtained the victory in my combats: but I have grown weary of loving God, and have loved Him only by fits and starts. Is it possible to be weary of loving Thee, O my God, Thou Who art infinitely lovely?

SIXTH DAY.

Statura tua assimilata est palmæ.

He whose love for God is only constitutional, is like those trees whose leaves fall as soon as winter begins: he, on the contrary, who has true charity, and that love which proceedeth from Grace, is like the palm tree, which never loses them. The one grows weary, and ceases to love, when his heart loses feeling for God: the other never wearies, and when he feels the least decay, by the sustaining Grace of God he makes successful efforts to love continually. Even the moments during which he appears not to love are not lost, or void of love. When the feeling ceases, the impression remains; it is less a cessation, than a tranquil repose, during which love is not idle. He feels in his heart a propensity, an habitual inclination to love, and he acts in all things as if in the actual exercise of the most ardent love. By this, my soul, thou mayest thoroughly know thyself, and discern if thou art in the paths of true Charity.

SEVENTH DAY.

Statura tua assimilata est palmæ.

My Spouse is Himself this mysterious Palm tree, ever loaded with leaves and fruits. His Love to me is continual; He loves me, and He does me good every moment of my life: there is not a single moment in which He has not supported me. If He had ceased an instant to love me, and to favour me with His Divine Regards, I should have returned immediately unto the abyss of nothingness whence I came forth. Let me say more, there is not a single moment that He has not sincerely desired my salvation and my glory, because He has always loved me. Alas! how have I replied to His continual Favours? Compare, O my soul, the way in which thou hast employed the moments of thy life with this perpetual thoughtfulness of thy God. What time lost! what terrible voids, what intervals, what hours, what days, in which thou hast not loved Thy God! Lament, and repair the past by continual love.

Thirtieth Week.

LOVE OF CONFORMITY.

When two persons of unequal merit are bound together by perfect friendship, it is right that he who feels in the other a genius superior to his own, should conform to his will. With how much more reason should we conform our will to that of God, when we desire to prove our love to Him; to Him Whose Knowledge and Penetration are infallible; to Him Who is the Best of all Friends; to Him Whose Will is always favourable to us; to Him Who inspires us to do His Will, only that He may reward our submission by doing ours.

Love is often defined by the holy Fathers as a will in common between two persons. The superior ought to prevail over the inferior; and to reign gently over him; the other ought to acquiesce; so that of two wills once separate, there shall result but one. We see, indeed, that when God promises a Saviour to Jerusalem, He says that He will reign over her, and she shall be called His Will: vocaberis voluntas mea in eâ. (Isa. lxii.) When we do this Will of God in all things, we are freed by degrees from our own will, the most insupportable of all burdens: that of God takes its place, says St. Augustine. Thus we will as God wills, and all that He wills, because we love Him; and He then does all that we will, because He loves us: quando facimus voluntatem Dei, tunc fit voluntas ejus in nobis. (Hom. xlii. ex. l.)

After the bride has been brought unresistingly into the chambers of her Beloved, she says to Him, We will be glad and rejoice in Thee, remembering that Thy Breasts are better than wine: exultabimus et lætabimur in te, memores uberum tuorum super vinum. (Cant. i.) A holy soul tastes the perfect joy of Divine Love figured by the Breasts of the Spouse, only when it suffers itself to be guided, and conforms itself in all things to His Divine Will.

She complains, indeed, in the third chapter, that she has sought her Beloved without finding Him. And how could she find Him, for she had slept tranquilly in her bed whilst her Spouse was labouring and walking swiftly: but when she obeys Him, rises, and follows Him, she finds Him and says, I found Him whom my soul loveth; inveni quem diligit anima mea. (Cant. iii.)

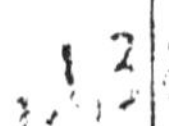

AFFECTIONS.

FIRST DAY.

Exultabimus et lætabimur in te, memores uberum tuorum super vinum. (Cant. i.)

We will be glad and rejoice in Thee, we will remember that Thy Breasts are better than wine. Yes, Lord, I acknowledge that I have never done my own will without remorse and grief, because I have never done it without sin, when it has been contrary to that with which Thou inspirest me: but I have never conformed to Thine by submission and love, however severe it appeared, that it has not caused me innocent pleasure, and produced calm in my soul. Mine is like a pernicious wine which overpowers the reason; Thine, like breasts which give abundantly the delicious milk of Heavenly Consolations. Let my self-will, then, which has caused me so many rebellions, and so much evil, perish. Do Thou, O Divine Will! live in me, and reign in me Alone, destroy and absorb mine. As I desire to love Thee only to death, from henceforth I will only what Thou Thyself willest.

SECOND DAY.

Exultabimus et lætabimur in te, &c.

I cannot feel true spiritual joy, nor delight in God Alone, unless I love Him perfectly; I cannot love Him perfectly if my mind is not entirely conformed to His Illuminations, and my heart to His Divine Will. This double conformity enlightens my mind and inflames my heart. By this Light I see what I have been, what I am, and what I ought to be; I humble myself, and I take precautions for the future. By this Heat I love what I ought to love, and hate what I ought to hate. What, then, hinders me now from having this love of conformity, in which I discover certain comfort and infinite advantage? Is it my mind? I will sacrifice its lights and have no other views than those of God. Is it my self-love? I will watch and combat it, so that it shall have no other will than that of God.

THIRD DAY.

Exultabimus et lætabimur in te, &c.

Why is my heart so often restless and troubled? Why can it find nothing capable of satisfying it? Because it is not united to God by love of conformity. The mind should make it its great object to study the Will of God, and the heart should make it a duty and a pleasure to follow it and to conform its own thereto; without this I shall never delight in GOD. To know the Will of GOD well, we must begin by loving Him. GOD reveals his Designs and His Secrets only to His friends. To execute the Will of GOD we need strength, and love again gives this. By this submissive and loving conduct I shall find my joy in GOD Alone. It is impossible to be calm or to feel any pleasure when we gainsay the Will of GOD, because nothing can prosper without it. Blind heart, thou understandest not thy true interest when thou wouldest follow other paths than that of the Will of GOD! it is thy Pilot, thy Compass, thy Light, and the Centre of thy repose. It shall be henceforth my rule, O my GOD. I will love Thee because Thou wilt have it, and I will suffer because Thou willest it, and as much as Thou willest, assured that Thou lovest me, and that Thou willest only my good.

FOURTH DAY.

Exultabimus et lætabimur in te, &c.

It is but too just, LORD, that it should cost my heart some sacrifices before it tastes the joy of possessing Thee, and that I should expose myself to suffer all that Thou art pleased, in order to conform my will to Thine. What did it not cost Thee to conform Thine to that of Thy Adorable Father? all Thy Blood! Couldest Thou suffer, Thou, Who art an impassible GOD, but at the expense of a miracle of Thy Almighty Power? Couldest Thou suffer, Thou, Who wert all filled with an essential happiness which could not quit Thee for a moment? It was necessary, by an unheard-of miracle of Thy Love, to suspend the outpouring of Thy Glory, which would naturally have flowed from Thy Divinity upon Thy Holy Humanity, and thus to deliver It to suffering. I am ready, LORD, to conform myself to Thine: whatever it may cost me, self-indulgence, aversions, repugnance, pain, natural affections, human respects, temporal advantages, pleasures, I will sacrifice all to the love of conformity, even though Thou shouldest exact the last drop of my blood.

FIFTH DAY.

Inveni quem diligit anima mea. (Cant. iii.)

I found Him Whom my soul loveth, says the bride. But she did not find Thee, LORD, till she had risen and sought Thee as Thou hadst commanded her. It is, indeed, loving Thee very imperfectly to conform ourselves to Thy Divine Will only when It agrees with the natural feelings of our heart, which seeks only pleasure and repose: and to find It bitter when It is opposed to our inclinations, and when It calls on us to awake from our indifference, and to rise and run after Thee amid sufferings and persecutions. The union of our will with Thine cannot be an evident mark of our love unless it be universal, courageous, tranquil, and resigned in all things, in prosperity, in pleasure, in pain, in abundance, in poverty, in glory, in shame, in health, in sickness, in life, and in death. I acquiesce, O Heavenly Spouse, I submit, I conform myself from duty and from love; I am content with all that Thou wilt do with me, provided that I love Thee, and that Thou wilt save my soul.

SIXTH DAY.

Inveni quem diligit anima mea.

How doth a "It is the Will of GOD," enable us to find Him Whom our soul loveth amidst the bitterest tribulations, when it is spoken by the lips, only because it is first felt in the inmost heart! How energetic is this one word! What a powerful charm, what an efficacious remedy is it in all the most unlooked for and most grievous troubles, vexations, and evils, when it proceeds from love of conformity and not mere necessity; when we speak it at the first instant, the first assault of grief, and not when the heart, exhausted with murmurs and complaints, regards it only as the last resource and refuge from the evils on which it has worn out all its sensibility! Try it, my soul, and thou wilt find effects that will agreeably surprise thee; unite thy will with that of GOD, directly thou sufferest pronounce an act of resignation and love, maintain it with steadfast courage; thou wilt never suffer, and wilt have all the merit of suffering.

SEVENTH DAY.

Inveni quem diligit anima mea.

The Will of GOD is GOD Himself; I cannot conform myself to it without finding Him Whom my soul loveth, without His reposing in me, and my finding rest in Him. By this conformity, I free myself from an insupportable burden, and deliver myself from the tyrannical empire of my own will. By this union of my will with that of GOD, mine is elevated, purified, and hallowed; it is happily lost to be found again in Him in a far more noble and more glorious manner. If I love Thee, O Heavenly Bridegroom! and if I truly love myself with a pure and spiritual love, I shall never strive to bend Thy Divine Will to mine; but to elevate, conform, and unite mine to Thine, however severe it may appear to me. Let Thy Adorable Will be done in Heaven and upon earth, in my mind, in my heart, in my body, in my soul, in all that I possess, in all that I desire, in all that I love, and in all that I am.

Thirty-first Week.

LOVE OF RESEMBLANCE.

We are naturally inclined to love our own likeness, and love is almost always founded on resemblance, for it either supposes it, or is not long in producing it. From this it is easy to conclude that we are placed on the earth only to love God, because we have borne His Image from our birth, and the Almighty Creator engraved it upon us only because He loves us and desires that we should love Him.

Our Adorable Saviour has given fresh clearness, fresh beauty, and fresh likeness to this Image, by uniting Himself to our nature. He has taken what was in man, that man might take what was in God, and that this admirable exchange, as the Church calls it, making of man a perfect Image of God, may establish and preserve perfect love in perfect resemblance.

But it is not enough to bear this Image on our face; it is not enough that our soul, by its spirituality and simplicity, be an expression of the being of God: it is further necessary that it strive to imitate His Justice, His Charity, and His other Perfections; it must become a living copy of the Virtues of Jesus Christ; and love must perfect and preserve the Features of this Divine Image.

The Spouse instructed His bride in this love of resemblance, when He said to her, Set Me as a Seal upon thine heart, as a Seal upon thine arm: pone me ut signaculum super cor tuum, ut signaculum super brachium tuum. (Cant. viii.) The heart is the seat of the feelings of love, and the arm denotes its actions. Set Me as a Seal upon thine heart; that is, according to the saying of an eminent bishop, Draw from My Heart all the feelings of inviolable love (Guillel. Paris. hic); receive and take My Form, as the yellow wax receives it from a seal, and, by an exact representation, retain My Image; et meam subtili expressione similitudinem trahas. The stronger is the impression of love, the more resembling shall My Image in thee be found. Set me as a Seal upon thine arm: ut signaculum super brachium tuum. (Cant. viii.) It is not enough to feel; in order to resemble, it is further necessary to act, to labour as I have done, and to make My Actions the only model of thine.

AFFECTIONS.

FIRST DAY.

Pone me ut signaculum super cor tuum. (Cant. viii.)

Set Me, says the Bridegroom, as a Seal upon thine heart. There is a natural Image of God hidden in the heart of rational man; there is a supernatural Image of God hidden in the heart of Christian man; love is the seal and the signet which has impressed it. Let me carefully seek them both. I must find them, for I have a heart, I am a rational man, and so honoured as to be a Christian. Let me seek it to engrave it more deeply, and to give it new features of resemblance by purer and more ardent love. Alas! I have reason to fear that this Image may be effaced or sullied by the innumerable earthly affections which have occupied my heart. Help me, Lord, to find it; help me to repair it; help me to seek out all its features; imprint Thyself upon my heart as the signet upon the wax, and grant me grace to love Thee so strongly, that I may never lose the Impression.

SECOND DAY.

Pone me ut signaculum super cor tuum.

JESUS CHRIST is the Seal; and the heart of the Christian ought to be a tender and supple wax, to receive its impression; after which it should be, according to the saying of Tertullian, the coin and image of JESUS CHRIST: Moneta et imago Christi. A coin becomes a lawful instrument of commerce in a kingdom, only when its metal is pure, when it has been violently cast in the image of the prince, and when it has passed through the fire, the crucible, the anvil, and the hammer. My heart can become the true coin of JESUS CHRIST only when its substance is pure, when it has passed through the fire, the crucible, and the trials of love, and has nobly sustained them without sinking or changing. Strive, then, my soul, to bear upon thine heart the Impress and Image of JESUS CHRIST Suffering; receive the impression of His Heart all burning with Love and Charity; resemble Him in every feature, and thou wilt become a coin of good alloy to purchase Heaven. Love in order to suffer well; suffer in order to love well; be pure, and never sully the Image of thy GOD. I am Thy Image, LORD; I am Thy coin: form in me so perfect a resemblance, that the love of the creature may never efface it.

THIRD DAY.

Pone me ut signaculum super cor tuum.

I have but to open the eyes of my soul, and I shall see in GOD all that I ought to love. I have but to open my heart, and I shall receive from Him all that is necessary to love Him well. He is not only the Object most deserving of love, but He is also the Model and Example of the most excellent Love, and an Exemplar Who, not content with showing Himself to my mind, impresses Himself upon my heart as a seal upon wax, if I oppose no resistance to His Divine Impressions. Open Thy Heart to me, Heavenly Bridegroom; open to me my own; bend down Thine, raise mine; unite them together, that mine may receive Thy Image and Thy Features, and that the resemblance may be perfect. Teach me to do for Thee what Thou hast done for me; discover to me more and more how Lovely Thou art; make me feel what I ought to love, and grant me grace never to love anything but through Thy Love and for Thy Love.

FOURTH DAY.

Pone me ut signaculum super cor tuum.

How blind and hard to itself would my heart be, if it did not love Thee with all the tenderness of which it is capable, and if it refused to open to receive the gracious impressions which Thou art pleased to make in it! It is the work of Thy Adorable Hands, it bears Thy Image and Likeness; Thou hast formed it only for an abode, a throne, an altar, and a tabernacle. Enter, Lord, into this abode, and purify it from all that does not bear the glorious features of Thy Love; rule as a sovereign on this throne, and give me all the docility which I need to obey Thee; receive sacrifices of love upon this altar; kindle on it a holy fire, which shall always burn, and never be extinguished; reside as a God of Majesty and Holiness in this living tabernacle that Thou hast formed for Thyself: but O Heavenly Spouse, perfect Thy copy in this image; engrave upon it all Thy Features, and efface all which do not resemble Thee.

FIFTH DAY.

Ut signaculum super brachium tuum.

Set me also, says the Bridegroom, as a Seal upon

Thine arm as well as upon Thine heart. It is not enough, then, to bear the image of JESUS CHRIST upon my heart by feelings of tenderness, it must be also imprinted upon my arm; I must strive to copy the actions by which He has proved His Love to me. Consider, then, O my soul, that the religion in which thou art placed is a learned academy. The fine Original that we have to copy there is JESUS CHRIST; it is impossible to copy Him well but by a love at once of the affections and of action; it is not enough to feel, we must act. Place thyself well, choose a good light, design correctly; begin with bold and noble strokes; take beautiful and rich colours, bright, durable, and unchanging. Be assiduous at thy task. The Original is well placed, He is elevated upon a mountain, and fastened upon a cross. He is there immoveable, He is there either dying or dead; choose one or other of these attitudes. Represent truly that Head defiled with Blood, those dimmed Eyes, that livid Mouth, those pierced Hands and Feet. Be not content with copying His outward appearance in thine, go to the Heart; It is opened by a spear that thou mayest see It more easily. Copy Its Love, and Its Actions of Love, and thou wilt make a perfect picture. Then lower thine eyes to the ground of Calvary, thou wilt see it all wet with His Blood; by this Blood poured forth thou wilt understand that Love shows itself more in actions than in feelings. This is the excellent Original which thou must imitate, and of which thou oughtest thyself to be a perfect copy, and a speaking likeness. Bear this Image upon thy heart and thy whole person till death.

SIXTH DAY.

Ut signaculum super brachium tuum.

Thou hast loved me, LORD; Thou lovest me, Thou desirest that I should love Thee, and should bear Thy Portrait upon my heart and upon my arm. This truth transports me, and I cannot read it in Thy Divine Word, where it is so often repeated, without being moved, or repeat it to myself without feeling new pleasure each time. My God and my Spouse desires that I should bear His Image in my heart, and His Divine Portrait on my arm: what a grace, and what a favour! He has formed me only in His own Likeness; He is Jealous of His Image; He will not have me lose it, or let it fall in the mire; He desires that I shall study to copy and to imitate it every moment of my life: can I have a nobler and more glorious occupation? To acquit myself of this duty, I must make it my great business to love Him as He has loved me, by doing for Him what He has done for me.

SEVENTH DAY.

Ut signaculum super brachium tuum.

Henceforth I will listen no more to the feelings of my heart, except when they are in perfect agreement with those of the Heart of God: I will bear His Image on my arm, and regulate my actions by His. I desire, O my God, that my love for Thee may be the image of that which Thou bearest to Thyself. Thou lovest Thyself supremely; and all that Thou lovest Thou lovest for Thyself Alone: Thou lovest Thyself wholly and undividedly, continually and uninterruptedly: by this love, Lord, will I regulate mine. Stamp all the characters of this Love upon my heart and upon my arm, as the seal on the wax: be Thou in such manner the Master of my heart, that it may love only Thee and for Thee: give it a single and unmixed love, give it a constant love, which will never weary of burning for Thee, which will suffer all, be never repulsed, undertake all, and resemble Thee in all things.

Thirty-second Week.

RENEWED LOVE.

In the love of God, more than in all other things, novelty has always charms; and frequent repetitions, far from being odious, are always pleasing. Jesus Christ did not content Himself with asking once of Peter, Lovest thou Me? Simon Joannis, amas me? (St. John xxi.) He asked him three times in the same discourse, and He took so much pleasure in the loving repetitions of the Apostle, that He then confided to Him the care of His sheep.

We cannot repeat too often to God that we love Him with all our heart. The feelings of this love, though sacred, are subject to decay, like other created things; they lose their strength, and are worn out; the different objects which the heart finds in its way often injuriously divert these feelings, and unless we are attentive and exact in renewing our acts and protestations of love, we cease to love.

Even if the heart feels itself dry and indifferent towards God, the lips should often pronounce these acts. By this pious industry they ordinarily pass from the mouth to the heart. Thus, says St. Gregory, we preserve our soul in its first beauty; and this continual renewal of fervour purifies it, and insensibly perfects it in love: Mens humana dum igne amoris excoquitur, semper in se servat claritatem pulchritudinis quotidianâ innovatione fervoris. (Mor. xxii. 2)

The Spouse compares His beloved, at one time, to a vine covered with flowers, which are renewed every year to bear new fruits, and says to her: The flowers of the vine are giving their sweet smell. Arise, my love, my fair one, and come away. Vineæ florentes dederunt odorem suum. Surge, amica mea, speciosa mea, et veni. (Cant. ii.) At another time He compares her to a delightful garden: thy plants, says He, are a garden of pomegranates, with pleasant fruits, with spikenard and myrrh: Emissiones tuæ paradisus malorum punicorum cum pomorum fructibus. (Cant. iv.) And He adds, that this mystic garden always reproduces its first perfumes: Cum omnibus primis unguentis (Ib.); to make us understand that the soul of the Christian, which is the spouse of JESUS CHRIST, should be ever renewing its first fervour, lest it become languid, and should unceasingly produce new affections and new acts of love.

AFFECTIONS.

FIRST DAY.

Vineæ florentes dederunt odorem suum; surge, amica mea, speciosa mea, et veni. (Cant. ii.)

The flowers of the vine give a sweet smell: Arise, My love, My fair one, and come away, says the Spouse. Flowers wither, their beauty fades, their scent passes away almost as soon as they are gathered; often the same sun which makes them blow, sees them die the same day; and nature repairs this loss only by daily renewing, and by furnishing the plants, which bear these flowers, with new vigour to bring forth more. The mysterious vine of my soul sometimes produces the pleasing flowers of Divine love when the Sun of Justice favours it with His Regards; it has happy moments, during which it is all on fire, and all perfumed with the sweet odour of this Divine charity, which God sheds abroad in our hearts. But, alas! these flowers pass away too quickly, because I am not careful to renew them. Thou, Heavenly

Bridegroom, must furnish my soul, Thy vine, with the sap and the vigour of an ever-new grace, that it may always produce new flowers; but it is my part to cultivate them, and I do it not.

SECOND DAY.

Vineæ florentes dederunt odorem suum, &c.

Arise, my soul, Thy Spouse calls thee, surge; and He calls thee as His beloved, amica mea. Repeat these words to thyself unceasingly; they are sweet to hear and to pronounce. Thou hast need of this frequent repetition, because thy love sinks unceasingly into faintness, and must unceasingly be renewed. Imagine that thou hearest these words from the Lips of thy God, and from thy God Who loves thee, since He calls thee His beloved. He speaks then to thy heart as to that of His bride, and He desires that thy love may be renewed like hers. Think not to have fulfilled the whole extent of the precept of charity, because thou hast given thy heart to God at the beginning of the day; but too often art thou guilty of acts contrary to this first gift of thyself, which are at least an implicit withdrawal, and hinder it from influencing all the other actions of the day. Thou canst not repeat too often to God that thou lovest Him with all thy heart.

THIRD DAY.

Vineæ florentes dederunt odorem suum, &c.

The vine would never put forth new flowers, if the Author of nature did not furnish it every year with new sap; the fire would soon go out, if fresh fuel were not incessantly substituted for that which is consumed; our bodies would perish if we did not give them each day new food; and every thing in nature subsists only by constant renewal; but this renewal is necessary no less in Grace than in nature, and above all in the exercise of Divine Love. This love is at once created and uncreated. It is uncreated in its Origin, which is God: but it is created in its continuance, and when it enters into the heart of man, it seems to contract the conditions of the creature to which it is communicated. It perishes if not renewed; or rather, it remains or withdraws, it is ardent or languid, according to the way in which it is received and preserved. Its infusion depends on God Alone; its preservation in part on myself; and I shall never preserve it if I am not careful to make acts of it often, and to renew them whenever I perceive that it begins to languish.

FOURTH DAY.

Emissiones tuæ paradisus malorum punicorum cum pomorum fructibus. (Cant. iv.)

Thy plants, says the Spouse, are a garden of delights, with all manner of fruits. The soul of the just is the mysterious garden of the Spouse; and to be a garden of delights, like that of the bride of the Canticles, it is not enough that the flower-beds are in good order, that pleasant flowers are found there, in constant succession, and having the charm of novelty; the garden must also be filled with innumerable good trees, bearing delicious fruits for all seasons, and above all for that of winter. These flowers are the affections of Divine Love; and these abundant and ever-new fruits are the acts of that love. How often, my soul, hast thou been almost discouraged in the severe season of internal abandonments, of dryness, of trials and of sufferings, for want of having laid up a provision of those delicious fruits which would have sustained thee in thy weakness and dejection! How many faults hast thou committed, how many good things lost, in a state in which thou mightest have practised so many virtues, and acquired so many graces, if thou hadst faithfully renewed thy love!

FIFTH DAY.

Emissiones tuæ paradisus malorum, &c.

The soul of the bride was a delightsome garden for her Spouse: the flower-beds and plants, the flowers and fruits, the affections and the acts of Divine love, made it a paradise of delights; the neatness, the order, the rich colours, furnished a charming spectacle to His Eyes; the odour of the different flowers was a sweet perfume for His Smell; but above all, the pomegranates, and the other fruits which He found there abundantly, delighted His Taste. Art thou, my soul, a paradise of delights for thy Spouse, CHRIST JESUS? Art thou not, on the contrary, a hideous desert, an ungrateful soil, which, instead of bearing daily the new flowers and fruits of charity, produces nothing but fresh thorns? Entreat the Heavenly Spouse to kindle in thee the fire of His love, to consume those monstrous productions of self-love which sprout and renew themselves unceasingly, that the soil of thy heart may bear nothing but the fruits of Grace and of the most excellent Charity.

SIXTH DAY.

Cum omnibus primis unguentis. (Cant. iv.)

In thy garden, also, My beloved, are all the first perfumes, says the Spouse; there are found all the ardour of those first affections, all the fervour of this first charity, all the exactness of this first devotion; nothing has become cold, nothing grown slack; thou hast preserved the first spirit of thy calling, because thou hast been careful to renew it often. When I gave myself to my GOD, I did it with all the ardour of which I was capable: weariness, contempt, trials, temptations; I conquered all, because my love was new. This first fire which inflamed me, sustained me against the most sensible evils, and I thought that nothing was capable of shaking or overcoming me: but the odour of these first perfumes has insensibly passed away through my negligence in preserving myself in my first spirit and in my first fervour. Renew me, LORD, and give me daily a new heart, which shall be always Thine.

SEVENTH DAY.

Cum omnibus primis unguentis.

It is no cause of surprise, that we should grow weary of loving a creature, however amiable it may appear; it fades as the flower of the grass; this passes away, and grows old, and we need not wonder that profane love does the same. But when I love GOD, I love a Beauty always new, and undecaying; I love an infinite and inexhaustible Goodness, Which daily begins anew, and is never weary of heaping new favours on me. I ought to have loved Him with all my heart, and to have offered to Him the first perfumes of my love, from the time I first knew Him: but this is not enough, I ought to offer them to Him every day of my life by new acts of love; I ought to love Him as He loves me. He never ceases to bestow new favours on me; if I am faithful to Him, I should be ever adding new fire to my love, lest it fail. New protestations of attachment, new confidence, a new mind, a new heart: this is my duty; without this my love will fail like profane love, and I shall soon find myself without love, the greatest evil which can befall me.

Thirty-third Week.

UNIVERSAL LOVE.

It is no cause for surprise that God, Who has loved us with an universal and unreserved Love, requires the same from us, and that, in the command that He has given of this Love, He demands that we love Him with all our heart, and not with a part, with all our soul and with all our strength. This is a very plain law of universal love.

He requires that we should love Him with all our heart; that is, that He shall be the only Object of all its affections, desires, and attachments; and He regards the least sensible tenderness which inclines it towards the creature, and finds its end in that, as a robbery.

He wishes that we should love Him with all our mind; that is, that all its thoughts, aims, projects, and study, should be devoted to Him; so that, if it is obliged sometimes to think of temporal things, it may always be with regard to Him Alone. He requires that we should love Him with all our soul, that all our faculties may be consecrated to Him, our memory filled with Him Alone, that our understanding be applied only to Him, and that our will determine nothing without Him. He desires, in short, that we should love Him with all our strength, and that outwardly as well as inwardly we may be unreservedly devoted to Him, that our eyes may see, our tongue speak, our hands labour only for Him, and that every part of us may strive to show Him our love; and in this consists the universal love which He has a right to exact of us.

It is also to establish its necessity, and to show its benefits, that the Spouse and the bride reciprocally describe one another's beauty, omitting nothing which can make it more striking. Behold, thou art fair, My love! exclaims the Spouse, without that which is hidden within. Quàm pulchra es, amica mea, absque eo quod intrinsecùs latet! (Cant. iv.) By this exclamation, He makes known to us that perfect beauty, which is nothing else but perfect love, results only from the universal harmony between the interior and the exterior of the bride.

The bride, also, in her turn, describes the wondrous Beauty of her Beloved; and after having said that His Head is as the most fine gold, His Eyes as those of doves, His Lips like lilies, dropping sweet-smelling myrrh, she unites all these touches in one, when she says, He is altogether lovely: totus desiderabilis. (Cant. v.)

AFFECTIONS.

FIRST DAY.

Quàm pulchra es, amica mea, absque eo quod intrinsecùs latet! (Cant. iv.)

Behold, thou art fair, My love, without that which is hidden within! When shall I attain that my Heavenly Spouse shall address these words to me as He addressed them to His bride? When both outwardly and inwardly I shall be wholly consecrated to His Divine Love. Charity only can procure for me this universal beauty, to please His Eyes, and to attract the praises of His adorable Lips, when for His love my eyes turn away from all objects of vanity, and pour forth tears of penitence and love; when my ears are closed to all the discourses of the world, and opened only to His Divine Word; when my mouth has renounced every excess, and unceasingly sings the mercies of my God; when my smell has renounced all sensuality, and when the odour of the poor and of dungeons shall be its delight; when my hands labour only for the Glory of God and for my own salvation. This is the outward beauty of the bride to which I aspire.

SECOND DAY.

Absque eo quod intrinsecùs latet.

Without that which is hidden within, says the Bridegroom. The outward senses, O my God! give Thee but feeble testimonies of love, when the inward senses are not entirely devoted to Thee. To love Thee with universal love, all that is within me must be unreservedly Thine. Bless the Lord, then, O my soul, and with all thy inward powers sing the praises of His Holy Name. But that I may do this, O Divine Spouse, exclaimed St. Augustine, give me a memory remembering only Thy Favours and Thy Goodness, my wretchedness and Thy Mercies; give me a mind thinking only of Thee, and occupied only with Thy Greatness and my littleness; give me a heart loving Thee only, and loving Thee universally and in all things, in exaltation as in abasement, in joy as in grief, in dryness and desertion, as in the most sensible delights. I desire that all that is within me and without me shall love Thee unto death.

THIRD DAY.

Quàm pulchra es, amica mea, &c.

Thou givest praise, Lord, to the universal love of Thy bride when Thou admirest all her outward and inward beauties: but Thou makest this love an express law in Thy Gospel, when Thou commandest me to love Thee with all my soul, with all my heart, and with all my strength. Thou wouldest have my soul to know that Thou art Lovely, wouldest have my heart feel it, and my works be answerable to my love. To know Thee is the happy prelude to charity, it is the introduction to love, because it is impossible to know Thee well without loving Thee. To feel Thee, to enjoy Thee, is the delight of love: but to serve Thee by inclination is the sublimity of this love; it is the love of the whole being; and thus, with the help of Thy Grace, I aspire to love Thee.

FOURTH DAY.

Quàm pulchra es, amica mea, &c.

In order to acquire this true beauty which the Heavenly Spouse admires in His beloved, we must love GOD at all times, in all things, and with one's whole being; the least reserve blemishes this beauty of the soul, and declares either the weakness or the falseness of the love. But, to know if we love Him universally, we must ask our heart, our mind, our tongue, and our hands. My heart, dost thou love GOD? Is He the only Object of all thy desires, and the Origin of all thy affections? Dost thou never hesitate when required to sacrifice to Him that to which thou art most sensibly attached? My mind, dost thou love GOD? Dost thou give all thy thoughts to Him? Dost thou give attention to His Divine Presence, and to all the ways of mortification that He gives thee? My tongue, dost thou love GOD? Dost thou consecrate all thy words to Him? Dost thou maintain His interest every where? My hands, do you love GOD? For what do you labour the most? Undoubtedly for what you love best; and is what you love best the Divinity That you adore? Ah! LORD, this examination confounds me. My heart, my mind, and my hands do not love Thee as they ought; and I am very far from that universal love which Thou demandest of me.

FIFTH DAY.

Totus desiderabilis. (Cant. v.)

My Beloved is altogether Lovely, says the bride,

and I ought to say and to feel it with her. He is altogether Lovely, because He is Beauty and Goodness itself. The excess of His Love, the tenderness of His Mercy, His Gentleness, and His Patience, are proofs of the Goodness of His Heart. He is, then, altogether Lovely, because He has all that can attract the most ardent love, which consists in Beauty and Goodness. But, happily for me, it is a Beauty impressed, and a Goodness poured out in my soul by continual grace. He imprinted on me, when He created me, the Light of His Countenance, says the prophet, to give joy to my heart (Ps. iv. 6); and in order to engage it to raise itself to the Original from love for the copy, He poured out His Goodness on me by loving me, not with part, but with the whole of His Heart; by redeeming me, not with part, but with all His Blood. How hardened must I be not to love so Lovely an Object! How ungrateful to make no return to so universal a Love!

SIXTH DAY.

Totus desiderabilis.

Is all our mind, our heart, and our soul, too much? Is all that we feel, that we desire, that we possess, and that we are, too much to mark our love to a God Who is altogether Lovely, and Who has given us the very last drop of His Blood? Ah, Lord! it would have cost Thee much less, if Thou hadst chosen, and if Thou hadst loved us less. But Thy Love is universal and without reserve; Thou carriest it to excess, and Thou knowest not what it is to spare Thyself when the interest of those whom Thou lovest is concerned. Thou hast given us Thy Labours, Thy Merits, Thy Sufferings, Thy Body, Thy Mind, Thy Soul, Thy Heart, Thy Blood, and Thy Life: what can we render Thee for so universal a love? and how answer to so many favours? Happy, indeed, that Thou wilt be satisfied with a heart that Thou hast formed Thyself! I offer it to Thee, LORD, with all the tenderness, the affections, the desires, and the ardours of which it is capable.

SEVENTH DAY.

Totus desiderabilis.

A creature altogether hateful, formed and redeemed by the Hands of a GOD altogether Lovely, what a frightful monster is this in the order of nature and of Grace! But am I not myself this hideous monster for which I appear to have such horror? To know certainly, let us examine what renders a creature lovely or hateful in the Eyes of GOD. Divine love undoubtedly is its whole beauty, and attracts the esteem and love of GOD: the want of this love makes it a monster, and draws down on it the contempt and hatred of GOD. But none can truly love who does not love as He has commanded; that is, universally, and with all his heart, with all his soul, and with all his strength. Ah, LORD! what reason have I to fear lest I have deserved Thy Hatred, rather than Thy Love! But I am resolved to love Thee henceforth with all that I am, and with all that Thou hast given me. Thou hast given me a mind, I offer to Thee all its understanding; Thou hast given me a heart, I present to Thee all its ardours, and I sacrifice to Thee all its attachments; Thou hast given me a body and a soul, I consent to lose both, provided that I love Thee in time and possess Thee in eternity.

Thirty-fourth Week.

CONSTANT LOVE.

Nothing is more inconstant than the heart of man; it is weaker than the reed, more fragile than glass, and lighter than the wind; it yields itself and is carried out of itself continually, to run blindly wherever its fickleness leads it; it builds and destroys, says St. Bernard; it loves, and hates that which it has loved; it promises, and retracts; it makes projects, and effaces them. A prey to its different passions, it is hardly ever in harmony with itself: hurried away by restless vivacity, by unquiet and rapid emotions, and by an infinite multitude of different desires, nothing is capable of fixing it but the love of God: and it is even to be feared that it may too soon grow weary of having loved Him, and, disheartened by the severe and continuous sacrifices which this love exacts from it, its natural inconsistency may resume its power.

Therefore it has need of great light, of powerful motives, and evident examples; of light to know well what it ought at once to love, which is God Alone; of motives to induce it to dwell for ever upon this supremely Lovely Object; and of examples to make it easier to practise this love without sinking under temptations to discouragement, or being moved by the seducing and flattering objects which we continually find in our path, and which strive to make an unjustifiable diversion of its love to themselves. The bride of the Canticles furnishes us with this light, these motives, and these examples. Hardly is she given to her Bridegroom before her mother's children are angry with her: Filii matris meæ pugnaverunt contra me. (Cant. i.) I know that some interpreters here speak of the persecutions which the early Church suffered from the synagogue; but many others apply these words to the faithful soul ill-treated by the world, by flesh and blood, when it desires to love God; and noble enough to find in these very sufferings new motives for firmness in the love of God. She says afterwards that she will be entirely her Beloved's, and that she will not cease to go to the mountain of myrrh, and to the hill of frankincense, until the day break and the shadows flee away: Donec aspiret dies, et inclinentur umbræ. (Cant. iv.) These shadows denote this present life, which is filled only with darkness: this day is that of eternity, where evidence will succeed to the obscurity of faith. Thus a true bride of Jesus Christ should labour, combat, and love constantly till death.

AFFECTIONS.

FIRST DAY.

Filii matris meæ pugnaverunt contra me. (Cant. i.)

My mother's children were angry with me, says the bride. But, Lord, she has remained faithful to Thy Love; the outrages she had received from her own brothers have not made her change; her veil has been taken away from her; she has been cruelly struck; and the more she was ill-treated, the more she loved Thee. How far am I from this noble firmness! The least disappointment has shaken my confidence and chilled my love; my protestations of courage have only lasted till the time of trial. My mother's children indeed were angry with me from the time that I entered on the career of Divine love; mockery, contempt, and criticism have assailed me, but should I not have been prepared for them? Did not the Apostle forewarn me on this point, when he said that all that will live godly in CHRIST JESUS shall suffer persecution? (1 Tim. iii. 12.) Why have I slackened my steps? Would it not have been far better to cleave fast to Thee, O my GOD? What hast Thou done that I should so soon cease to love Thee? and what good thing can I hope from the world that I should prefer its love to Thine?

SECOND DAY.

Filii matris meæ pugnaverunt contra me.

It is not only my mother's children who have risen against me to withdraw from the dominion of GOD the heart that I had given Him; it is my own children, the monstrous productions of my heart; it is I who have risen against myself; it is I who am the source of my own inconstancy; it proceeds more from my own heart than from outward causes. It is my self-love which has brought me often back to myself. If I had constantly hated myself, I should have always loved my GOD. It is my own feebleness which could not maintain a continued love, has wearied too soon of that which ought to be my whole delight; it is my indolence which has refused to undertake the laborious duties to which this love engaged me; it is my criminal preference for creatures which has brought me down, and borne me towards them, because I have not been careful to repress its first emotions; it is the natural fickleness of my heart which seeks for pleasure in novelty, and which would fain love at one time GOD, at another the world. I know my inconstancy, O my GOD! I know the wounds that I have given myself; help me to heal them.

THIRD DAY.

Filii matris meæ pugnaverunt contra me.

What a gross delusion is it to love GOD and to draw back as if we repented of having loved Him; or to love Him and to refuse to endure all the trials of love, whencesoever they come, whether from God, from our brethren, or from our self! To love GOD is not merely to say to Him, My GOD, I love Thee; but it is to say it constantly every moment of our life, with the lips, the heart, and the actions, at once; it is to overcome ourselves nobly for His love, in dejection, in weariness, in desertion, in privation of joy, in pain, and to persevere in this till death. Ah, LORD! how happy is he who feels sufficient constancy in his love to be enabled to say, with the Apostle: Who shall separate us from the love of CHRIST? Shall tribulation, or distress, or famine, or nakedness, or peril, or persecution, or sword? (Rom. viii. 35.) Make me worthy, Heavenly Spouse, to use this language.

FOURTH DAY.

Filii matris meæ pugnaverunt contra me.

My mother's children have indeed fought against me, to turn me from the love which I owe and which I have promised to my GOD; and I have been base enough to yield to their attacks. My love has become inconstant, and this is what they desired. They have made use now of mockeries, which have disconcerted me; now of calumnies, which have disgusted me; now of persecutions, which have overcome me; sometimes passing from one extreme to the other, they have employed false promises, which have made me forget the true promises of my GOD; often have they made use of caresses, and disarmed me; now of vanity, which has dazzled me; now of pleasures, which have moved me. I had told my Heavenly Spouse that

I loved Him with all my heart, and that I would love Him to the last breath of my life; and I have become inconstant; a trifle has changed me, a nothing has cooled my first fervour. How, then, LORD, shall I dare now to make Thee new protestations of love, after having a thousand times violated all the old ones? Form them Thyself in my heart, and give me strength rather to die than to change.

FIFTH DAY.

Donec aspiret dies, et inclinentur umbræ.

I will get me to the mountain of myrrh, and to the hill of frankincense, and I will be wholly my Beloved's, says the bride, until the day break, and the shadows have given place to light. I also will love Thee, LORD, and constantly endure all the toils of life, to prove my love to Thee, till the Great Day of Eternity, when all the shadows of this mortal life shall be dispelled. But, alas! can I promise it, after having so often broken my word to Thee? Have I not reason to distrust the constancy of my love? To-day I promise to love Thee; perhaps, alas! I shall not do it to-morrow. The least affliction dispirits me, and slackens my ardour; my heart escapes from me at every moment; I am its dupe whenever it is in my hands. Take it into Thine; I give it Thee, O Heavenly Spouse; it is far better there than in mine; take it, that none may deprive me of it, and that it may be safe from the creature and from myself.

SIXTH DAY.

Donec aspiret dies, et inclinentur umbræ.

I am in the obscurity of faith, and I aspire to sight; I am in the shadows and clouds of a transitory life, and I aspire to eternal brightness; I love, and I desire to love, that I may become worthy of possessing everlastingly That Which I love, and I cannot possess this unless I love It constantly. How can it be, then, that of all the different objects which present themselves to my heart, there is nothing which it has more difficulty in loving constantly than God? and that of all the different occupations of life, there is none of which it wearies sooner than of the duties to which this love engages it? I feel that there is in my heart a perpetual changefulness of thoughts, desires, and impulses; it varies according to the different objects that it meets; that which is spiritual and above it fatigues it; that which is apparent and within its reach fixes it more easily. Raise this carnal and earthly heart, my God; amend these defects, make it perceive Thy Worth, fix it unchangeably on Thee Alone for time and for eternity.

SEVENTH DAY.

Donec aspiret dies, et inclinentur umbræ.

We promise the creature to love it till the shades of death; and whatever protestations of fidelity we make to it, the attachment must pass away, and inconstancy must succeed, because the creature is imperfect, and has not qualities to be always loved, and because the heart grows weary, discerns its faults, and because, besides, it has not capacity always to love. Is it possible to deal thus with God, Who makes His Goodness to be felt every day in a thousand different and ever-new manners, and who provides the faithful heart daily with new zeal to love Him? Base and inconstant creature! what dost thou find wearisome and capable of disquieting thee in the love of Thy God? Why, then, change so often and so shamefully? Why descend to the earth after ascending to Heaven? Why love the dust after having loved God? Why knock unworthily at the heart of a vile creature, after having taken possession of the Heart of Thy God. Amend thy fickleness, then, if thou wilt merit the crown of love, which is given to constancy alone.

Recapitulation of the Seventeen preceding Weeks.

PRAYER TO OBTAIN THE LOVE OF GOD IN THE ILLUMINATIVE LIFE.

Almighty God, Fruitful Source of light and ardour! Sun of Righteousness, Who enlightenest and inflamest all minds and all hearts upon which Thou dartest Thy Divine Rays; enlighten my intellect with a light giving at once clearness and unction, that it may know Thee only to love Thee (Eighteenth Week). Inflame my heart with a Heavenly Fire, which shall purify and hallow it (Nineteenth Week). Render it attentive to that Divine language which Thou speakest so often to the heart of those whom Thou lovest, and who love Thee (Twentieth Week). I need the sweetness and the strength of this Voice to detach me completely from creatures and from myself, and to make me love Thee with disinterested love (Twenty-first Week), which shall seek and esteem nothing but Thee (Twenty-second Week). Instruct me, Lord; teach me to love Thee wisely and without indiscretion (Twenty-third Week). Give me living lessons in this chaste and unmixed love (Twenty-fourth Week), which looks to Thee Alone, and which preserves an inviolable faithfulness till death (Twenty-fifth Week). Be Thou, O Celestial Spouse, the Beginning, the Centre, and the End of all the desires of my heart (Twenty-sixth Week). Be Thou the only Model of all its ardours and of all its eagerness (Twenty-seventh Week). Thou hast given Thyself wholly for me; what can I do to acknowledge Thy Liberal Love, but give myself wholly to Thee (Twenty-eighth Week); and give myself to Thee continually, as often as I breathe (Twenty-ninth Week). Thou thinkest unceasingly of me, and lovest me; and wert Thou for one instant to cease to do so, I should cease to be what I am. I cannot better mark my love to Thee than by an entire conformity to all that Thou hast done for me, and to all that Thou desirest of me (Thirtieth Week); and by dedicating myself to copy Thy Heart so carefully, that mine may worthily bear Its image and Resemblance (Thirty-first Week). Do Thou often retrace Its glorious features; renew them in characters of fire upon my memory, my mind, my heart, and my soul (Thirty-second Week), and universally upon my whole being (Thirty-third Week), that this precious impression may never be effaced, and that I may resemble Thee, and love Thee constantly till the last breath of my life (Thirty-fourth Week). Amen.

AFFECTIONS

FOR THE

UNITIVE LIFE.

Thirty-fifth Week.

LOVE OF ATTACHMENT.

When we have faithfully profited by the light which is inseparable from Divine Love, and when by this light the paths which lead to the Heart of God have been gradually discovered to the soul that sought it with its utmost ardour, it soon passes from the Illuminative to the Unitive Life. Its love, formerly subject to decay and inequality, becomes more perfect, more constant, and more continuous. Having seen and tasted how gracious the Lord is, it will part from Him no more. Having nobly completed the destruction of all the too sensible and imperfect ties which bound it to created things, God lays on its hands stronger and more glorious chains, those of a more perfect charity, and its love becomes one of true attachment.

The bride had already given testimonies of true tenderness to her Heavenly Bridegroom; she had entreated Him to draw her after Him, that she might run to the odour of His Perfumes; and the Spouse had praised her love in praising her beauty. Yet, for fear that this bride should escape Him, He desires that she shall love Him with a love of attachment, saying: We will make thee chains of gold, with studs of silver. Muraenulas aureas faciemus tibi, vermiculatas argento. (Cant. i.) These chains denote inviolable attachment, and gold and silver are the symbols of the most excellent charity.

But as it is impossible to love God without being loved by Him, or to attach ourselves to Him unless He attaches Himself to us, the bride thus gloriously enchained, boasts in her turn that she also holds her Beloved, that she has happily stopped Him after a long pursuit, and that she will not let Him go: tenui eum, nec dimittam. (Cant. iii.) If we hold firmly to God, and He holds to us by the bands of reciprocal charity, we never separate from Him, and we regard other attachments as filth.

AFFECTIONS.

FIRST DAY.

Muraenulas aureas faciemus tibi, vermiculatas argento. (Cant. i.)

We will make thee, says the Bridegroom, chains of gold with studs of silver. Make them so strong, O my God, that they may never break; bind me to Thee so closely, that I may never part from Thee in life or death, in time or eternity, for the pleasures, the riches, the honours, or the vain amusements of the earth. Heavenly Bridegroom, put these glorious chains on my neck, as on that of the bride, for an eternal mark of my servitude, and of my inviolable attachment to the laws of Thy Divine love. Put them on my hands, that they may never labour for vanity or for the world, but for Thy Glory Alone. Put them on my feet as on those of a willing slave, who desires to serve Thee Alone, that they may take no steps contrary to those inspired by Thy love.

But, since these chains of gold are chains of love, and are made rather for the heart than the body, chain mine in such manner that it may never attach itself to any but Thee.

SECOND DAY.

Muræenulas aureas faciemus tibi, &c.

It is by excessive charity, says St. Augustine (Conf.), that God has attached Himself to rational beings; this charity is a chain as strong as God Himself. He has thus attached Himself to this creature, that reciprocally attached to Him, it might draw from His Adorable Heart, as from a plenteous Fountain, desires and ardours which might lead it to repose, and to an anticipated possession of the eternal pleasures which God prepares for it; and that, like a bee, settled upon a flower, it might draw out all the honey, the juice, and the sweetness. Suck, then, my soul, says this Father; taste the ineffable sweetness of thy God. Attached to this Fountain, open thy whole heart to receive its sacred Stream; take boldly, fill thyself, enjoy at thy ease, be swallowed up in this Ocean of delights, satisfy thyself unceasingly, and be never weary. The chain which binds thee to God is not thy work, but His; respect it, love it; it is of the purest gold, which is the symbol of charity: beware of losing it; it is an inestimable treasure: beware of breaking it; the Heavenly Workman Who formed it would no longer be to thee a Spouse, a Lover, or an affectionate Father, but an inexorable Judge.

THIRD DAY.

Muræenulas aureas faciemus tibi, &c.

I have but too much cause to say mournfully, with the Prophet, The chains of sinners compassed me about; I have borne them but too long. It is then just, O my God, that I should now bear those which

Thou offerest me. Those were shameful, and I gloried vainly in that real disgrace: these are bright as gold, it is glorious to wear them; yet I have been ashamed of them, and have despised them. Those are hard and cruel; yet I have loved them, and have gladly burthened myself with them: these are soft and pleasant, yet I have regarded them with horror, and have refused them. Those shamefully deprive us of liberty, and make nothing but slaves, because they are chains of profane love: these preserve and sanctify liberty; they free all slaves, because they are the chains of Divine love which bringeth liberty everywhere, and because they are made by the Hand of God. Load me then, Lord, with these chains of gold, not of that perishing gold which dazzles, and feeds the greediness of the avaricious, but of that pure gold of Charity which destroys covetousness, and which sanctifies the hearts of the children of God.

FOURTH DAY.

Muraenulas aureas faciemus tibi, &c.

My sins were bands and cords to bind the Hands of my Saviour and my Spouse; thus was He led to the punishment of Death; and He has revenged this outrage only by making for me chains of charity and love, to bind my heart to His. I bound Him to a shameful tree to give Him death; and the chains which He offers to me bind me to a Saving God, to give me a life of grace and of glory. I have cruelly chained the Hands of my Deliverer, to hinder Him from doing me good; and These Divine and Almighty Hands Which could crush me and reduce me to ashes, break those chains only to heap favours upon me. What a powerful motive is this for eternal attachment to my God! what an inducement to respect and to cherish the glorious chains which He gives me, and to bear them with pleasure till death!

FIFTH DAY.

Tenui eum, nec dimittam. (Cant. iii.)

I hold my Beloved, says the bride, and I will not let Him go. It is in vain, O my soul, that thou hopest to hold thy Spouse and thy God, if thou hast not sought Him as ardently and perseveringly as the bride. Thou must walk, run, and never stop. Like her thou must suffer thy veil to be taken away, and attach thyself to nothing perishable, if thou desirest that thy love for God shall be a love of true attachment. If thou still holdest to any thing, thou holdest not yet to God. Thou art moved and filled with emotion in a prayer, or in a Communion; thou lovest Him then, He has come bodily to dwell with thee; but this is yet but a transient love; or if thou holdest thy God, thou art not yet sufficiently advanced to say with the bride, I hold Him; and I will not let Him go. For if thou art not careful to preserve the precious Treasure which thou possessest to-day, perhaps to-morrow thou wilt lose it amidst created things.

SIXTH DAY.

Tenui eum, nec dimittam.

Sacred Love, exclaimed a Father, how great is thy strength, and how powerful are thy chains, for thou canst chain an Immortal God, bind Heaven to earth, the Creator to the creature, and bind them together for eternity! To bind a God, what a prodigy! To bind His Heart to man, what a miracle of love! Divine Charity, how powerful, how active art thou! Thou gainest us at first skilfully, thou takest us gently, thou engagest us tenderly, to bind us powerfully; and when we are thine, thou givest thyself wholly to us, thou teachest us in our turn to bind the Strong, to disarm the Almighty, and to overcome the Invincible. Thou holdest our hearts only that we may hold that of God; thou bindest us to Him only to bind Him to us. Who can render these bonds indissoluble? Ah, Lord! make my heart feel that I hold Thee by a Love of attachment, and give me strength never to forsake Thee!

SEVENTH DAY.

Tenui eum, nec dimittam.

I cannot hold to my God by a love of attachment, without being so happy as to hold Him like the bride. I cannot hold Him without possessing in Him and with Him all the treasures which accompany Him. If I adhere to Him in all things, and if I am strongly attached to Him, I become, according to St. Paul, of the same mind with Him. (Phil. ii.) I leave my low estate to share His Greatness; I strip myself of all the miseries of my mortal existence to enter into the participation of His Immortal Being. I am nothing if I am not bound to Him by the cords of love; I am every thing if I hold Him. United to Him, I hear, touch, see, feel, taste Him; He pours into my bosom all the sweetness of His Grace; He diffuses over my heart all the unction of His Divine Word, and all the ardour of His Love: the more I am attached to Him, the more I love my bonds, and my attachment, and then I say with the bride, "I hold my Beloved; and I will not let Him go:" tenui eum, nec dimittam.

Thirty-sixth Week.

FERVENT LOVE.

As it is the property of fire to warm all that approach it, and to burn all that touch it, we cannot be attached to God, Who is a consuming Fire, without feeling His ardour, and loving Him with fervent love. To be attached to God and to burn for God, is one thing, says a celebrated author: ardenter Deum amare, ipsum tenere est. (Thom. à Kempis Med.)

I know that our fervour is not always equal, and that into the love which the most perfect feel for God, there creeps from time to time a slight drowsiness, which must be daily aroused, lest, being neglected, it shall at last cause the total extinction of Divine Love. Yet, when we have the substance, the habit, and the impression of this Love, we have no difficulty in awakening its fervour. Our heart is like to a half-extinguished torch, still smoking and burning; directly another lighted torch is brought to it, it instantly receives the flame, and burns with the fire of that which re-kindled it. In the Heart of God is a Divine and inextinguishable Flame: this fire of Charity attracts our hearts when they begin to grow dull; it restores their fervour by re-kindling them with its own fire; it takes fresh possession of them, and inflames them with a more ardent and delicious fire, says a Father: totum igne suavissimæ dilectionis reaccendit. (D. Bonav. Sent.)

The bride strove to raise herself to the Heart of her Beloved, to renew her fervour, when the Bridegroom exclaimed on seeing her: Who is this that cometh out of the wilderness, like pillars of smoke, perfumed with myrrh and frankincense? Quæ est ista quæ ascendit per desertum, sicut virgula fumi ex aromatibus myrrhæ et thuris? (Cant. iii.) She was in the wilderness, the place from which we most easily rise to God; and it was the fire of her love which raised the smoke of her perfumes towards the Heart of her Beloved, to gain from It new ardours.

The Bridegroom says also, at the end of His Canticle, that the lamps of His bride are lamps of flames and fire: lampades ejus, lampades ignis atque flammarum. (Cant. viii.) This expression, "flames and fire," is no useless repetition, but a mystery and an instruction. The one denotes the affections, the other the works, of fervent love. These lamps are of fire, because charity burns in her heart; they are of flames, because this charity, too fervent to be inclosed within the narrow limits of the heart, should also inflame others, and shine outwardly by noble actions.

AFFECTIONS.

FIRST DAY.

Quæ est ista quæ ascendit per desertum, sicut virgula fumi ex aromatibus myrrhæ et thuris? (Cant. iii.)

Who is this that cometh out of the wilderness, like pillars of smoke, perfumed with myrrh and frankincense? says the Bridegroom. I understand, LORD, by these words, that to acquire true fervour, we must love solitude, we must have courage always to go onwards, without stopping; we must rise unceasingly towards Thee, and love Thee with all our heart. Thy bride was in the desert; Thou Thyself hadst led her there to speak to her heart. Separate me like her from sensible things; separate me from myself, that I may listen more attentively to Thy Divine Word, which is, according to the Prophet, as a burning fire. (Jer. xx. 9.) The bride proceeded courageously, and I proceed faintheartedly, or I stop too soon, after having run for a time. She was ever rising, ever loving; and the fire of this excellent charity which burnt in her heart, sent up to Thine the odour and the pleasant smoke of its perfumes. Is it then surprising that her love was fervent? Raise me, LORD;

give me strength to ascend unto Thee, and never to return.

SECOND DAY.

Quæ est ista quæ ascendit, &c.

Teach me, LORD, how to follow the footsteps of the bride to go to Thee; direct my steps, take me by the hand, draw me after Thee, lest I wander, or stop. I learn from a holy penitent (D. Aug. Conf.), that I cannot go to Thee but by the fervour of my love, and that I shall never reach that happy end so long as I am cold and slothful. My perfumes cannot ascend to Thee unless they proceed from the fire burning in my heart. Give this weak heart all the ardour which it needs to rise unceasingly towards Thee. Go forward, my soul, without diverting thyself with the creature; forsake it finally for the Creator Who calls thee; be all fire, and be so till death; lament that a dull and cold charity has succeeded thy first ardour; strive to the utmost to acquire new fire, and never suffer it to be extinguished or to diminish. Fly to GOD, thou hast wings; if thou hast them not, love with all the ardour of which thou art capable; fervent love gives them.

THIRD DAY.

Quæ est ista quæ ascendit, &c.

O for the fervour of the bride to hasten to the midst of the most frightful deserts, and to rise at last to Thee, O my GOD, like the smoke of precious spices! I will run the way of Thy commandments, said the prophet, when Thou shalt enlarge my heart. (Psa. cxix. 32.) It is by coldness and indifference that the heart contracts, and becomes too heavy to rise to GOD; it is by the fervour of love that it enlarges, and acquires a sort of immensity, in order to contain, in its own manner, Him for Whom the infinite space of

Heaven and earth sufficeth not. The fire of Divine Love gives it the activity of a glorified body to rise more easily towards its Centre, the Heart of God. Thou then, Lord, must give more enlargement to my heart; Thou must expand it by Thy Love, to render it capable of containing Thee; Thou, Who art a Divine Fire, must enable me always to burn; Thou must keep me thus fervent to the last moment of my life.

FOURTH DAY.

Quæ est ista quæ ascendit, &c.

We must always proceed, and always rise, if we desire to secure our salvation, and these two things can be done only by fervent love. The heart of the Christian cannot fix for itself any point of steadfast continuance, where it may abide. As soon as its fervour ceases to augment, it must relax; as soon as it ceases to love God, it must love the creature to the prejudice of its duties; when it ceases to rise, it must sink; when it is no more all fire, it is but a little way from becoming all ice; when it flies no more towards Heaven, it will very soon creep miserably on the earth. Leave thy lukewarmness, then, immediately, my soul; let there be always a holy fire in thy heart, to raise to Heaven the pleasing smoke of thy perfumes. This is not the abode of indolence, it is but a pilgrimage; thou hast little time, and hast a great journey to make, and very extensive duties to fulfil: thou hast many passions to combat, many virtues to acquire, many rocks to avoid, and many monsters to overcome. The only means of success is always to love God, and to love Him fervently.

FIFTH DAY.

Lampades ejus, lampades ignis atque flammarum. (Cant. viii.)

The lamps of the bride are lamps of flame and fire. The fire burns and consumes, the flame shines and enlightens. We must not only burn for God, but the light and fire of our love must also lead others to God. Why are so few fervent Christians, and why are the greater part so slack? Is it actually that their heart is of ice? No, but it is that in this heart there are strange fires. A heart all ice is easier to warm with the love of God, than a base heart that loves the creature. Nothing is more contrary than these two flames. When one is stronger than the other, it gets possession of the whole heart, and excludes the other. If my love is feeble towards God, there must be in my heart some little imperfect attachment to the creature. Let me seek it carefully to extirpate it finally; let me beware lest it be hidden in my self-love, or lest it be my self-love itself.

SIXTH DAY.

Lampades ejus, lampades ignis, &c.

Happy are those, Lord, who, like the bride, are always flames and fire, and who have hardly any moments in their life devoid of Divine love! Yet I sometimes experience that my love is speechless, and sends scarcely any thing to my lips to testify that I love Thee. But it feels, it enjoys, it sighs, it sobs, it sends tears to my eyes; it desires its Beloved, it labours, it is all fire. It is enough, it needs not other expressions to be heard by the Heart of my God. Silence sustained by true fervour, is much more eloquent than the best arranged words. Grant to my heart, Heavenly Spouse, grace to be silent, and always to speak in this manner; give endurance to those precious moments which pass away so quickly. How happy should I be, if I could enjoy them without intermission till death.

SEVENTH DAY.

Lampades ejus, lampades ignis, &c.

O eternal Truth! exclaimed St. Augustine. O true Charity! O beloved Eternity! Thou art God Himself, and Thou art the whole delight of my heart. O Charity, all flame and fire, all ardent and luminous! when shall I burn, and be consumed by Thy Divine Ardour? If here below Thou appearest so sweet and so delightful to my heart, what will it be when it has the happiness of possessing Thee eternally in Heaven! If I sometimes feel such violent ardour in loving Thee, what will it be when this heart shall find no more obstacles to the entire enjoyment of the Supreme Good which it loves! If a single spark of Thy Divine Love sets it all on fire, what will it be when it is wholly inflamed by the infinite ardour which is the delight of the blessed! Let us, then, here serve the apprenticeship of that fervent love which will be our whole happiness in Heaven. If God is a consuming Fire, let us approach Him as nearly and as frequently as we can; far differently shall we burn when we have the happiness of being immediately united with Him throughout eternity.

Thirty-seventh Week.

HEROIC LOVE.

True heroes are found only in the religion of Jesus Christ, and love alone forms, produces, animates, and sustains them. The hero of the world looks only to men, from whom he hopes but for transient glory; the Christian hero looks only to God, from Whom he awaits immortal Glory. Thus, as his motives are more urgent, his views more pure, and his aim more illustrious, it is not surprising that his enterprises are more daring, his actions more splendid, and his success more glorious. The former, being destitute of true love, which alone is the strength of true heroes, is now overwhelmed by grief, now vanquished by luxury, and always dazzled by false glory; the latter, says a holy man (Laur. Just.), being established in the faith, consoled by hope, and sustained by ardent charity, is always master of himself, and nothing is able to shake him. The more he suffers, the happier is he; the more he is oppressed, the more is he free; the more he is pressed down, the higher he rises; the more he is persecuted, the more tranquil is he, because he is convinced that he combats only to triumph more surely, that he labours only to rest in Heaven, and that he shall die only to live eternally with the GOD Whom he loves.

The bride, showing the bed of Solomon to her companions, tells them that threescore valiant men are about it, of the valiant of Israel: en lectulum Salomonis; sexaginta fortes ambiunt ex fortissimis Israel. (Cant. iii.) She adds, that they all hold swords, because of fear in the night, and that they are expert in war: omnes tenentes gladios, et ad bella doctissimi. (Ibid.)

Solomon is here the type of JESUS CHRIST; the bed in which He reposes, is the soul of the just, His bride; or His mystic Body, the Church; or His natural Body, His Holy Humanity. These valiant men of the valiant of Israel, are the Apostles, those first heroes of Christianity, who, once weak as other men, became very strong by their love, and have made wonderful conquests with the sword of the Divine Word. They are also the martyrs, who gave undoubted proofs of heroic love by the effusion of their blood. They are, lastly, the holy men and women of the

Church militant, who boldly walk in the footsteps of those great men, and who love Jesus Christ with all their heart.

AFFECTIONS.

FIRST DAY.

En lectulum Salomonis; sexaginta fortes ambiunt ex fortissimis Israel. (Cant. iii.)

Behold, says the bride, the bed of Solomon; three-score valiant men are about it, of the valiant of Israel. It is not enough, then, to be valiant; we must be valiant among the most valiant to possess heroic love, and to be worthy to guard the mysterious bed of the true Solomon. We must be like those heroes, insatiable for conquest, who go forward constantly without stopping, and without desiring to taste the pleasure of their victories as long as there remains one inch of ground to conquer, and one enemy to overthrow. Whatever thou hast done for God, O my soul, think not of it. Pause not a moment, lest thou lose the fruit of thy labours by reflections in which self-love will have but too large a part. Do not amuse thyself with counting thy past victories, whilst thou hast many more to obtain; a true hero should never rest. Seek, press forward, force thy enemies even in their last intrenchment. If thou lovest truly, thou wilt always find passions to combat, virtues to acquire, and heroic labours to undertake.

SECOND DAY.

En lectulum Salomonis, &c.

Remember, O my soul, that thou art thyself the mysterious bed of the true Solomon of the new law, as often as He reposes in thee by the Holy Communion. Heroic love is necessary to guard carefully the nuptial bed of this Heavenly Spouse, and to preserve in it that angelic purity which He deserves and demands of thee. Never slumber: be like those valiant men of Israel, who, says the bride, watch unceasingly, and are always armed, because of surprises and fears in the night. Be indefatigable in labours, intrepid in peril, bold in enterprise, resigned in suffering, invincible in combat, and tranquil in the most violent tempests. What fearest thou? JESUS CHRIST is with thee; He sleeps in the vessel of thy soul, and in the bed of thy heart. He will awake in the time of need, and when thou callest Him to thy assistance. He trusts Him to thee; He gives Himself, abandons Himself wholly to thee; guard Him well, lest His enemies, who are thine, despoil thee of this precious Treasure. They will despoil thee as soon as thou ceasest to love Him with all thy heart; thou wilt preserve It, and He will preserve thee, as long as thou lovest Him with heroic love.

THIRD DAY.

En lectulum Salomonis, &c.

After the numberless mercies that I have received from my GOD, I ought to be valiant among the most valiant of Israel, and I am, perhaps, the weakest among the weak. Labour deters me, dangers terrify me, afflictions overcome me, and, far from being capable of great enterprises, the smallest alarms me; or, if I begin something great, I lose courage, and draw back in the midst of my course. Where are the victories that I have obtained? the fatigues that I have endured? the monsters that I have overcome? What mastery have I gained over my mind and my heart? What good have I done to my neighbour? What increase have I procured to the Glory of GOD? All my protestations of courage have lasted only till they were tried. I imagined roaring lions in the paths of my love; I expected an entire defeat from them, and was terrified. When, LORD, shall I have that heroic love which overcomes all and fears nothing?

FOURTH DAY.

Omnes tenentes gladios. (Cant. iii.)

Heroes have their swords always in their hands to guard themselves, to preserve their conquests, and to gain more. Worldly heroes take the sword only to shed the blood of others; that of the Christian hero strikes only to do good, and he employs it only to cut off his own passions, or to gain Glory for GOD. It is two-edged, says a Father (S. Ant. p. 3, l. 4), therefore it never strikes unsuccessfully. It gleams through Charity, it is sharpened by Truth, it strikes by the Power of GOD; it casts down only to raise more gloriously; it wounds only to heal, and slays only to give life. It pierces, says St. Paul, even to the dividing asunder of soul and spirit (Heb. iv.), to unite both under the dominion of Divine Love. Let us use this sword against ourselves; let us cut away all that is not heroic in our love; let us separate from it, by this mystic sword, inconstancy, weakness, uncertainty, daintiness, natural sensibility, and vain terrors. Let us not fear even death; a true hero regards it less as a punishment than as a reward.

FIFTH DAY.

Omnes tenentes gladios.

My Heavenly Spouse is a Divine Hero, Who has conquered Heaven and Earth. He carried an Invincible Sword, not by His Side, like profane heroes, but it went out of His Mouth, says the beloved Disciple (Apoc. i. 16), and this terrible Sword is His Divine Word. He carried the Sceptre, not in His Hand, like earthly sovereigns, but on His Shoulders; and this Sceptre is none other than His Cross. Yet this Hero subdued the most barbarous nations, humbled the proudest heads, overthrew the most formidable enemies. But He desires that I shall imitate Him, and become by my love a hero like Himself. He gives me no less than a whole kingdom to conquer; and though it is eternal, and of infinite worth, He gives me arms sufficient to conquer it. With the spiritual sword, which He puts in my hand, I have only to cut off all my carnal desires that I may embrace suffering, and I render myself worthy of tasting pure and eternal pleasures. I have but to cut off in my heart greediness for riches, and I shall acquire immense treasures. Henceforth I will have only the Sword and the Sceptre of my Heavenly Spouse, which are His Cross and His Divine Word: these are my arms; with them I must become a violent hero, to take Heaven by force.

SIXTH DAY.

Et ad bella doctissimi. (Cant. iii.)

And these valiant men of the valiant of Israel, says the bride, are expert in war. I have received the holy unction of Baptism, because I am the champion and the soldier of JESUS CHRIST. A second anointing has confirmed the former. I ought, then, to be expert in war. I have been often wounded, and the ministry of penitence has healed me: I have often received the Bread of the strong, I have fed upon the Substance of the LORD of Hosts: my sacred anointings, my combats, my very defeats, my wounds, the wise Teaching of my Divine Master, His Promises, His Example, and the continual assistance which He has given me when I fought for His Love, should have made me a true hero of Christianity: and I am but a coward, who have yet done nothing for my GOD, because I have not loved Him enough. Heroic love mocks at peril. The fire, the sword, and death, far from intimidating it, give fresh edge to its courage.

Let me, then, amend my cowardice, let me love heroically: GOD desires it, I can do it, and Heaven is its reward.

SEVENTH DAY.

Et ad bella doctissimi.

Examine thyself, my soul, on the different characteristics of true heroes, expert in the spiritual war of Divine love. Observe those marks which thou wantest, and labour to acquire them. A true hero undertakes all for the Glory of GOD; he continues his enterprise to the end with the same ardour with which he began it, never discouraged; and when things become desperate, he has most confidence and firmness. All things appear difficult to thee, and the least obstacle hinders thee. Nothing can trouble the hero; his courage and his prudence increase in proportion as persecutions and difficulties augment; and tranquil in the midst of the most furious tempests, he looks for the help of GOD Alone, without ceasing to labour for His Glory, whilst thou art alarmed by the smallest dangers! He bears the heaviest burthens without feeling their weight, because he loves; fatigues sustain him, labour increases his strength instead of diminishing it; and thou complainest of thy weakness when any thing difficult is imposed on thee! Love heroically, all things will be sweet and easy to thee; and the hardest combats will be but a pleasing exercise of thy love.

Thirty-eighth Week.

ZEALOUS LOVE.

As ardent charity produces and sustains zeal, so zeal causes charity to act, and gives it perfection and splendour. This zeal, which proceeds from love, or is love itself and perfect love, is, according to the Holy Fathers, a lively and continual movement, and a violent transport of the heart towards the Object which it loves and would make all creatures love, if it had the power, and which willingly offers itself to undertake all, and to suffer all, to bring it about. It is composed of desires, of fear, of joy, of sorrow, and sometimes even of holy wrath. It ardently desires the salvation of souls, and the increase of the Glory of God; it fears lest He should be dishonoured; it feels joy when His Kingdom increases; sorrow when it sees its decrease; and it is inflamed with just wrath against the sinners who outrage Him. These are the characteristics by which thou wilt know if thou hast love and zeal for God.

These happy marks of zeal are easy to perceive in the bride. For why does she say, in the singular number, to her Spouse, Draw me after Thee: trahe me post te (Cant. i.); and afterwards add, in the plural, We will run to the odour of Thy Perfumes: Curremus in odorem unguentorum tuorum? It is, say St. Ambrose and St. Bernard, because she is the type of the most perfect and zealous souls, who, not content with loving God, strive also to draw all the world to His love. It is not, then, sufficient for this zealous bride to love Him alone, but she desires also to gain for Him the hearts of all her companions, when she says to them: Go forth, O ye daughters of Zion, and behold King Solomon with the crown wherewith His mother crowned Him in the day of His espousals: Egredimini, filiæ Sion, et videte regem Salomonem in diademate quo coronavit mater sua in die desponsationis illius. (Cant. iii.)

Indeed, her love and her zeal increase in such manner, that the Bridegroom Himself gives it perfect praise by a most astonishing comparison, for He says,

"It is strong as hell:" Dura sicut infernus æmulatio. (Cant. viii.) This expression appears extravagant; but it is impossible to say any thing too strong to mark the ardour of a soul burning with zeal and with love for God.

AFFECTIONS.

FIRST DAY.

Trahe me post te, curremus in odorem unguentorum tuorum. (Cant. i.)

Draw me after Thee, said the bride; we will run to the odour of Thy Perfumes. No, Lord, I would not love Thee alone, but I desire that all creatures should have but one heart with me to love Thee. Inflame me with such ardent love, that I may inflame others, and run with them after the odour of Thy Perfumes. I will labour to do this with all my might; by my desires, my prayers, my good works, and my example. I am ready, Lord, to immolate myself for the enlargement of the empire of Thy Divine Love, and for the increase of Thy Glory. There is no peril to which I will not expose myself, nothing too difficult for me to undertake, nothing too dear to sacrifice, to draw to Thee the homage and the heart of the whole earth. Speak Thyself within my heart, Heavenly Spouse; what dost Thou require of my zeal? My property, my health, my reputation, my life? Happy should I be if I died of the suffering! I could not make a more glorious sacrifice of this mortal life than by losing it for Thy Love.

SECOND DAY.

Trahe me post te, &c.

Is it not presumption, O my God, to entreat Thee to draw me after Thee? What interest hast Thou to do so? What wilt Thou gain by it? What is the motive of Thy Love for me, but Thy Love Itself, and Thy Love of free Grace? What am I, LORD? and what art Thou? I am a worm of the earth, a sinner, a miserable nothing, and Thou art the GOD of Heaven and earth. Of what value, then, is this heart which Thou lovest as a Jealous GOD? Ah! it must be of some worth, since Thou desirest to draw it to Thee, to repose there, to fill it, and since Thou forbiddest me to give it to any besides Thee. I give it Thee, Heavenly Spouse, or, rather, I return it to Thee, for it is Thine Alone. Draw it effectually to Thee; consume and destroy, by the fire of Thy Divine Zeal, all impurity and earthliness that yet remain in it; kindle there a pure and ardent zeal, which shall burn unceasingly for Thy Glory, and which will draw all the earth to run with me to the odour of Thy Heavenly Perfumes.

THIRD DAY.

Egredimini, filiæ Sion, videte regem Salomonem in diademate quo coronavit eum mater sua, &c.

Go forth, O ye daughters of Sion, and behold King Solomon with the crown wherewith His mother crowned Him in the day of His espousals, says the bride to her companions. Go forth first thyself, O my soul! go forth from thy sloth and indifference; go forth from thy cowardice and lukewarmness, which are opposed to the zealous love which thou owest to Thy GOD; go forth from the prison of thy fleshly senses; first love with all thy heart, then bring others to love and admire the true Solomon, CHRIST, in His double Crown; the one Bloody, the other Glorious. The Synagogue, which is His mother, crowned Him with a bloody and painful Crown on the Cross, the nuptial bed where He immolated Himself to make thee worthy of being His bride, and where love was the priest of this Divine marriage. Show Him in this state to all the daughters of Sion; draw all their hearts towards this most lovely Object, when thou hast given Him thine own. Admire Him, adore Him, love Him afterwards in the glorious Crown with which He was crowned in Heaven by His Father in the day of His Triumph. In CHRIST Alone Thou hast a Spouse of Blood, and a Spouse of Glory; hasten first, with zealous love, to the Bloody Crown, if Thou desirest to see Him one day in His Glorious Crown. He gained one by the other; follow His Footsteps; He is thy Pattern.

FOURTH DAY.

Egredimini, filiæ Sion, et videte regem, &c.

To invite all the earth to love GOD, to desire this with all possible ardour, to follow up this desire on occasion by bold and noble actions, to grieve with the Saints at seeing Him dishonoured by sinners; this is the true character of holy, not of profane, love. This last dreads rivals, the other desires them, because it knows that the Heart of GOD is large enough for all; and this holy jealousy is nothing else than that zeal which would have all the world love GOD. LORD, inflame me, consume me with this ardent zeal. I would desire that all creatures had the hearts of Seraphims to love Thee, that all lips resounded with Thy praises, that all minds were occupied with Thy Greatness. I join in all the homage which Thou receivest from the Angels, from the Saints in Heaven, and from the righteous upon the earth: I would that all who love and adore Thee were infinitely multiplied; and I would give all my blood to prevent a single offence against Thy Divine Majesty.

FIFTH DAY.

Dura sicut infernus æmulatio. (Cant. vi.)

Zeal as strong as Hell, says the Spouse. Thine

was stronger, for it delivered me from it, and broke its gates to open to me those of Heaven. It was stronger than death, for it deprived Thee of life to give it to me. Carefully protecting me against the enemies of my eternal happiness, Thou hast hidden me, like the royal Prophet, in the secret of Thy Presence (Ps. xxxi.), and under the shadow of Thy wings. Thou hast declared that he that touches me, touches the apple of Thine Eye (Ps. xvii.). Thou hast been so jealous of my soul, that Thou hast kept me in Thy Hands, assuring me that none can tear me thence. Thou hast opened Thine Heart to me, and it depends only on myself to enter, to dwell there, and never to leave It. This zeal is stronger than death and hell. Withdraw it not from me, Heavenly Spouse, as Thou didst from the ungrateful people whom Thou hadst threatened. I know that the extinction of zealous love in my heart has power to chill Thine for me: let me rather die than cease to love Thee.

SIXTH DAY.

Dura sicut infernus æmulatio.

Can we now say that the zeal of men for God is strong as hell? Alas! nothing is weaker, and it is now a virtue hardly known. Where do we find a David who can boast of being consumed with the ardour of his zeal; an Elias or a Phineas who, in the presence of the great ones of the earth, exposes himself to all risks for the Glory of God? A false zeal, destitute of love, has taken the place of the true, and the real interests of God are now more abandoned than they have ever been. Lord, revive this fainting love and zeal in the hearts of men; revive it in mine, and give me ardour enough to maintain Thy Glory at the expense of my life. I count it as nothing, provided Thou art loved and honoured; I count it as much, if, by losing it, I may obtain for Thee the honour which is Thy due: I cannot employ it, sacrifice it, or lose it more gloriously.

SEVENTH DAY.

Dura sicut infernus æmulatio.

How can I know the strength of my love and my zeal for God? I know that, were I asked if I truly loved a friend worthy of my esteem, to whom I was under essential obligations, I should examine myself on the following points, which are the most manifest proofs of zealous love. 1st. If I take his part warmly against his enemies. 2nd. If I am ready to undertake all, both labour and fatigue, for his good. 3rd. If I suffer for him joyfully and without complaining. 4th. If I am grieved when he himself suffers, and when he is insulted; and rejoice when I see him honoured by all. These are the essential marks of a zealous love. It is too much, O my God! this detail declares my coldness and indifference. This examination confounds me, and these heads are so many proofs against me, which convince me that I have not yet a zealous love. From henceforth, Lord, I will take Thy part, at the expense of that which is dearest to me. I will give all, undertake all, suffer all, and sacrifice all for Thy Love.

Thirty-ninth Week.

BLIND LOVE.

In the sensual life, there is a blindness which is a sin, and the punishment of sin: in the spiritual life, there is a blindness which is a virtue, and the path which conducts to the most eminent virtue. The one is the most infallible symptom of the hardness of the heart towards God; the other the most evident proof of its docility and of the strength of its love. Sinners fall into blindness because they follow the false lights of a carnal reason, which is but darkness; and the just acquire blind love by renouncing their own lights, to allow themselves to be guided through the happy obscurities of faith to the Source of true Light, which is God. Thus, in the practice of Divine Love, we must be blind in order to see; must renounce our own intellect and reason, to have them; acquiesce in our ignorance and darkness, to attain assuredly to true light.

There is a blind love which is the work of the creature sustained by the Grace of God. This is when, in spite of its most natural feelings, and of its own wisdom, it submits without delay, and without reasoning, to all which God enjoins, however severe, and says like the bride, Behold, my Beloved speaketh unto me: En dilectus meus loquitur mihi (Cant. ii.); or when in the midst of dryness, of inward desolation, and privation of light, it fails not to seek God as faithfully as if the soul were overflowing with delights: like the bride who seeks Him Whom her soul loveth amid the darkness of night: In lectulo meo per noctes quæsivi quem diligit anima mea (Cant. iii.). There is another blind love, which is rather the work of God than of the creature; this is when He elevates a soul to a simpler and more sublime contemplation, in which He is known more by Himself than by His works; less by the efforts of the imagination and the mind, than by a simple regard of the entire soul; less by the contemplation of some particular attribute, than by a confused but delightful view of His whole Divinity; which the holy Fathers call a sacred obscurity. We turn towards this Supreme Being as towards an Ineffable, Incomprehensible, Infinite, and infinitely Lovely Object; we regard ourselves as swallowed up, absorbed, and lost in the vast Ocean of this Infinite Essence, seeing Him only through that mysterious cloud of which the prophet speaks, in which He takes pleasure in hiding Himself, without ceasing to make Himself felt, and to speak to His friends as He did to Moses: a sublime state, in which the bride was when she said, Behold, He standeth behind our wall, He looketh forth at the windows, showing Himself through the lattice: En ipse stat post parietem nostrum, respiciens per fenestras, prospiciens per cancellos (Cant. ii.); or when she said: Until the day break, and the shadows flee away, I will get me to the mountain of myrrh, and to the hill of frankincense: Donec aspiret dies et inclinentur umbræ, vadam ad montem myrrhæ, et ad collem thuris. (Cant. iv.)

AFFECTIONS.

FIRST DAY.

En dilectus meus loquitur mihi. (Cant. ii.)

Behold, my Beloved speaketh unto me, says the bride: en; behold Him. I ought like her to see Him with the eyes of faith, which, though dim, will not fail to discover Him to me if it is accompanied by love: Loquitur mihi; He speaks to me; I must hear Him, and lend the ear of my heart to His Divine language, which, though not articulated, fails not to make itself inwardly felt by a calm and attentive soul. He commands me to go onward. But how? I am wholly surrounded by darkness. It matters not, I am sure of the Heart of my God; He will not lead me to destruction, but to eternal salvation. Go forward then, my soul! suffer thyself to be blindly led; be not perplexed at sometimes losing thy star, like the Magi; thou hast seen It once, that ought to suffice thee; go on boldly across precipices by the obscure ways of faith. Thy Heavenly Spouse, which is Light Itself, will hold thee by the hand as long as thou lovest Him. Follow His adorable movements in the midst of thy darkness; see only with His Eyes, see only as much as He will have thee see. Such darkness, and such blindness, are far better than thine own light.

SECOND DAY.

En dilectus meus loquitur mihi.

I ought to keep profound silence when my Beloved speaks to me; otherwise, I am wanting in respect to Him, and I risk the loss of some of His Divine Words, which are all Words of Spirit and of Life. I should impose this silence, not only on my mouth and my outward senses, but on my soul and all its powers. When He has spoken, I must act and run blindly where He leads me, without hearkening to myself; I must lose and absorb my own will in His, I must annihilate it, that that of my God may be the only motive of all my actions. Human reason, constitutional eagerness, natural wisdom, self-will, prejudices, sloth, cowardice, repugnance, self-love, imperfect affections, sensible attachments, self-interested designs, ye shall all die in me; I am about to sacrifice you to the blind love which I owe to my Celestial Spouse.

THIRD DAY.

En ipse stat post parietem nostrum, respiciens per fenestras, prospiciens per cancellos. (Cant. ii.)

Behold, says the bride, He standeth behind our wall, He looketh forth at the windows, showing Himself through the lattice. Thou art then truly a hidden God, O Heavenly Spouse. Thou Who art

Light, and the Source of light, hidest Thyself in darkness, says the Prophet (Ps. xviii.); lest our eyes be dazzled, Thou lettest Thyself be seen, says the Apostle, only through a glass darkly (1 Cor. xiii.). Thou art above, around, and amidst us, with Thy most brilliant light, and we see but its faint reflections. Thus Thou exercisest our faith and our love, to make them more acceptable to Thee; yet Thou failest not to see me, and to speak to me through this mysterious wall which Thy skilful love has placed between Thee and me; and Thou wilt have me see Thee, speak to Thee, and amidst the dimness of faith love Thee, with a blind and submissive love. I accept it, LORD: I will adore Thee as reverently as if the wall were destroyed and I saw Thee openly: I will obey Thee as exactly as if I heard the sound of Thy Divine Word, and I saw the motion of Thy Lips distinctly articulating the orders which Thou givest me. Speak to my soul, O Divine Spouse; I am ready to obey Thee blindly in order to prove to Thee the fidelity of my love.

FOURTH DAY.

En ipse stat post parietem nostrum, &c.

How long, LORD, shall the wall of separation, which hinders the perfect union of my heart with Thine, subsist? When shall light come forth from the depth of my darkness? When shall evidence succeed to faith, clearness to dark sayings, the reality to the reflection, and the Original to the image? When shall I be able to say, like the Prophet, With my GOD I shall leap over the wall (Psalm xviii.), to be inseparably united with Him? Who shall deliver me from the body of this death; from this fleshly wall which hinders me from openly seeing my GOD? But, LORD, I will wait mourning for the revelation of Thy Divine Countenance; then shall I be like Thee, for I shall see Thee as Thou art (1 John iii. 2). Till that happy time, I will profit by my own ignorance, I will rejoice that Thou dwellest in inaccessible light; I will blindly run wherever Thou orderest, that by this submission I may one day become worthy of seeing Thy Brightness.

FIFTH DAY.

In lectulo meo per noctes quæsivi quem diligit anima mea; quæsivi illum, et non inveni. (Cant. iii.)

I sought my Beloved, says the bride, during the darkness of the night, and I found Him not. To seek God and not to find Him, is the terrible punishment of the ungodly who have not sought Him in a time when He may be found: but to be faithful to Him, and to seek Him with all possible ardour during the darknesses of this mortal life without finding Him, is not a punishment but a trial. I seek Thee often, Heavenly Spouse, and Thou takest pleasure in hiding Thyself; I strive to unite myself to Thee, and it seems that Thou removest from me. In my prayers I find only darkness, ignorance, and dryness; and often my heart, notwithstanding all its efforts, is harder than the rock of the desert. I could not find comfort for this affliction, if one of Thy most perfect lovers who often experienced it (D. Bern. de naturâ amoris Dei) did not teach me that Divine Love profits by its own defects, that it takes fire from its own coldness, that the most brilliant light proceeds from the depth of its thickest darkness, and that its blind and submissive ignorance conducts it to the clearest knowledge. I consent, Lord, to the privation of a transitory light, if Thou wilt not deprive me of Eternal Light.

SIXTH DAY.

In lectulo meo per noctes quæsivi, &c.

I will seek Thee, Lord, till death, notwithstanding

the darkness of my ignorance. It is enough for my soul to know that it is Thou; it is enough for my heart to feel that it is my God, to love Thee with a blind love. Sitting in darkness and in the shadow of death, Thou failest not to visit me; and if I see not the light of Thy Countenance, which will be revealed to me only in Heaven, yet I feel its happy influence, and its Divine Looks. I find myself amidst this sacred darkness, in which I feel Thee, without seeing Thee. My eyes are too weak to look upon the sun at mid-day, though it is but a faint image of Thy Divine Brightness; how, then, could they see the infinite splendour of Thy Being? Yet I feel the heat of that sun which I cannot look upon. I entreat Thee, Lord, that through this cloud which hides Thee from my eyes, my heart may feel the warmth of that sacred fire which Thou hast come to kindle upon the earth, till I possess Thee, and see Thee without clouds in Heaven.

SEVENTH DAY.

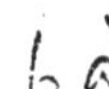

Donec aspiret dies et inclinentur umbræ, vadam ad montem myrrhæ et ad collem thuris. (Cant. iii.)

Until the great Day of eternity appears, and until the shadows of this mortal life are dispelled, I will get me to the mountain to gather the myrrh of privation and of suffering, and to breathe the sweet odours of the incense of Divine Love. I am content to love without seeing, since Thou willest it, Lord; if I may feel what I love, it is all that I ought to wish. I will hasten, like Moses, to the sacred darkness of the mountain, to hear the words of my God; I will love and adore Him as a hidden God. I shall see nothing, but by love I will embrace Him Who is All, and apart from Whom, and without Whom, there is nothing. Like the bride, my ignorance and my darkness will be the bitter myrrh that I shall gather: but my love, my affection, my desires, my transports, and my anticipated possession, will be the delightful odour of the incense which I shall breathe. I shall be lost, absorbed, swallowed up in this Ocean of Light, and I shall not see its brightness; I shall vividly feel His Adorable Presence, and shall not see His Face: I shall experience His Sweetness, and shall not see His Beauty: I shall burn with this consuming fire, and shall not see the flame: I shall closely clasp Him by the arms of an ardent charity, without having a distinct knowledge of Him; yet through this obscurity I shall see an infinitely Perfect, and infinitely Lovely Whole. The less I am permitted to see, the more I shall sigh after the happy moment which will for ever raise the veil which now hides from me His Divine Face, the sight of Which will be my eternal happiness.

Fortieth Week.

SUPREME LOVE.

To love God, and not to love Him supremely, is neither loving Him as He merits, nor as He requires; on the contrary, it is offending Him, because it is making an odious comparison between Him and a created being. Wherefore, when Jesus Christ delivered the great precept of love, He immediately gave that of supreme love, and united both in the same words. Thou shalt love, says Jesus Christ, the Lord Thy God; this is the precept of love: with all thy heart, with all thy soul, and with all thy strength; this is that of supreme love.

The reason of this great precept is, that, as God Alone is our Sovereign Lord, and our Sovereign Good,

He also only is the supreme Sovereign Object of love. He is our Sovereign LORD because He has created us, because He has redeemed us, and because He is the absolute Master of our life and death, both temporal and eternal. He is our Sovereign Good, because He is the only Author, the Centre, and the End of all imaginable good, and because, without Him and apart from Him, there never existed any true good.

Divine Love is often typified in the Holy Canticles by incense, and by the perfume whose pleasant odour ascends even to the Heart of GOD; but sovereign love is a perfume composed of the most precious spices which contains and surpasses them all. This leads the Bridegroom to say, that the smell of the garments of His bride is better than all spices: odor vestimentorum tuorum super omnia aromata. (Cant. iv.)

The bride responded perfectly to the praise which the Spouse gave to her love, because she loved Him sovereignly, and above all things. Indeed she was seen to run after Him Alone in the desert with so much ardour, that her companions, astonished by her eagerness, said to her, What is thy Beloved more than another beloved, O thou fairest among women? qualis est dilectus tuus ex dilecto, ô pulcherrima mulierum? (Cant. v.) She answers immediately, that He is the chiefest among ten thousand; electus ex millibus (Ibid.); and adds, that His Head is as the most fine gold; caput ejus aurum optimum (Ibid.) These are the motives of her sovereign affection for her Beloved.

AFFECTIONS.

FIRST DAY.

Odor vestimentorum tuorum super omnia aromata. (Cant. iv.)

The smell of thy garments, says the Spouse to His beloved, is better than all spices. All virtues are so many precious garments which protect the bride from the insults of her enemies; they are the ornaments which render her pleasing in the Eyes of her Bridegroom; they are perfumes which cause her to breathe out and to diffuse around the good odour of CHRIST JESUS. But if love does not preside over these virtues as a sovereign, these garments are but weak defences, these ornaments are worthless, and these perfumes are neither exquisite nor delicious. This love is a strong cuirass which prevents her soul being wounded; a precious stone which gives relief and brilliancy to her ornaments; a fire which calls forth and enhances the odour of her perfumes, which dissolves them, diffuses them, and causes their sweet-scented smoke to ascend to the Heart of GOD. Submit, then, with pleasure, O my soul, to the supreme dominion of Divine Love. Without this, count all thy virtues as nothing; with it, count upon the Heart of GOD, which is all that thou shouldst desire.

SECOND DAY.

Odor vestimentorum tuorum, &c.

If Divine Love is not the chief ornament of my soul, if its perfumes are not better than all other spices; i. e. if It does not preside over my virtues, if It is not their soul, their life, and their main-spring; in a word, if It is not in my heart as a Sovereign upon His throne, I am nothing, I merit nothing, and consequently I can aspire to nothing, because I cannot be pleasing in the Eyes of my Heavenly Spouse. Without this supreme Love, it will be vain for me to practise the most profound humility, it will be but meanness of spirit; my hope will be but rashness and presumption; my faith but a frightful carcase; my imagined magnanimity only real pride; my zeal only wrath hidden under holy pretexts; my prudence worldly policy or carnal prudence; my justice hardness of heart, and my energy a vain phantom of devotedness. Reign, then, Thou Alone, O Divine Love! reign over my heart, over all its desires, and all its attachments; reign over my soul and all its powers; reign over all my virtues; melt, dissolve, burn all these perfumes, and give them all the power which they need to sanctify my soul, to edify my neighbour, and to send up their good odour to God Himself.

THIRD DAY.

Odor vestimentorum tuorum, &c.

Divine Love is a delicious perfume which ought to prevail over all other perfumes: it is a Heavenly Manna, which contains the sweetness of all the most exquisite aliments; it is the salt which preserves them, and which gives them that flavour which they need to satisfy all different tastes. To love God sovereignly, says a holy writer (de document. salut. c. i. ap. St. Aug.), is consequently sovereign blessedness. Love, then, the One Good in which are all other goods, and that will suffice for thy happiness: in this One Good wilt thou find all that thou lovest, all that thou oughtest to love, and the way to love It. If I love God sovereignly, I shall find myself in God, because I shall love but for God's sake: I shall find my brother whom I love in the Heart of God; I shall find all in God, and God in all things. I shall find Him in my poverty, my sufferings, my darkness, my dryness, as well as in my tenderest affections, because I shall refer all to this sovereign Love. He shall be my Beginning, my Centre, my End; I will think and act by Him, for Him, and with Him, always and in all things.

FOURTH DAY.

Qualis est dilectus tuus ex dilecto, ô pulcherrima mulierum? (Cant. v.)

What is thy Beloved more than another beloved, O thou fairest among women? said the bride's companions. Their astonishment at seeing her run with so much ardour, and at seeing in her eyes, her steps, and her whole person, such eager emotion, made them conclude that this Beloved must possess extraordinary merit. They saw her entirely engrossed with the only Object which her heart loved; she saw and spoke to creatures only to ask where He was. Thus, says a holy writer (Man. c. 20, ap. St. Aug.), a soul that loves God sovereignly, can think of nothing but Him, and cannot act but for Him. Nothing created affects it; all that is not God, and does not lead it to God, is burdensome; all the soul, the memory, the mind, the heart, the will, the desires, incline only towards Him Who reigns Alone and sovereignly within. When shall I be wholly devoted to my Adorable Master? When shall I love sovereignly this only Sovereign of hearts?

FIFTH DAY.

Qualis est dilectus tuus ex dilecto, &c.

I ought to love the creatures which God enjoins me to love for His sake alone; I ought to give them that place in my heart that He will have them occupy; but my Sovereign Lord shall ever have the first place, and shall be its absolute Master. He shall not only be the Beloved of my heart, but beloved more than another beloved; otherwise I should reverse the law of Charity. Not to enthrone this Charity as a sovereign, wherever it is found, is not to know that she is, in the words of St. Augustine, the eldest daughter of the Heart of God, and God Himself. Ask thyself now, O my soul, what place thou hast given to Divine Love in thy heart; what place It holds there, now that thou knowest Its merit; and what place It will henceforth hold there. Ah, Lord! the past makes me lament; I am not sure of the present; but I feel in truth that I am resolved to love Thee sovereignly till death.

SIXTH DAY.

Electus ex millibus. (Cant. v.)

My Beloved, says the bride, is chosen among ten thousand. His Election is eternal; His Adorable Father chose Him from all eternity to be my Saviour, my Mediator, my Spouse, and my King. He acquiesced in His Election; but He had to buy all these characters of love at the price of His Blood and of His Life. If I love Him above all things, in Him freely I possess what cost Him so dear. He saw that He could not fulfil the character of a Sovereign of hearts if He did not love sovereignly; He did it first, and at the time when I had incurred His hatred and when I deserved hell; He does it still, and will do so always, if by my love I acknowledge His Sovereign Dominion. He loved me more than His temporal Glory, more than His Life, for He lost it for love of me. He is infinitely Lovely, infinitely Perfect; yet He asks my heart, and offers to recompense my love with an Eternal Crown by sharing His Sovereignty with me. How many powerful motives, O Heavenly Spouse, for loving Thee sovereignly!

SEVENTH DAY.

Caput ejus aurum optimum. (Cant. v.)

The Head of my Beloved, says the bride, is as the most fine gold. The head is the symbol of Sovereignty, because it rules the whole body. Gold is the symbol of Charity; for this is the Queen of Virtues, as that is the King of metals. My Heavenly Spouse is my Sovereign, and a Sovereign Who will reign only by Love. He has no Ambition but to reign over my heart, and to make me reign with Him if I love Him above all things. Let me see if I truly acknowledge Him as my Sovereign. A sovereign rules everywhere, and is ruled by none : he establishes laws, he rewards ; but he is so jealous of his authority, that he suffers not the least revolt. He is obeyed, loved, courted, reverenced, the least look of his eyes is valued, none of his words are suffered to be lost, men fear to displease him, they anticipate his wishes, they risk their health, their property, and their life for his glory. This men do, Lord, for the sovereigns of the earth : this at least should I have done for Thee, if I had always loved Thee sovereignly.

Forty-first Week.

SOLITARY LOVE.

It is very astonishing, says St. Gregory, (Moral.) that while there is nothing nearer to us than our heart, there is yet nothing more fugitive and less given to solitude. It escapes us, and it continually goes forth from itself to follow its different inclinations, and to pour itself out amongst the objects which it meets on its way, or which itself goes to seek ; so much so, that to recal it from its wanderings and to fix its fickleness, it is necessary that God should speak to it ; but it is also necessary that it should retire as soon as it hears His Voice.

I speak here of a solitude of heart which is that of perfect souls and of the true spouses of Jesus Christ, not of that which consists only in a simple corporeal departure from creatures ; and of this I find two sorts. In the first, the faithful soul, after having withdrawn from the world, strives to withdraw into itself, and to enter into its own heart to enjoy God Alone, like the bride to whom her Beloved addressed these words: O my dove, that art in the clefts of the rock, and in the cave of the wall, let me see thy countenance, let me hear thy voice: columba mea in foraminibus petræ, in cavernâ maceriæ, ostende mihi faciem tuam (Cant. ii.): a solitude which had become so sweet to her, that she wished to leave it no more, for fear of interrupting, for a moment, the converse of her heart with her Beloved, Who said to her, My sister, My spouse is become a garden enclosed, a fountain sealed: hortus conclusus, fons signatus (Cant. iv.); a solitude, in short, in which her love makes such great progress, that she will no more open her heart but to God Alone, Whom she invites unceasingly to come and repose in her as in a garden of delights, and to come there to eat the fruits which He planted there Himself: veniat dilectus meus in hortum suum, et comedat fructum pomorum suorum. (Cant. iv.)

But there is another and more sublime solitude, which is the recompense of the first: God Himself draws His bride to this inward solitude, which may be called the secret garden of the Heavenly Spouse. She almost ceases to act, but God acts in her; she keeps silence, and God speaks to her; an exquisite feeling with which she is altogether filled is her whole language: attentive, calm, she is detained in the inward recesses of her heart by a superior but delightful power; she cannot go forth without extreme violence; the Spouse detains her in His garden of delights, He gives her honey, milk, and wine, and He makes her sit down at a table of light and of love: veni in hortum meum, soror mea, sponsa. (Cant. v.)

AFFECTIONS.

FIRST DAY.

Columba mea in foraminibus petræ, in cavernâ maceriæ. (Cant. ii.)

"O my dove," says the Spouse, "that art in the clefts of the rock, in the cave of the wall, let me see thy countenance, let me hear thy voice." The dove is in safety when she is in the clefts of the rock; elsewhere she is in peril. Flee then the world, O my soul! thou knowest not how destructive its intercourse is to thee. What canst thou do in the world, thou who art greater than the whole world, since thou canst contain God Himself, though He be Infinite? Thou art solitary, thou enjoyest pure pleasures with Jesus Christ Alone; He is the mystic Rock in which thou reposest with safety and delight. Uneasiness, fickleness, weariness, or dissatisfaction tempt thee to come forth from this solitude to see the world: I pity thee; thou art about to lose all that thou hast acquired,—composure, devotion, affections, love of God. In their place thou wilt bring back from the world an inclination for that deceiver, and a taste for its amusements and customs; thou wilt return wholly filled with the spirit of this world, and pitiably empty of the Spirit of God.

SECOND DAY.

Columba mea in foraminibus petræ, &c.

Die, O my soul! die unceasingly and finally to all creatures which turn thee from the Creator; be solitary; flee this world, it will seduce thee, if thou seekest it. Hide thyself, like the dove, in the clefts of the rock, and let this Rock be Jesus Christ. Where canst thou be better than with Him? Where canst thou be well without Him? Practise solitude of heart; open it but to Him Alone, and never suffer any stranger to enter there. The Heavenly Spouse, Who calls thee to this inward solitude, will have thee show Him thy countenance, that is to say, thy whole soul; He desires to hear thy voice; speak to Him freely, as to a friend; listen to Him with reverent attention, dwell alone with Him Alone; thou wilt peacefully enjoy God in thyself, says St. Bernard, and thou wilt enjoy thyself in God.

THIRD DAY.

Soror mea, sponsa, hortus conclusus, fons signatus. (Cant. iv.)

My sister, my spouse, is a garden enclosed, and a fountain sealed, says the Bridegroom. An open garden is too much exposed, its flowers and fruits are not in safety; and a fountain not shut up runs the risk of seeing the purity of its waters defiled. To wish to love God without being solitary, to be solitary in the body and not to close our mind and heart against creatures, or not to occupy both with God in solitude, is a delusion. Be then, O my soul, a garden enclosed, and a fountain sealed, of which Jesus Christ Alone has the key. Inhale, and make thy Spouse inhale the delicious odour of the flowers of this mystic garden, which are the desires and affections of a heart imbued with love of Him; fill thyself with its fruits, which are acts of love; drink deep draughts of the waters of this fountain; enclose thyself for ever in this mysterious garden; God is there, that is enough for thee. There wilt thou love purely, and feel that thou lovest; thy whole delight will consist in loving, and this chaste delight will purify and consecrate the loving heart. That love which is not distracted by the world, causes sweet transports: the heart, without leaving itself, runs with happy swiftness towards the Object Which inflames it; it speaks, though the mouth keeps silence; it makes itself plainly heard, because creatures are silent; it speaks of God, with God, and to God Himself; it hears God speak; and in this delightful solitude it is transformed into God.

FOURTH DAY.

Soror mea, sponsa, hortus conclusus, &c.

It is by the heart, said St. Augustine, that I am what I am; and I can neither know nor govern this heart well but in solitude, which is the mystic garden of the spouse. There the Sun of Righteousness darts His rays perpendicularly to enlighten it, and to make it known to me; but it must be carefully shut, otherwise the world will enter, and the dangerous objects which accompany it, will divert and distract it; I lose sight of it, and its movements escape me; in vain do I seek there the love of my God, I find only the love of the creature; I strive to love this infinitely lovely Object, and I find an unworthy creature which takes Its place. I would fain speak to Him Alone, and, unawares, I speak to the world; I would shew myself to Him Alone, and a feeling of vanity tempts me to show myself to the world. Guide this heart into solitude, O my God! enlighten it, Thou art the Light; kindle it, Thou art a devouring fire; open it to Thyself, close it to sensible objects; open Thine to me, that it may be to me a delicious solitude in time and in eternity.

FIFTH DAY.

Veniat dilectus meus in hortum suum, et comedat fructum pomorum suorum. (Cant. iv.)

Let my Beloved come into His garden, says the bride, and eat His pleasant fruits. Come, Heavenly Spouse, come to Thy own dwelling in coming to me; come alone into my soul, as into a garden of delights; come to eat Thine own fruits, they are Thine, they come from Thee; Thou art the Spring of Living Water that waterest them; Thou art the Divine Sun which hast given them increase; come to visit a solitary heart which is Thine, which thinks only of Thee, which loves Thee Alone, which exists but by Thee, and sighs only after Thee. Thou Alone fillest to me the place of the most delightful companions; I hold Thee in my solitude, and I will never leave Thee. What glory for thee, O my soul, to be enabled to prepare in the garden of thy heart a delicious banquet for thy God, to be enabled to be alone with Him, to be enabled in thy solitude to unite thy heart for ever with His!

SIXTH DAY.

Veni in hortum meum, soror mea, sponsa. (Cant. v.)

Come into My garden, My sister, My spouse. When a solitary soul has made every effort to acquire recollectedness, and is prepared for the work of God, God acts in it; He calls, attracts, draws it with gentle violence into His mystic garden; it is suddenly carried away by a Superior Power; all the senses, both external and internal, retire into the inmost recesses of the heart; this inward operation crowns all its efforts; it feels God Alone acting within it; it feels itself wholly in God, and God wholly in it, in an ineffable manner; He seems to speak to her these words: My sister, My spouse, thou hast invited Me to enter into thy garden, come thou into Mine; thou hast presented thy fruits to Me, I give thee, therefore, fruits far more exquisite; taste the infinite sweets of a more sublime and more perfect love; come into My Heart which I open to thee; I have given calmness to all the powers of thy soul, taste this peace which is found in Me Alone; thou hast acted in order to unite thyself to Me in solitude, I will act in My turn, and act in the inmost recesses of thy heart; thou spakest, and I kept silence to prove thee: now keep silence, and hearken unto Me. Ah, LORD! can one who has tasted so delightful a solitude, speak to any but Thee?

SEVENTH DAY.

Veni in hortum meum, soror mea, sponsa.

Address these words to my soul, O Divine Spouse! call this recluse, Thy sister, Thy spouse, and make her merit these two characters. Thou hast promised me by a prophet to lead me into solitude, and to speak to my heart; draw me, then, to Thee, or come to dwell in me, that I may find Thee without going forth from myself, that I may feel Thee inwardly in the most hidden recesses of my heart, that I may hold and possess Thee there without fear and without alarm: I cannot seek Thee among creatures without the risk, either of not finding Thee, or of losing Thee as soon as Thou art found. Speak in the depth of my soul; I love much better to hear Thee, than to speak to Thee. Make in me so vivid an impression of Thy Adorable Presence, that I may never go forth void of Thy Divine operations. Collect, in the inmost recesses of my heart, all my senses, all my desires; calm them, purify them, consecrate them by the fire of Thy love in this delicious solitude, in order that they may never have any object but Thee.

Forty-second Week.

LOVE OF SYMPATHY.

WHAT we commonly understand by sympathy, is nothing but a secret propensity and a natural inclination which carries us towards an object which we find deserving of love; and this sympathy results now from proximity of blood, now from resemblance, and from certain conformities with our humour, our affections, and our customs.

From which it follows, that if this purely natural sympathy, proceeding only from the senses, often produces the closest ties, that which exists from our birth, between the substance of our soul and the God Who created us, and which is afterwards increased by Divine principles, that is, by grace, by the Sacraments, and by the Blood of Jesus Christ, ought to produce in our hearts an eternal charity and indissoluble bonds.

The causes of sympathy between relations and friends will appear weak, if we examine that which exists between God and us. He is our Father, and the Adorable Principle from Which we emanate; He is the Centre in Which we rest, and the End at Which we aim; He is our Life, our Support, our Saviour, our Brother, and our Friend; and if sympathy is often founded upon resemblance, He gave us His when He created us, and took ours when He made Himself Man. These are great motives for sympathy and love.

The bride had an exquisite feeling of this most intimate and most spiritual sympathy, for, though asleep, the first moment that her Spouse calls her, she opens her ears to hear His Voice, her mouth to speak to Him, and her eyes to see Him. Ah! I hear, says she, the Voice of my Beloved: behold, He cometh: vox dilecti mei; ecce iste venit. (Cant. ii.)

To maintain the sense of this sympathy, the Spouse takes pleasure in often calling her His sister; He says to her, Thou hast wounded My heart, My sister, My spouse; vulnerasti cor meum, soror mea, sponsa. (Cant. iv.) She replies to this Divine favour by saying tenderly to Him, O that Thou wert as my brother, that sucked the breasts of my mother! quis mihi det te fratrem meum, sugentem ubera matris meæ? (Cant. viii.)

Lastly, as reciprocal love is the work of this Sympathy, she boasts that she is wholly her Beloved's, and that her Beloved is wholly hers: Ego dilecto meo, et dilectus meus mihi. (Cant. vi.)

AFFECTIONS.

FIRST DAY.

Vox dilecti mei; ecce iste venit. (Cant. ii.)

The Voice of my Beloved, says the bride: behold, He cometh. By these words, the bride marks a perfect and universal Sympathy. Her ears, her heart, her eyes, all have a deep sense of it. Her ears hear Him, and even when asleep, the least sound of the Voice of This much-loved Spouse awakens her, and renders her attentive. I hear, she says, the Voice of my Beloved. She calls Him her Beloved as soon as she hears Him, because in perfect sympathy the heart moves as quickly as the ears, or rather, the ears of the heart hear better than those of the body. This Beloved Voice instantly awakens those most tender affections which Sympathy had engraven there: to hear Him and to love Him is the same thing. She adds: Behold, He cometh; it is He, it is no other. It is impossible to mistake when we hear and love none but our God. The world, vanity, pleasures, speak in vain; feeling nothing but antipathy to them, we do not hear them, and we know them only to avoid them. Thee Alone, then, O my God, do I desire to hear, to know, and to love.

SECOND DAY.

Vox dilecti mei; ecce iste venit.

I hear Thee, Heavenly Spouse; my collected soul

feels that it is her Beloved Who speaks to her, and I see Thee instantly, by the eyes of a living faith, full of Love. It is Thy Voice, LORD; I am too much accustomed to It to forget It, and to be deluded; It is too sweet and too delightful to be mistaken; the creature hears the Voice of its GOD, the daughter that of her Father, the sister that of her Brother, and the bride that of her Bridegroom. Directly Thou speakest to me by the Voice of inspiration, I feel Thee and see Thee present to my mind and to my heart; I awake like the spouse, and I say with her: I hear the Voice of my Beloved: behold, He cometh. This sweet and friendly Voice steals gently into my heart; and this feeling is not so much the effect of reasoning as an impression of sympathy, which Thou hast Thyself engraven in the depth of my soul. Can I fail to hear with pleasure the Voice of my Saviour, my Father, my Friend, and my Spouse?

THIRD DAY.

Vulnerasti cor meum, soror mea, sponsa. (Cant. iv.)

Thou hast wounded My Heart, My sister, My spouse. Is it indeed possible, O Heavenly Spouse, that Thou also feelest this Sympathy with me, that Thou gloriest in it as a character which Thou hast purchased at the price of Thy Blood, and that Thou callest me Thy sister and Thy spouse, tenderly saying to me, that I have wounded Thy Heart? It is so, LORD; my soul is Thy sister by Grace, Thy spouse by Love. By Grace I partake of Thy Divine Nature; Thy Apostle teaches me, that by it I proceed from the Same Father from Whom Thou art by Nature. I am also Thy bride by love and by attachment to Thy Divine Will; and these two glorious characters establish perfect Sympathy. What glory for thee, O my soul, to be the sister and the spouse of GOD! Thou wouldst be but an unnatural sister and an adulterous spouse, if thou didst not cleave all thy life, by chaste and ardent love, to the most Perfect of all Brothers, to the most Exalted and most Faithful of all Spouses.

FOURTH DAY.

Vulnerasti cor meum, soror mea, sponsa.

I have wounded Thy Heart, O my God! but what arms have I employed to wound this Adorable Heart, Which was once pierced for me with a spear upon the Cross, but the chosen arrow of Divine Love? Can a sister otherwise wound a brother whom she loves, and for whom she feels an unchangeable sympathy? Can a faithful bride inflict another wound on the Heart of a Spouse Who is God? Ah! I comprehend that since Thou hast taken my flesh, and given me Thine, the Sympathy which results from this union has wounded Thee with Love for me; but in wounding Thee, it has healed me; in piercing Thy Heart, it has given life to mine. Bear this wound, Lord, bear it for ever; it shows Thy Goodness, it is the triumph of Thy Divine Love, and the source of all my happiness and of all my glory. Wound, pierce my heart with the same arrow. Happy shall I be, if I cherish my wound! more happy if it is never healed!

FIFTH DAY.

Quis mihi det te fratrem meum sugentem ubera matris meæ? (Cant. viii.)

O that Thou wert as my brother, that sucked the breasts of my mother! said the bride. My sympathetic love, Lord, delights not to see Thee always seated on the Throne of Thy Majesty, nor armed with thunderbolts, ready to crush the guilty, nor as the Lord of Hosts, subduing the nations which are Thy enemies: Love does Thee more honour; and it is more in accordance with the inclinations of Thy Heart than fear. I desire to love Thee as a Brother with Whom I partake of the same milk and the same blood; I desire, like the bride, to caress Thee, as an infant brother who sucks the breasts of my mother. Love has humbled Thee even to take upon Thyself this low estate, in order to render Thee nearer, lovelier, and better suited to me; I am permitted to seek Thee out of Heaven, and in the Manger to adore Thy Divine Infancy, and to embrace Thee, like this favoured spouse, with the utmost reverence and tenderness of which I am capable.

SIXTH DAY.

Quis mihi det te fratrem meum, &c.

It is at the Holy Table that I perceive in Thee, Heavenly Bridegroom, all the tenderness and the sympathy of an affectionate Brother. Thou givest me there Thy Flesh, Thy Blood, Thy Heart, Thy Spirit, and Thy Soul: Thy Flesh sanctifies mine, Thy Blood purifies and consecrates mine; my heart is inflamed by Thine, and Thy Soul a second time quickens and redeems mine: there all that is Thine becomes mine, and I am transformed into Thee. Desire then, ardently, O my soul, to draw near to This Divine Brother, This Adorable Bridegroom, to give Him the chaste kiss of a sister and a spouse, and to stain thy lips with His Blood; there caress tenderly this Infant Brother, Who abridges His Immensity that He may be contained in the elements; there suck the milk of the children of God, which is the grace of the Sacrament; run eagerly to feed on this most pure Flesh. The more worthily thou receivest It, the more wilt thou strengthen thy Sympathy with This Adorable Brother, Who is Thy Spouse and Thy God; and the impression which He will make in thee will render thee firm against the torrent of vice.

SEVENTH DAY.

Ego dilecto meo, et dilectus meus mihi. (Cant. vi.)

I am my Beloved's, says the bride, and my Beloved is mine. How insensible must I be, if I did not hold this language with the bride, since my soul has as much sympathy as she had with her Spouse, Who is also mine. Yes, LORD, I am altogether Thine: I am the work of Thy Hands, the breath of Thy Mouth, the production of Thy Spirit, and the price of Thy Blood; I exist in the order of Nature, only by Thy Providence; and in the order of Grace, only by Thy Divine Mercy. The life which animates me, the air I breathe, the food which sustains me, the blood which flows in my veins, all come from Thee, and all are Thine. Thou sustainest me, Thou surroundest, fillest me; this connexion, these close ties, form in me a natural and supernatural Sympathy, which I cannot do otherwise than feel, know, and love. Can I fail to love a Spouse Who has given Himself altogether to me? Is it too much to be altogether His?

Forty-third Week.

LOVE THAT DELIGHTS IN GOD.

To love GOD, and to make it our great object in all things to please Him, is the same thing. In order to acquire this love of delight, we must destroy and build up; destroy our tendency to delight in ourselves, and build up a great esteem for GOD.

Study thyself seriously, that thou mayest know thyself well; know thyself well, that thou mayest thoroughly despise thyself; and as soon as thou shalt begin to be unpleasing to thyself, thou shalt begin to be pleasing to God. Empty thy heart of this vain esteem, of these frequent returns of self-love and vanity; God will fill it; thou wilt feel, enjoy, esteem, and love Him; He will please thee, and thou wilt strive to please Him in all things.

Why dost thou go forward so little in perfection? Because thou stoppest so often in the way. What stopped thee? says St. Augustine; one single feeling of self-satisfaction. Thou hast secretly applauded thyself for a good action, and hast gone no further: Ubi tibi placuisti, ibi remansisti. (Serm. xv. de verb. Ap.) Dost thou seriously desire, then, to please God? Permit thyself no delight, either in thyself or in the world; and labour unceasingly, says St. Gregory, till there remains in thee nothing of thyself: Qui perfecte placere Deo desiderat, in se nihil de se derelinquat. (Lib. x. Mor. c. 4.)

In the second place, conceive a high idea of that Supreme Being Whom thou seekest to please: fill thy memory, thy mind, and thy heart, with His Greatness, His Goodness, and the remembrance of what His Love has done for thee: thou wilt esteem Him, thou wilt love Him; He will be pleasing to thee, and as soon as He begins to please thee, says St. Augustine, thou wilt also please Him, and thou wilt delight in Him Alone: Ille placet Deo, cui placet Deus. (Ps. xxxii.)

It was this delighting love that made the bride so beautiful and so lovely in the Eyes of her Spouse, that He exclaims admiringly: Behold, thou art fair, My love; behold, thou art fair; thou hast doves' eyes: Ecce tu pulchra es, amica mea: ecce tu pulchra es! oculi tui columbarum. (Cant. i.) If she was pleasing to her Spouse, He was also infinitely pleasing to her, for she replies by the same expression, saying to Him: Behold, Thou art fair, my Beloved, yea, pleasant! Ecce tu pulcher es, dilecte mi, et decorus. (Ibid.)

She supports the feelings and words of this love of delight by heroic deeds, which prove it. She suffers her veil to be taken away, herself to be beaten and wounded in seeking Him; and her companions are so surprised, that they say: What is thy Beloved more than another beloved, O thou fairest among women? Qualis est dilectus tuus ex dilecto, ô pulcherrima mulierum? (Cant. v.)

AFFECTIONS.

FIRST DAY.

Ecce tu pulchra es, amica mea, ecce tu pulchra es! oculi tui columbarum. (Cant. i.)

Behold, thou art fair, My love; behold, thou art fair; thou hast doves' eyes, says the Spouse of the Canticles. What praise, Lord! How spoken? Admiringly. By what Lips? By those of a Spouse, Who is God. God Who admires and praises His own work! Whom dost Thou praise, whom dost Thou admire, Lord? A creature formed by Thy Hands. What dost Thou praise in it? What Thou hast given it of free mercy. What has it capable of attracting Thy Praise and Thy Delight? Purity, love, eagerness to please Thee Alone; and these virtues are Thy Gifts, which it has but from Thee. Take from me, then, Lord, cried St. Augustine, all that injures me and displeases Thee; give me all that is requisite to please Thee: give me words, affections, desires, and works, which may draw upon me Thy Eyes, Thy Delights, and Thy Love.

SECOND DAY.

Oculi tui columbarum. (Cant. i.)

Thou hast doves' eyes, says the Spouse to His

beloved. The eye is taken, in Scripture, for the desire of pleasing. The dove has eyes only for her mate. She is tender, pure, and single-eyed. The Holy Bridegroom says that His bride has doves' eyes, that is, according to the Hebrew text, eyes that delight Him, ravish Him, and seize upon His Heart, because they are always fixed on Him Alone; seeking to please Him in all things. The eye has power to transform itself into that which it sees, and to take its image in miniature. The Heavenly Spouse sees and admires this Image in the eyes of His bride, who looks unceasingly on Him. He loves Himself in her, and their delight is reciprocal. Is thine eye, my soul, as pure as that of the dove? What image does thy Spouse now see in it, His own only? Does He find none beside? Take, and bear away this Image of God; never efface it, and never wear another.

THIRD DAY.

Oculi tui columbarum.

In order to discover perfectly the full beauty of an object, we must draw near to it, and there must be nothing between it and our eye. If thou desirest, my soul, to see God, and to be seen of Him; if thou desirest to please Him, and to take delight in Him; thou must draw nigh to Him by continual adherence of the mind and heart, and carefully clear the space between Him and thyself of all created things, which prevent thee from seeing Him distinctly. Is thy intention of pleasing Him pure and unmixed? Hast thou not, by thine own fault, placed some obstacle between God and thee? Is there not in that interval some little interested motive, some small self-applause, some secret vanity, some desire of pleasing men, some regard for self, some self-love, or some other view wanting in purity? Cast out all these motes, which darken thine eye, while they hinder thee from discovering all the beauty that thou mightest see in God. He cannot please thee, and thy whole delight cannot be in Him.

FOURTH DAY.

Ecce tu pulcher es, dilecte mi, et decorus. (Cant. i.)

Behold, Thou art fair, my Beloved, yea, pleasant, said the bride. If the beauty of created things has charms, if they cause some delight, they pass away, they fade, and they are filled with repulsive defects: but Thy Beauty, Lord, is ever perfect and ever new; it ought to attract all eyes, delight all minds, and charm all hearts. Henceforth, Lord, I desire to look on no beauty but Thine; I desire to please none but Thee, or for love of Thee: it shall be my great study to avoid all that might displease Thee, and to comply blindly and exactly with Thy Will in all things; and if delight in that which pleases us and which we love, leads to imitation, I desire, henceforth, to suffer for Thee as Thou hast suffered for me; to humble myself as Thou didst humble Thyself for love of me: in a word, I will strive, without presumption, to think, will, speak, labour, and love as Thou hast done. Give me grace to copy this excellent pattern throughout my life.

FIFTH DAY.

Ecce tu pulcher es, dilecte mi, et decorus.

This Spouse, though so Perfect, so Holy, so Powerful, so Majestic, and so Fair, is yet altogether mine, provided that I am altogether His. He has been so gracious as to impress on me the Brightness of His Adorable Face, in order to communicate to me an Image of His Beauty. Preserve it carefully, my soul; never efface its precious features. But thou canst not preserve it, except by striving to please

Him in all things. His readiness to serve thee was infinite: it cost Him His Life. Why shouldest not thou make Him a like return? I know, LORD, in truth, that because Thou lovest me, Thine Eyes are ever looking on me to do me good; and that I cost Thy Love as much care and solicitude as if I were alone in the world, and Thou hadst no creature but me to guide. I desire that the ready compliance of my love may correspond to this. I desire to think of Thee, to love Thee, to serve and to please Thee, amidst the creatures that surround me, as if they existed not. As I have none but Thine Eyes to fear, so have I no others to seek.

SIXTH DAY.

Qualis est dilectus tuus ex dilecto, ô pulcherrima mulierum? (Cant. v.)

What is thy Beloved more than another beloved, O thou fairest among women? say the bride's companions. What is the Beauty, the Merit of Him for Whom thou art in such emotion? Thou runnest after Him like one frantic; thou sufferest thy veil to be taken away, thyself to be beaten and covered with wounds: does He deserve this active affection, which costs thee so much fatigue and so much blood? The Heavenly Spouse deserves it; it is even glorious to die in endeavouring to please Him. My Beloved, says the bride, is White and Ruddy; His Head is as the most fine gold; His Eyes are as the eyes of doves; His Lips drop sweet-smelling myrrh; His Hands are as gold rings; the sound of His Voice is most sweet; yea, He is altogether Lovely. This, LORD, justifies the delighting love of Thy bride: this is the portrait of the Beauty of Thy sacred Humanity, which was fair only by the reflection of the infinite Beauty of Thy Divinity, Which filled it. I rise from one to the other, and adore the splendour of Thy Divine Being, the brightness and light of Thy Intellect, the depth of Thy Wisdom, the excess of Thy Goodness; this, Heavenly Spouse, shall induce me to please Thee, whatever it may cost me, and if possible to make the acts of that delighting love which I owe Thee, equal in number to the moments of my life.

SEVENTH DAY.

Qualis est dilectus tuus ex dilecto, &c.

It is no longer time for weak compliances with the world, when we have learnt, by our own experience, that it is a traitor that deserves them not, a deceiver who makes no return for them: It is not fitting to have any for ourselves, when we are convinced of our own worthlessness. My Spouse Alone, Who is Beauty and Goodness Itself, shall be henceforth the Object of all my delight, my care, my eagerness, and my application. But if I am resolved to please God Alone, the whole world will declare itself my enemy, and turn me to ridicule. Its enmity and esteem matter not; its mockery and applause shall make no impression on my heart. It will consider me ridiculous and foolish; but its blame shall be to me as praise: the folly of which it will accuse me shall be the beginning of that true Wisdom to which I aspire; and my Heavenly Spouse, Whom Alone I desire to please, shall be all things to me. If He repaid the compliances of my whole life by but one of His looks, I should be better paid than by all wealth, honour, and pleasure that the world can give.

Forty-fourth Week.

FAMILIAR LOVE.

A COMMON charity truly renders the soul pleasing to GOD; but a perfect charity affectionately constrains this Supreme Greatness to descend from the Throne of His Majesty in order to become familiar with a bride, and to bind Himself in close affection with her. All that can be said of the strongest affections does not approach to that between GOD and the soul which loves Him heartily. These affections are considered to consist either in the pleasure of conversation, in the communication of secrets, in reciprocal liberality, in conformity of sentiments, or in courage to suffer all things for one another. But, in the first place, what is more familiar and tender than the converse between GOD and the soul which loves Him Alone? What outpourings of heart! what Divine caresses! what chaste pleasures! what reciprocal complacencies! In the second place, what secrets does He not confide to her, as a Friend to His intimate friend! and what confidence has not this bride to open her whole heart unreservedly to Him! In the third place, if He gives her all His treasures, His light, His graces, this bride also gives Him all that she hath; and the more she gives, the more she receives. In the fourth place, a close union of feelings is formed between GOD and this beloved soul; it no longer wills anything but what GOD wills and as He wills; and GOD humbles Himself also to will only what it wills: so that from these two wills there results but one. Finally, they mutually support each other's interests; the bride remembers that her Bridegroom exposed Himself to death for her; and there is nothing which she will not sacrifice for His Love.

The bride of the Canticles gloried much in this familiarity when she said that the King had brought her into His secret chambers: introduxit me rex in cellaria sua. (Cant. i.) Proud of this favour, she is resolved not to leave Him till she has in her turn introduced Him into the house and chamber of her mother: donec introducam illum in domum matris meæ, et in cubiculum genitricis meæ. (Cant. iii.)

Lastly, after having depicted all the beauties of this Spouse to her companions, she says to them: This is my Beloved; that is, majestic, rich, and beautiful as He is, He is nevertheless my Friend: talis est dilectus meus, et ipse est amicus meus. (Cant. v.)

AFFECTIONS.

FIRST DAY.

Introduxit me rex in cellaria sua. (Cant. i.)

The King hath brought me into His secret chambers, says the bride. Thy Love was not satisfied, O Divine Spouse, with giving me the Sacred Kiss of Thy Mouth to reconcile me to Thee; Thou hast also drawn me after Thee to the odour of Thy perfumes, and hast taken me by the hand, as a bride, to introduce me into Thy secret chambers, there to speak to me heart to heart, and to load me with caresses. Thou sufferedst me not to dwell any longer in the tabernacles of sinners, as a stranger; but in Thy house as a servant, a friend, and a bride, where I have the comfort of finding Thee, and of conversing with Thee every moment of the day. There Thou openest Thy heart to me, and with the same tenderness and freedom I may open mine to Thee. There Thou layest aside the splendour of Thy Majesty, and descendest from Thy Throne to converse familiarly with me. Who am I?

and what art Thou, O my God? How astonishing is the power of Divine Love!

SECOND DAY.

Introduxit me rex in cellaria sua.

Where is it well with us but in the house of God? And when we have been brought as a bride into the secret chambers of the Spouse by the Spouse Himself, is it possible to be weary there? is it possible to resolve to go forth? How glorious is it to open our whole heart when this Sovereign, now become a Spouse, is so gracious as to knock at it! How sweet is it to receive Him, to feel, to hear, to converse with Him in all freedom as a Brother, a Spouse, and a Friend! What chaste pleasure to receive the tender outpourings of the Heart of a God, and to pour out ours to Him, without fearing that this familiarity may offend Him! I will have this boldness, O Divine Spouse, for it is Thyself Who inspirest me with it: I will enjoy this glorious familiarity, since Thou offerest it to me so graciously; and to make myself worthy of it, the door of my heart shall be closed against all creatures, and open to Thee Alone; it shall speak only to Thee and of Thee; it shall love only Thee, or Thy Love.

THIRD DAY.

Introduxit me rex in cellaria sua.

People are eager to make friends in the world; they often fail, or when they think they may reckon on their hearts, they find only faithlessness. Let us cultivate but one Friend; He is faithful, He is easy of access; He comes more than half way to meet us; He has no caprice of temper, no vexing pride, though He is Greatness Itself: He is tender, and desires to be tenderly loved; He is lovely, for He is Love Itself; in Him is no harshness, no severity, no repulsiveness;

and when we have once become familiar with Him, He never withdraws His Heart unless we withdraw ours. This Friend alone, then, is far better than all the friends in the world; for He knows better how to love; it is safer to confide to Him the secrets of the heart; there is more pleasure, more purity, and more advantage in loving Him; and in loving Him we may give full scope to the tenderness of our heart without fear of exceeding His and displeasing Him.

FOURTH DAY.

Introducam illum in domum matris meæ, et in cubiculum genitricis meæ. (Cant. iii.)

I held my Beloved, says the bride, and would not let Him go until I had brought Him into my mother's house and chamber. I have God for my Judge; this truth makes me tremble, because I am a sinner, and He has a right to punish me: I have God for my Father, my Saviour, my Spouse, my Friend; this truth re-assures me, it dispels my troubles, allays my fears, and is my whole confidence. Not content with giving me admittance into His secret chambers, He is pleased to enter familiarly into mine; He places me in His Heart, and Himself in mine; He speaks to me with cordiality, He listens to me with pleasure, He is gracious enough to enter into all my wants, to console me in my sufferings, and to be with me in tribulation. Render thyself worthy, O my soul, of this sublime familiarity; nothing can do thee greater honour: reply to it as thou oughtest, and as He demands; profit by it, and it will be all thy glory and all thy happiness.

FIFTH DAY.

Introducam illum in domum, &c.

What honour is it for us to bring God under our roof! What Mercy, and what Love of God, to be pleased to enter His creature's abode, and to take delight therein! What nations can boast of having a God so nigh unto them as ours? of having divinities who humble themselves, and who love only in order to be loved? Ah, Lord! exclaims St. Bernard, I perceive that love has overcome Thy Heart, and that, dazzling as is the Greatness which Thy Divinity gives to Thee, Thou takest pleasure in obscuring it, to show us Thy tenderness, and to draw ours to Thee. Thy Divinity gives us evident tokens of affection. Thy Majesty is softened towards us. What fearest Thou, then, my soul? Draw near confidently and boldly to the Throne of a loving God. If it is a Throne of devouring fire to His enemies, they are flames of love for those who have given Him their Heart: go to Him, or bring Him into thine abode: converse with Him, hearken to Him, love Him, and He will never depart.

SIXTH DAY.

Et ipse est amicus meus. (Cant. v.)

Yes, daughters of Jerusalem, says the bride, He Whose Greatness, Whose Perfection, Whose incomparable Beauty I have described, is nevertheless my Friend. Can a creature be so happy as to have its God for a friend? Is it not over-boldness to flatter ourselves that it is so, and to boast of it? Is it not even presumptuous to dare to think it? No; if we love, we may do so. I know that a sort of miracle is needed to establish this strict familiarity between God and His creature: but love will work it, for it is as powerful as God Himself. It has power to bring down this Supreme Being to the nothingness of the creature, to elevate the creature to Him, to unite them together, and to make of them but one mind, one will, one soul, and one heart. I will, therefore, speak boldly to my God if I love Him, and I will say loudly that He is my Friend; I will speak familiarly to my

God, though I am but dust and ashes; He permits me, He solicits me, He commands me: I will rather abandon myself wholly to the feeling of His Goodness and of His Love, than allow myself to be overwhelmed by the fear of His Justice, or dazzled by the splendour of His Majesty.

SEVENTH DAY.

5/15

Et ipse est amicus meus.

What can more powerfully invite us to love, says St. Augustine, than to be anticipated by the tender solicitations of God Who is infinitely lovely; above all, when He humbles His Supreme Greatness even to treat us as friends, and to ask our heart with the familiarity of an equal? The Heavenly Lover Who offers me His Affections, and Who demands mine, is Greatness Itself; He is pleased to descend from the glorious Throne which He occupies, to make me ascend thither with Him; the profit which I shall find in the holy exchange which He desires to establish between His Heart and mine, is an eternity of glory and of ineffable delight: let me, then, fearlessly accept the familiarity of so illustrious a Friend, since He offers it freely; let this boldness be a merit in His Sight; it is to His Taste, it ought to be to ours: let me love Him with all my heart, and then boldly say, This God, so Holy, so Majestic, so Powerful, so Perfect, and so Beautiful, is, nevertheless, my Friend; and I will strive to the utmost that He may be so in the whole compass of His Divinity.

Forty-fifth Week.

CONSECRATING LOVE.

As the love of God is God Himself, it partakes of the honour of His priesthood; it has power to consecrate the hearts in which it resides, and which are faithful to Him, and to make them so many living temples and sanctuaries, which shall henceforth serve for no other purpose than to contain Him, to adore Him, to love Him, to render Him continual homage, and to burn unceasingly with His Divine Ardour.

A feeble and transient love warms the heart for a time, but it does not set it on fire, and it has not the privilege of consecrating it for ever; but when we have long loved, and love has been continually increasing in the heart, its flames, which are purity itself, consume even the least defilements; little by little it makes it its temple, it carefully adorns it, then consecrates it; lastly, takes entire possession of it, abides in it, fills it, delights in it, and never departs. There might be confusion or inconstancy in the love of the bride while she was yet a neophyte; and the Spouse, Who desired to consecrate her unchangeably to Himself, begins by separating her from creatures. Having separated her, He brings her into His banqueting-house; there He inebriates her with the mystic wine of a more excellent charity, which she had not yet known; in this happy inebriation she lost the human mind to act in future only by the Mind of God; and the Spouse chooses the time of this happy alienation to consecrate and to regulate in her His love; ordinavit in me charitatem. (Cant. ii.)

It is not surprising that after this special consecration, made by the hands of the Celestial Spouse, of the Divine Priest, the bride cannot refrain from saying, I am my Beloved's; ego dilecto meo. (Cant. vi.) Could she be any other's than His who had formed, regulated, and consecrated love in her heart?

But the Spouse also exacts of her, at the end of His canticle, that she keep herself in this consecration; and that the impression of this consecrated love may never be effaced, He says to her, Set Me as a seal upon thine heart; pone Me ut signaculum super cor tuum (Cant. viii.); because love is not love, if it is not strong as death. This is the seal of this consecration set by the Hand of God upon the heart of His bride.

AFFECTIONS.

FIRST DAY.

Ordinavit in me charitatem. (Cant. ii.)

My Beloved, says the bride, has regulated in me my love. When the soul has long loved God, and its ever-constant charity has never grown cold or relaxed, God, in His turn, acts upon the soul; He elevates its charity to a superior order; He works all things in it, and consecrates it entirely to Divine love. So far it was the work of God and of the creature together; in this consecration it is the work of God alone. Self-love, which is a distracted and disorderly love, is almost wholly extinguished; and Divine love, which is a consecrating love, a regulated and ordained love, takes possession for ever of the heart. In this sublime state wouldest thou now be, my soul, if thou hadst never relaxed in the practice of Divine love, and if thou hadst faithfully replied to all the tenderness of thy Heavenly Spouse. Think, then, seriously of what thou art, think of what thou couldest and oughtest to be, and strive to attain to this consecration.

SECOND DAY.

Ordinavit in me charitatem.

Bring me, Lord, into Thy Divine Banqueting-house as Thou broughtest Thy bride, and make me feel that Thou art at once the Spouse and the Priest. As the Spouse, inebriate my soul with the delicious wine of Thy charity; as the Priest, ordain, regulate, and consecrate in me Thy love, that Thou mayest ever be the only Object of its ardour, and its only Consecrator. Adorable Priest, Thou hast already conferred upon me the unction and consecration of Baptism, which set on me the seal of Thy predilection, which bedewed me with Thy Blood, and gave me a right to aspire to the heavenly inheritance. By a second ordinance of grace Thou hast added a new unction, which confirmed the first, and which should have given me courage enough to maintain my consecration to the shedding of my blood. Thou hast renewed this consecration as often as Thou hast come into me in the Holy Communion; I have received within me the Spouse and the Priest in person: should not my soul, then, be wholly consecrated? Ah, LORD! nothing more is wanting to my happiness but the entire conrecration of my heart by a more ardent and never-changing love: give it me!

THIRD DAY.

Ordinavit in me charitatem.

Entreat, then, O my soul, of JESUS CHRIST, Who is thy Spouse and thy Sovereign Priest, that He will consecrate thee for ever to His Divine Love. Thou art His temple, and it is time that it be solemnly consecrated. Is this mystic temple in a state to be consecrated? Are its foundations laid deep enough in humility? has it elevation enough through the hope of Heavenly joys? has it the right length, by lively faith in the truths most removed from the senses? has in due breadth and width by true charity? Is this temple sufficiently purified from the least defilements? is it sufficiently adorned with virtues to receive this Heavenly anointing? Is its altar, the heart, ready to receive all the victims? will it allow itself to be bedewed with their blood, whatever it may cost? Does the fire of Divine love burn continually upon this altar, in order to consume the Holocausts? Receive, then, O my soul! this Adorable Consecrator; but after thy consecration remember that this temple can no longer serve for any profane purpose, and that it is destined for God Alone.

FOURTH DAY.

Ego dilecto meo. (Cant. ii.)

I am entirely consecrated to my Beloved, says the bride. Happy should I be, Lord, if I could make this noble declaration of love as boldly and as truly as she, and if I could say, at this moment, from the bottom of my heart, that I am wholly Thine! But what hinders me from holding this language? What is there within me opposed to my total consecration? Is it not some vain delight in the creature, some weakness which I have not yet overcome, some remains of vanity, some little secret attachment, or some hidden love for myself? Yet I am the temple of my God, and I ought to be wholly His: I must, then, continually purify it from all its secret defilements, and so effectually shut its doors, that nothing profane may ever enter it, no earthly desires, no imperfect affections, no sensible attachments. I desire to be wholly Thine, Lord, and to make myself worthy to be consecrated to Thy love and by Thy love: and I hope, by the help of Thy Grace, to be so faithful to Thee, that I shall never commit anything unfitting the purity of my consecration.

FIFTH DAY.

Ego dilecto meo.

Remember, O my soul, that to be entirely consecrated to the Divine love, there must be an election, a separation, and an application. For thine election, thou must suppose it, and act accordingly. If God had not chosen thee to be His bride, He would not have done for thee what He has. Thy separation is no less evident: He has separated thee from this sinful world, which He has rejected, which would have corrupted thee, if thou hadst abode in it; He has brought thee into His own sanctuary to serve and to love Him. It rests not, then, with thy Heavenly Spouse to make thee wholly His, and to complete thy consecration; thou must reply to it in order to its completion. Reply, then, to thine election. This manifest choice of God honours thee too much for thee to make any other. Live in noble separation from all that is not God, and in continual fixedness of mind to follow His Divine movements; thus wilt thou nobly sustain the honour of thy consecration.

SIXTH DAY.

Pone Me ut signaculum, &c. (Cant. viii.)

Set Me, engrave Me as a seal upon thine heart. To produce from time to time some transient acts of Divine love, when the heart finds pleasure in that sweet exercise, and to neglect the practice of them when lassitude, dryness, desertion, or adversity are felt, is not so much true consecration as mere love of temperament. This is not an impression like that which a seal makes on wax, where the lines are deeply marked, and are difficult to erase. Sacred love, thou art this Divine seal, which bears and which imprints the Image of my Celestial Spouse. Imprint it Thyself, not on the surface, but in the inmost recesses of my heart. Press Thy Almighty Hand, Lord, on this Divine seal, to engrave it better; and to render my heart more yielding and more susceptible of its impression, warm it like wax by Thy Divine Ardour, to soften its hardness. When it bears all Thy Features, and they are deeply impressed, my consecration will be perfect.

SEVENTH DAY.

Pone Me ut signaculum super cor tuum.

My soul, dost thou bear the token and the image of thy God upon thy heart? Is this impression very deep and well marked by constant and immoveable love? If so, thy consecration is made, and thou art no more thine own. No; thou art no more thine own, but God's Alone. Consider, then, that this consecration has worked in thee a total alienation from all that thou hast, and all that thou art; all has passed under the absolute dominion of Him to Whom thou art consecrated; thy memory and thy mind, thy will, thy natural and supernatural affections, all are His, and thou hast no longer a claim on anything but His Heart. Thine external senses are as much alienated as the internal: thine eyes, thy hearing, thy smell, thy taste, thy hands, all should bear the glorious marks of thy consecration; thou must no more love, desire, think, will, speak, act, but with God, for God, and in God; in a word, there must remain in thee nothing of thyself. Happy consecration, happy alienation, which makes us give all that we are, to possess and to become all things in God.

Forty-sixth Week.

PURE LOVE.

The abiding place of Pure Love is not this mortal life. Religion, which leads us to God as to an Object infinitely deserving of love, guards us against forgetting that He is infinitely just: it requires us, therefore, to render homage now to His Goodness, now to His Justice, and will have our love sometimes mixed with fear and alarm. God is, nevertheless, so gracious, that, condescending to our weakness, of this fear which He prescribes, He makes a virtue which He recompenses; He makes it even serve to increase our love, when we strive to purify it from all servile and mercenary views.

Moreover, though love comes from God, Who is Purity Itself, it is also the production of the heart of man. The heart feels it; it makes acts of it; and as it is a heart of flesh, says St. Augustine, whatever purity it may have acquired, it will find in itself, till death, some defilements to purify.

Yet there are degrees of this purity which may be acquired, and by which we may approach more nearly to that Supreme purity of Love which we shall possess only in Heaven. I speak not of a common purity, which consists in not making in one's heart an odious mixture of the love of the Creator with that of the creature; that regards the Purificative Life, and I have treated of it in Chaste Love; but of a more sublime purity, which consists in separating from this love all imperfect and too mercenary views, all looking to self as our object, all attachment to sensible joys, and the least division of the heart; in a word, in loving God only in order to love Him; and in desiring Heaven only in order to love Him more purely.

The wonderful praise which the Spouse gives to His beloved, proves that she had acquired great purity of love, for it is impossible to please this Spouse of Virgins, Who is Purity Itself, or to become the subject of His satisfaction and praise, but by a most pure love. After a pleasing relation of her beauties, He says to her: Thy lips, O My spouse, drop as the honey-comb: Favus distillans, labia tua, sponsa. (Cant. iv.) He adds: Honey and milk are under thy tongue, and the smell of thy garments is like the smell of incense: Mel et lac sub linguâ tuâ, et odor vestimentorum tuorum sicut odor thuris. (Ibid.) Honey and milk are the symbols, the one of sweetness, the other of purity; they are united on the lips and the tongue of the bride, because sweetness without purity is only cloying. This honey is always dropping, because the heart, which is the centre of love, unceasingly produces new sweets when it loves with purity. It is from this excellent model that we must copy the purity of love, in order to give satisfaction to our Heavenly spouse.

AFFECTIONS.

FIRST DAY.

Favus distillans, labia tua, sponsa.

"Thy lips, O my spouse, drop as the honey-comb." Pure love, so far as a creature is capable of feeling it, is this delicious honey-comb which produces infinite sweets; and it is not so much attached to these sweets as to Him Who causes them. It has no ambition, and is content with itself, because God is always with it. It asks no earthly recompense, and is never disappointed. It requires nothing, says St. Bernard, and it obtains and possesses all; without having mercenary views, there is nothing to which it may not aspire. When it is pure, it alone is itself its own reward, and nothing can equal it; it is itself its recompense and its own crown, because it loves only in order to love God as its good, and to possess That which it loves, and it possesses It in loving It. My lips, O Heavenly Spouse, would now drop the delicious honey of pure love. I should even find sweetness in the midst of suffering and bitterness, if I had been always faithful, and if I had been attentive to purify my love from all the imperfect and mercenary views which have alloyed it. Henceforth, I will love Thee Alone; I will love Thy very gifts only for Thee; I will love Thee for Thyself Alone, and that I may enjoy Thee eternally as my Sovereign Good.

SECOND DAY.

Favus distillans, labia tua, sponsa.

As the sweetest and most exquisite honey is obtained only from the sweetest and most odoriferous flowers which contain it, my lips cannot sing hymns that shall please my Heavenly Spouse, unless my heart, from whence they emanate, and which produces them, be pure, and my love for Him undivided and without alloy. Yet, O God of Purity, I cannot labour alone for the purification of this heart, because I am weak and blind. Assist me, enlighten me, to know and to cleanse the least stains which are displeasing to Thine Eyes, and which escape my self-love. Sprinkle me with hyssop (Psalm li.), that I may be clean, and that this salutary bitterness may destroy in me the taste of every sweet which comes not from Thee. Wash me also with the pure waters of victorious Grace, that I may become whiter than snow: or rather, Lord, send from the Throne of flames and fire whereon Thou sittest, Divine ardours which may instruct, enlighten, and inflame me, and which may consume in my heart even the smallest defilements with which it is stained.

THIRD DAY.

Favus distillans, labia tua, sponsa.

To love God only from interested motives, and with reference to any other end, is not to present to Him a honey sufficiently pure, or sufficiently exquisite, and is not to love Him with chaste love. The most urgent motive which should engage us to love Him is Himself; otherwise, we set a higher value on that which we desire to receive as the recompense of our love, than on Him Who has the power and the will to give All to the soul that is disinterested in its love, and that seeks Him Alone as a reward. Nevertheless, Lord, I hope for Heaven, I desire it; and Thou wouldest have me sigh after that happy abode: but I ask it only because it is Thy command, because there I am sure of loving Thee eternally, and of possessing Thee without alarm and without fear of losing Thee. I would not breathe one sigh for that abode, if by an impossibility Thou wert not there: it would be even a terrible prison to me if Thou wert not loved there; because Thy Love alone is able to make my whole happiness; and I renounce all other to possess Thee as my ultimate aim.

FOURTH DAY.

Mel et lac sub linguà tuâ. (Cant. iv.)

Honey and milk are under thy tongue, O My beloved, says the Spouse. What sweetness and purity at once in the love of this chaste bride! She could neither open her mouth, move her lips, nor speak to her Divine Spouse, without manifesting the sweetness of odoriferous honey, and the purity of milk of incomparable whiteness; and both were under her tongue, because her heart was full of them. Her lips dropped, and her mouth was filled only from the abundance of her heart. She loved Thee Alone, then, Lord, and in this consisted the purity of her love. Is it indeed a pure love that loves something with Thee, and not for love of Thee? No, my God; it is, on the contrary, an impure mixture which can but displease Thee: but pure love of Thee is to love Thee Alone, or to love nothing but with regard to Thee and for the love of Thee. This, Lord, is the pure and chaste love which Thou demandest of me, and I give it Thee.

FIFTH DAY.

Mel et lac sub linguâ tuâ.

I acknowledge, LORD, that my love is not pure enough to deserve to have, like the bride, the honey and milk of Thy Divine consolations in my heart, and on my tongue, because I have not yet nobly endured all the trials of this love, and because I have not made a holy use of my dryness and of my inward sufferings. I ought to know, that if honey comes from flowers, it must also pass through the sting of the bee; and that if milk has whiteness and relish, it was once blood. If it is in privations and in weariness that love acquires all the purity and all the disinterestedness of true charity; if it is when most ill-treated, and most destitute of sensible graces and of spiritual joys, that it is purified as gold in the furnace provided that it perseveres faithfully, I acquiesce in all these severities. O Heavenly Spouse! deprive me not of Thy Love, but of the feeling of Thy Love; try me, purify me, but support me, lest I sink; lead me through thorns and blood, till my love be pure enough to deserve the mysterious honey and milk of the bride.

SIXTH DAY.

Et odor vestimentorum tuorum sicut odor thuris. (Cant. iv.)

The smell of thy garments, says the Spouse to His beloved, is like the smell of incense. As the smell of this perfume can be brought forth only by fire, which is the symbol of love and of purity, the good odour of the soul can ascend unto JESUS CHRIST only by the fire of a love wholly purified from all sensible attachments, and from all that is earthly and perishable. The least mixture corrupts this good odour, and destroys all that is pleasing and delicious in it; and the Spouse, Whose delicacy with regard to love and purity is infinite, does not breathe this incense with pleasure. Examine thyself therefore carefully, O my soul! Seek out, exactly, all the defects of thy love, all its inequalities, all its reserves; purify it from the petty views of earthly interest, from all self-seeking; permit not thyself the smallest burst of self-love; it is by studying this purity of love, that thou wilt become thyself the sweet savour of Christ.

SEVENTH DAY.

Et odor vestimentorum tuorum, &c.

I will labour for the purification of my love with such care and such fixedness of mind, that at last I shall follow the counsel of the Apostle, and put on the LORD JESUS CHRIST. (Rom. xiii. 14.) Clothed with this Adorable Saviour, Who is a GOD of love and of purity, the smell of my garments will surpass that of incense and of the most exquisite perfumes. I shall ever have this excellent Original before my eyes; and from my eyes it will pass into my heart, never to depart thence. On my body I will wear mortification as a precious garment, and I will make it a cuirass which shall guard my purity. I will strive to copy all the features of this pure Spouse, to imitate all His virtues, and above all, the purity of His love. I will remember that He loved me with a love so strong, so lofty, and so disinterested, that He valued His life less than mine, for He gave it to preserve me from death. In imitation of this purity and noble disinterestedness of love, I will count my life for nothing, and will be ever ready to give it for His love, the first moment that He shall require it.

Forty-seventh Week.

PERFECT LOVE.

It is not presumptuous for a mortal creature to aspire to the perfection of Divine Love, since Jesus Christ has traced its paths, provided its rules, given the means, and commanded us to labour for its acquisition. He gave the precept of this love when He said, "Thou shalt love the Lord thy God;" but He gave the rules of Perfect Love when He said, "Thou shalt love Him with all thy heart, and with all thy soul, and with all thy mind." (Matt. xxii. 37.)

These words alone, "with all thy heart," comprise all the perfection of Divine Love, since they exclude all reserve, all division and inequality. In demanding the whole heart, says St. Bernard, He exacts all the feelings, the affections, and the tenderness of love; He desires to be Alone its whole delight and pleasure, without permitting it to be affected by any created thing.

When He says, "with all thy soul," we must remark, that in the Holy Scriptures the soul is almost always taken for the life, and that thus He will have us love Him throughout our life, and more than our life. Thus He requires us to live, to breathe, and to act for Him Alone, and to be ever ready to sacrifice this life for His love.

By the words, "with all thy mind," He desires an appreciating love, a love of esteem, which shall lead us to consecrate to Him all our reason, our designs, our thoughts, our application. Thus all the heart, all the soul, and all the mind, contribute together to the perfection of love.

The figure of this Perfect Love is plainly marked in the Canticles, where the Spouse, after having gone up to the mountain of myrrh, and to the hill of frankincense, says to His bride, Thou art all fair, My love; there is no spot in thee: tota pulchra es, amica mea, et macula non est in te. (Cant. iv.) Since CHRIST went up to Calvary, the faithful soul, which is His bride, may attain perfection; and His Adorable Blood, with Which it may be unceasingly washed, has power to cleanse all her stains.

He adds, in the sixth chapter, My dove is one and perfect: una est columba mea, perfecta mea. (Cant. vi.) She had been so assiduous in the Divine lessons of her Beloved, so faithful, and so ardent in putting them in practice, that her love had become perfect.

AFFECTIONS.

FIRST DAY.

Tota pulchra es, amica mea, et macula non est in te. (Cant. iv.)

Thou art all fair, My love, says the Spouse, there is no spot in thee. I perceive, LORD, by this most pure praise which Thou givest to Thy bride, that in order to acquire Perfect Love, it is necessary to cut off and to add; to cut off the smallest faults, and to add unceasingly new ardours to this love: the bride had carefully washed all her stains, and had become all fair. She had perfectly imitated both the sculptor and the painter, and had united these two beautiful arts in a sublime manner, in order to attain to perfect love. The sculptor gives perfection to his statue only by cutting off the superfluous parts, and removing that which conceals it; the painter only finishes his picture by adding to it some fresh touches. But, O Heavenly Spouse, since Thou Alone workest all in all things, supply my weakness, and do these two things in me. Cut off in my heart all that is opposed to the perfection of Thy Divine Love; add fresh touches of beauty to this image which Thou hast formed Thyself, till my love become a perfect copy of Thine.

SECOND DAY.

Tota pulchra es, amica mea, &c.

To be without spot, to be Thy love, and to be fair in Thine Eyes, O Divine Spouse, is to have acquired Perfect Love. But how can I acquire it, if Thou dost not assist me; I, who can do nothing without Thee? I see in Thy evangelic oracles that this perfection is now a mystic Mountain, now a Pearl, now a hidden Treasure, now a Gift, now a Prize, now a Crown, and now a Kingdom. I cannot ascend this Mountain unless Thou takest me by the hand; I cannot buy this precious Stone unless Thou givest me the means; I cannot find this hidden Treasure, unless Thou enlightenest me with Thy Divine Light; I cannot merit this Gift, Thou must therefore give it me freely; I cannot gain this Prize unless Thou helpest me to run like a giant; I cannot obtain this Crown unless Thou sustainest me in my combats; I cannot, lastly, take possession of this Kingdom, unless Thou givest me arms, strength, courage, and perseverance to conquer it.

THIRD DAY.

Tota pulchra es, amica mea, &c.

Be not terrified, my soul, at the name of perfect Love, like the cowards of the world; do not regard it as too sublime a state to aspire to: thou canst attain to it if thou wilt; all is within thy reach. Become spotless, like the bride, by washing thyself daily; acquire, like her, the beauty of the soul, by exercising thyself in all Christian virtues, and thou mayest become perfect. The rules of this perfect Love are neither numerous, perplexing, nor abstruse; they are written simply in the Gospel; Christ Himself spake and wrote them for thee; bear them, read them, follow them. Thou shalt love the LORD thy GOD, says this Adorable Saviour, and thou shalt love Him with all thy heart, with all thy soul, with all thy mind, and with all thy strength. This is the epitome, this the height of perfect Love: happy if thou canst engrave this rule and this law in thy heart in eternal characters. It will be no sooner engraven in thy heart, than thou wilt possess That of Thy Divine Spouse. Dost thou desire any thing beside?

FOURTH DAY.

Tota pulchra es, amica mea, &c.

Besides the theological, I must also practise the cardinal Virtues, if my soul desires to be without spot, and all fair in the Eyes of my Heavenly Spouse. But let me seek a shorter way; let me love Him with perfect love, and I shall possess all these virtues in the most eminent degree. What, indeed, is Christian Prudence, but love enlightened, vigilant, and attentive to discern whatever may draw us nearer to GOD, or estrange us from Him? What is Justice, but exact love, which omits nothing that it owes to GOD, and deals in like manner with its neighbour? What is Fortitude, but generous and intrepid love, which sustains itself in perils, and exposes itself to all rather than depart from GOD? What, lastly, is Temperance, but chaste love, which finds its whole pleasure in GOD Alone, and deprives itself of all that delights the senses, in order to obey and to please Him? Study single love and perfect love, O my soul: it is the surest means to be spotless, like the bride, and to be all fair in the Eyes of GOD.

FIFTH DAY.

Una est columba mea, perfecta mea. (Cant. vi.)

My Dove is one and perfect, says the Spouse: and I may become so too, if I labour with equal fidelity. Ah! how shameful it is for men, and for Christian men, to be daily making new discoveries in profane arts, and to be so ignorant as they are, after so many ages, in the Art of arts, that of loving God! Those arts, at first so imperfect, have acquired extreme perfection in the course of years, because they are studied for the sake of vanity or temporal lucre: and the art of loving Thee, O my God, decays daily instead of gaining perfection, because it is neglected. Remember, therefore, O my soul, that the bride is called perfect, only because she has neglected all in order to learn to love God perfectly. This science shall be henceforth thy only study: happy, indeed, if thou knowest it in all its extent before thy death, for it is the study of a whole life!

SIXTH DAY.

Una est columba mea, perfecta mea.

I cannot perfect myself in Divine Love, without also advancing in the other virtues, because that is their soul and main-spring; and my virtues cannot advance towards perfection but in proportion to my love: one is a proof of the other. If I wish to know how far my love has advanced in perfection since I began to give myself to God, I have but to examine if my heart is more humble and more pure; my mind more submissive and more diligent; my senses more restrained and less subject to sensuality; my body less inclined to daintiness, and more dead through the Spirit; if I suffer with more patience and resignation; if I have less uneasiness with regard to temporal wants, am less sensitive to insults and contempt: happy if this examination does not cover me with confusion, and if, after making it without self-flattery, I do not conclude, that instead of loving God as perfectly as I ought and might have done, I have not yet begun to love Him!

SEVENTH DAY.

Una est columba mea, perfecta mea.

It is enough for a soul to love the Lord as He prescribes, in order to become the Dove and the perfect one of the Heavenly Spouse. Indeed, if the natural law of Divine Love is written in the heart of the natural and reasonable man, the perfection of the Super-natural law of this love is written in the heart of the Christian man ; it ought to be imprinted there, both by the words of the Gospel, which contain all its extent and perfection, and by the Blood of Jesus Christ, Which is the Holy Ink that wrote it in characters which ought to be indelible, and Which, in writing it, gave strength to practise it in all its perfection. If I cannot find this law of perfect love in my heart, it is my fault, and I have effaced it by my unfaithfulness. What do I say, effaced it? Ah, Lord! I understand that it cannot be wholly effaced; Thou hast engraven it too strongly in the substance of this heart. I have felt it there many times; it is there, but obscured and hidden by some attachments foreign to this love. Assist me, O Heavenly Spouse, to uncover these precious characters, in order that it may be preserved there till my death in all its splendour.

Forty-eighth Week.

LOVE SACRIFICED.

The heart of man is placed between two very different sacrificers, who have each an altar, a victim, a fire to consume it, and an object to which it is offered.

These two sacrificers are the love of God and the love of the world; and the heart must declare for one. If it claims the first, it ought to know that its altars are Calvaries, its victims pure and spotless, its fire a Holy fire; that the sweet odour of its sacrifice ascends to Heaven, and it is received by God with pleasure. If it is so unhappy as to prefer the second, it ought to know also that its altars are theatres of abomination, its victims impure and detestable, and that the smoke of this horrible sacrifice, far from ascending to Heaven, descends to Hell, to be the delight of devils.

Suppose, then, that the heart of the bride has decided for the first: it remains then only to show her wherein this sacrifice consists, to make known to her its merit and value, to teach her how to offer it so purely, that from a simple sacrifice it may become a perfect Holocaust, and to make her understand that the most glorious title to which she can aspire in this life, is that of a victim of Divine love.

The bride of the Canticles was so inflamed with this love, that it raised her up from the desert, and that it made of her whole being a sacrifice worthy of her Bridegroom's Heart; so that her companions, who saw her so ardent, exclaimed with admiration, Who is this that cometh out of the wilderness like pillars of smoke, perfumed with Myrrh and Frankincense, and with all powders of the merchant? Quæ est ista quæ ascendit per desertum sicut virgula fumi, &c. (Cant. iii.) An excellent figure of sacrificed love, whose ardour sends forth its delicious smoke to Heaven. The Myrrh from which it proceeds shows that the mortal condition of the bride does not hinder her from rising to God to offer Him the incense of her love; and all these powders of the merchant are the symbols of all the virtues which should accompany the sacrifice of her love. She regarded this sacrifice as a debt which it was necessary to pay to her Spouse, Who had first sacrificed Himself for her. It seems, indeed, that she is wholly filled with the Spirit of prophecy, when she says to her companions: My Beloved is white and ruddy; dilectus meus candidus et rubicundus. (Cant. v.) He is white, say the Holy Fathers, by the incomparable purity and by the splendour of His Divinity; He is red, because, in the Sacrifice which He offered for love of us on Calvary, He trod the wine-press alone, according to the word of the Prophet (Isa. lxiii. 3), when He shed His Blood to spare ours.

AFFECTIONS.

FIRST DAY.

Quæ est ista quæ ascendit per desertum sicut virgula fumi? (Cant. iii.)

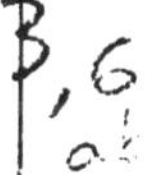

Who is this, say the companions of the bride, that cometh out of the wilderness like pillars of smoke, perfumed with myrrh and frankincense? Let us resemble this bride; let us make ready all the preparations for a sacrifice of love, whose sweet savour shall ascend to the Heart of God, Who sacrificed Himself for love of us. Let our whole self, with all that we possess, be the victim; our heart the altar; our separation from the world and from all sensible things, the instrument of sacrifice; our love, the fire; our desires, our eagerness, our sighs, the breath which kindles it. Let us put on this fire the myrrh, the incense, and the perfumes of all virtues, to render the odour more delightsome; let us bring all our attachments to this mysterious pile; let us offer all, burn, consume all, and reserve nothing for ourselves. Sacred Love, Who art God Himself, receive this sacrifice which I offer Thee to-day, and which I desire to offer Thee every moment of my life.

SECOND DAY.

Quæ est ista quæ ascendit, &c.

In order to offer to God a perfect sacrifice of love, it is not enough to give Him our property, our body, and our soul, we must also sacrifice to Him even the joy and the pleasure of Divine Love. The bride's sacrifice was perfumed, not only with frankincense, but also with myrrh, which is bitter; and the more her Bridegroom hid Himself from her, the more she redoubled her eagerness for Him. To love God in the absence of joy, of feeling, and of pleasure; to seek Him with all our strength amidst desertion, dryness, and inward desolation; above all, when we have done nothing to incur them, to claim none of the sensible delights of love, this is a noble sacrifice, which costs the heart much. It is a virtue to sacrifice sensual pleasures to Him; but it is a well-pleasing holocaust to sacrifice even the innocent delights of this love. Remember, then, O my soul, that as the most perfect faith believes without seeing, and still continues ardent in the midst of darkness, sacrificed love must love without feeling, because it loves only in order to love, and to love in such manner as God will have it, and not in order to find pleasure in its love.

THIRD DAY.

Quæ est ista quæ ascendit, &c.

I consent, Lord, to present to Thee the myrrh, the frankincense, and the powders of the merchant with the spouse; like her, to put them on the fire of my love, that they may ascend to Thy Throne; and I renounce all the sensible sweetness of these perfumes. I am willing to be deprived of it; and it suffices for me that Thou smellest them, and that it is pleasing to Thee. I consent, like her, to rise to Thee in privation and in the wilderness. I willingly renounce for the time to come all my sensible delights; far from being troubled about them, I rest on Thee, persuaded that Thou wilt make me full amends. I consent even that that time be delayed till eternity. As I am altogether carnal, and as I fear the delusions of the senses, I far prefer the love which comes solely from Thy Grace to sensible love. When Thou sendest me these delights, I will regard them as helps to my weakness; I will use them for a time, but I will not desire them, I will never become attached to them, and will be ever ready to sacrifice them to Thee when it pleases Thee to deprive me of them.

FOURTH DAY.

Quæ est ista quæ ascendit, &c.

I understand, O Heavenly Spouse, that in order to pay what I owe to Thy Supreme dominion, I must not now offer sacrifices of animals, but sacrifices of love, and sacrifices of the heart; I must not now immolate to Thee a strange flesh, but myself; I must not make use of material fire, kindled by men, but of the holy fire of love which Thou kindlest Thyself in our hearts; that I must not offer Thee sacrifices in the midst of a tumultuous world, but in solitude and in the wilderness, like the bride; I must not even touch the earth of this wilderness by any sensible attachments, but must ascend above the earth like her; I must not now offer Thee common odours, but the most precious perfumes; that is, the myrrh of continual mortification, the incense of most ardent prayers, and all the most exquisite powders of the merchant; that is, all the most heroic virtues. Of this, Lord, shall my sacrifice of love consist; and this sacrifice shall be accompanied with that of my whole being; render it worthy of Thy Divine regards, and receive it as a sweet-smelling savour.

FIFTH DAY.

Dilectus meus candidus et rubicundus. (Cant. v.)

My Beloved, says the bride, is white and ruddy; He is white as the lily, because He is Purity Itself; but He is ruddy as the rose, because in His Passion He was entirely covered with His own Blood when He sacrificed It for my love. These two mysterious colours, which are the august livery of my Heavenly Spouse, shall be henceforth my lot, and I will make it my great glory to wear them till death. When I shall be clothed in them, they will procure to my soul a perfect beauty, and they will give value to my sacrifices. Whiteness and ruddiness, that is, purity and blood, innocence and mortification; these must compose my sacrifice of love. I will, then, strive to the utmost to acquire true purity. I shall acquire it by sacrificing to my God all that might cause it the least blemish; but Divine Love shall ever be the principle and the soul of my sacrifices. I will love in order to purify my holocaust; I will sacrifice myself continually, in order to learn to love my God better.

SIXTH DAY.

Dilectus meus candidus et rubicundus.

Canst thou, O my soul, be a deformed bride, full of stains, whilst thou flatterest thyself with having a Bridegroom whiter than the lily? Canst thou be a dainty bride, while thy Bridegroom is ruddy only because He is a Bloody Husband, and because He made Himself a Victim for thy love? A sacrificing God is an astonishing prodigy, because every sacrificer is a subject, and God is an Almighty Sovereign: but God sacrificed for love, God a bleeding Victim, and a Victim by the hands of men, is an incomprehensible mystery of His love. God, Who is Holiness and Purity Itself, covered with His own Blood in the sight of His creatures, by His creatures, and for the love of His creatures; this is the astonishing prodigy of sacrificed love. Yet, O my God, Thou hast completed this rigorous sacrifice. Thou hast died an innocent and bleeding Victim; I desire to live and to die a penitent and loving victim. Receive this sacrifice, Lord, and give me courage enough to offer it Thee during all my life.

SEVENTH DAY.

Dilectus meus candidus et rubicundus.

Shall I now refuse the character of a victim, however terrible it may appear to my tenderness, since my God has taken it for love of me, and since He has fulfilled all its duties and sustained all its rigours? He has been Himself, by the excess of His love, the Sacrificer and the Sacrifice, the Victim and the Oblation; He has offered His whole Self, and His Holocaust was perfect, because His love was extreme. Can I be so unjust and so ungrateful as to set bounds to my love, and reserve any thing to myself? No, my God; I immolate to Thee all that I have, and all that I am; I sacrifice to Thee all my thoughts, my desires, my affections, my attachments, my memory, my mind, my heart, my love, and my blood; I offer Thee to-day, as a whole burnt-offering, my reputation, my possessions, my health, and my life: happy if all my faculties became an universal and perpetual burnt-offering to Thy love! I should then do but a part of what Thou hast done for love of me.

Forty-ninth Week.

LOVE IN REPOSE.

True repose in God is, according to the holy Fathers, an image and a foretaste of the happiness of the Saints, in which GOD is enjoyed without trouble, alarms, or desire of any thing beside Him. When the faithful soul has long desired and sought its GOD, its desires are crowned even in this life by an anticipated possession, its disquiet by profound repose and peace, and its seeking by a close and tranquil union. Having found in GOD its Centre, its End, its Perfection, and its Happiness, it is satisfied, and fixed, and reposes in Him: like a child who, after many cries, at last finds the bosom of his mother, he embraces and clings to it, the milk which he sucks from her breasts pacifies him, and he sleeps tranquilly in her arms.

But it is here important to observe the precaution of which I have made use in my Preface on the Divine Attributes, and to say, with St. Augustine (De Civ. Dei), that this love of repose is not an idle tranquillity, but a sweet and peaceful action: Ineffabilis quædam tranquillitas actionis otiosæ: an action which does not interrupt repose, a repose which does not dispense with action; but, on the contrary, gives strength for works of charity, and which is but the shadow of that which the Saints enjoy in Heaven.

The bride had found this pleasant shadow when she said: I sat down under the shadow of Him Whom I have desired, and His fruit was sweet to my taste: Sub umbrâ illius quem desideraveram sedi, et fructus ejus dulcis gutturi meo. (Cant. ii.) She had asked for the light of noonday, which is only for the blessed, says St. Bernard; but the Bridegroom will have her content herself with the shadow for her repose. Yet this shadow is refreshing; the bride will repose there tranquilly, and her Bridegroom will there fill her with fruits delicious enough to content her in this life.

Whilst the bride is thus reposing, her Beloved charges the daughters of Jerusalem not to awake her until she wishes it: Ne evigilare faciatis dilectam quoadusquè ipsa velit. (Cant. ii.) And this repose so strengthens her, that at the end of her Canticle she has become like a wall, since she came into the presence of her Beloved as having found peace in Him: Ex quo facta sum coram eo quasi pacem reperiens. (Cant. viii.) By the enjoyment of this Divine repose, she is so firmly established in God, that nothing can shake her.

AFFECTIONS.

FIRST DAY.

Sub umbrâ illius quem desideraveram sedi. (Cant. ii.)

"I sat down," says the bride, "under the shadow of Him Whom my heart had desired." What is sweeter to a weary traveller, scorched by the heat of the sun, than to find the shade of a tree wherein to repose and refresh himself; above all, when he finds on this tree delicious fruits to nourish him! What more sweet to a soul, which formerly lived amidst troubles and alarms, than to repose in God by a love of enjoyment, so far as the creature is capable of doing so in this life! What sweeter than to be able to count upon the Heart of an Almighty God, and to pour out ours to Him as to our most faithful friend! But before reposing on His Heart, it is necessary to repose under His Cross; before being inebriated with the torrent of His Love, we must be bedewed by His Blood. Cross of my Saviour, thou shalt be the mysterious tree under whose branches I will repose. Adorable Blood, thou shalt be the salutary and life-giving Fruit which shall support me. Faithfully bearing one, bedewed by the other, and loving with all my heart Him Who presents them to me, I shall soon find the means of reposing, as His favoured one, upon His Sacred Heart.

SECOND DAY.

Sub umbrâ illius quem, &c.

Where can I find true repose but in the love of my God? Where can I satisfy all the desires of my heart but under the shadow of Him Who Alone can fill them in time, and Whom I am to possess in eternity? Where can I find tranquil and profound peace but in the love of a Spouse equally lovely and powerful, Who now, as a Friend, lends me His Arm to support me; now, as a good Shepherd, offers His Shoulders to carry me to His Fold, from which I have strayed; now, as a Spouse, offers me His Breast to repose on; now, as a Saviour, presents me His Cross, under whose shadow I find a sure refuge; now, as a Delicious Nourishment, gives me, instead of fruits, His Flesh and Blood, to satisfy me and to fortify my soul against its troubles and temptations? Thou Alone, then, Lord, shalt be henceforth the Centre of my repose. Give me Thy Arm as my Support, Thy Shoulders as my Shepherd, Thy Breast as my Spouse, Thy Cross as my Saviour, Thy Flesh and Thy Blood as my Nourishment; or, rather, give me all at once in giving me Thy Heart and Thy Love.

THIRD DAY.

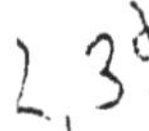

Et fructus ejus dulcis gutturi meo. (Cant. ii.)

"And His fruit," says the bride, "was sweet to my taste." What fruits are more delicious than those of true charity? The beloved Disciple had learnt, in reposing upon the Heart of His Divine Master, that he that dwelleth in love dwelleth in God, and God in him. (1 St. John iv. 16.) If I love my God, I not only repose in His shadow, but I repose and dwell in His Heart; there I enjoy at my leisure the delicious fruits of His Love, and I draw Him into mine to repose there, and that I, in my turn, may feed Him with my fruits, that is, with the affections and the acts of my love. The Heart of my God is a Refuge, a Sanctuary, a Fortress: who can trouble me there henceforth? Love alone has its key, love alone can bring me in, keep me there, and procure me the happy repose to which I aspire. Sacred Love, open to me the Gates of this Sanctuary, and inflame me in such manner that I may never repose but in the Heart of God.

FOURTH DAY.

Ne suscitetis, neque evigilare faciatis dilectam quoadusquè ipsa velit. (Cant. iii.)

"I charge you, O ye daughters of Jerusalem," said the Spouse, "that ye stir not up, nor awake My love till she please." What care, Lord, for a soul that loves Thee, and reposes in Thee! What attention to preserve this Divine repose which Thou givest her Thyself, and to remove all that might distract and trouble it! What pleasure, indeed, could this bride have tasted with her companions, while she was absorbed in delight with Thee? Give wings, then, Lord, to my love, to flee away and repose in Thy Heart; it is better to be there than in the tents of the ungodly, full only of trouble and confusion. Put away from me all these daughters of Jerusalem; that is, all those worldly conversations which speak not of Thee; remove all thoughts which would interrupt the innocent repose which I ask of Thee; let no creature ever awake me; I desire to leave my repose and my sleep only to obey Thee, to please Thee, and to apply myself to the works of charity which Thou shalt prescribe.

FIFTH DAY.

Ne suscitetis, neque evigilare, &c.

I am troubled, and I do not yet taste that Divine repose which Thou givest to the souls that love Thee Alone, and that thou permittest not to be awaked from their mystic slumber; but suffer me to say with one of those who loved Thee most perfectly, (D. Aug. in Psalm xciv.) Open me Thy Heart, Heavenly Spouse, to give a place of rest to mine. I feel, said he, that my heart is full of billows and of tempests, which agitate it unceasingly. Thou hast commanded the wind and the sea, and Thou hast made a great calm (Mark iv.); come and enter upon the billows of my heart; so calm it, that loving Thee with all its tenderness, it may embrace Thee tranquilly as its only Good. Remove from my memory every recollection which is opposed to the tranquillity of my soul; purify my mind from all its unquiet thoughts; burst in my heart the smallest ties which might bring trouble into it, and render me worthy to say to Thee with the Prophet: "I will lay me down in peace, and take my rest" (Psalm iv.); my repose shall be interrupted only by my sighs, and by the labours which Thou shalt require of my charity.

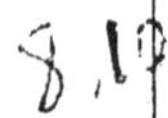

SIXTH DAY.

Facta sum coram eo quasi pacem reperiens. (Cant. viii.)

I have become immoveable, says the bride, since I have appeared in the presence of my Beloved, as one who has found peace in Him. How much thinkest thou, O my soul, that the bride had striven, and how much had she loved, before finding repose and peace in God? Her passions troubled her no more, for she was become their mistress; her love was no longer subject to inequalities, for she had been faithful in arousing its langour in spite of dryness and desolation. Let those dainty souls depart, who think true repose in God to consist in certain sensible joys, during which they imagine that God acts in them. This repose is often a delusion, this sleep is not always the mystic sleep of the bride; it is often a lazy repose which favours indolence and indifference. Man cannot enter the true repose of Divine Love but after a hard conflict; he comes forth from it immoveable by the torrent of vice. Like the bride, we are strong as a wall and as a tower when we have found our repose in God.

SEVENTH DAY.

Facta sum coram eo, &c.

When shall I rest in Thee Alone, O my God? When shall I taste with Thee, and in Thee, the delicious fruit of a profound peace? When I shall be strong as a wall against all the events of this life; when I shall be incapable of being moved by my passions; when I shall be insensible to the allurements of this world; in short, O my God, when I shall love Thee Alone, and with all my heart. It rests only with myself to acquire this peace and this repose, and I have not done it. I have understood a thousand times, that all the most brilliant and most flattering things which the world boasts, can only bring trouble; yet I am not entirely detached from it. I have felt only turbulent emotions every time that I have gratified my self-love; yet I have not sufficiently resisted it. I have never come forth satisfied from worldly conversations; yet I have not avoided them with sufficient care. I have never experienced true repose except in conversing with Thee in solitude, in thinking of Thee, and in meditating upon Thy Greatness and Thy Goodness. Why then do I not enjoy this true repose of love, since I know all the means of obtaining it?

Fiftieth Week.

INEBRIATED LOVE.

As excess of wine causes a shameful inebriation which gives death to the soul, so the pious excess of Divine Love causes to the soul a wise inebriation which gives it life. The one is an inebriation of intemperance; the other an inebriation of soberness, grace, and love. The one weakens and disfigures the body; the other sustains, purifies, and consecrates it. So was it with the Apostles on the day of Pentecost: they were all filled with fire kindled in their hearts by the Holy Ghost, Who is a Spirit of Love; this fire burnt in their eyes, their gestures, their words, and their whole persons. It is not surprising that the gross people supposed them drunken with new wine. (Acts ii.) It is indeed, says St. Bernard, the new wine of Divine Love which causes to the soul a holy inebriation and a most wise folly: mustum divini amoris in sapientem compellit insaniam (De dign. div. Amor.); this happens when burning more than ordinarily in prayer, it is now surprised and carried away by fresh and delightful discoveries; now dazzled by a brilliant and insupportable light; now tastes an exquisite sweetness which delights it, carries it away, and transports it out of itself; now is, as it were, overwhelmed by an excessive abundance of affections, joys, and caresses. These torrents of Divine Consolations inundate, absorb, and deprive it of sense; it knows no more what it says or does: in a word, it is inebriated with the delicious excess of what it sees and of what it feels.

The King, says the bride, brought me into His wine-cellar: introduxit me rex in cellam vinariam.

(Cant. ii.) There He so inebriated her with His Love, that she swooned and required support. Inebriated with this mystic wine of the Spouse, she says these admirable words: Eat, O friends; drink, yea, be inebriated, O beloved: comedite, amici, et bibite, et inebriamini, charissimi. (Cant. v.) A soul inebriated with the Love of God, far from losing true reason, is filled with ardent zeal for the Glory of God, and for the salvation of man: it would have its Beloved the Beloved of all the world, and would have all its friends inebriated with His Love.

AFFECTIONS.

FIRST DAY.

Introduxit me rex in cellam vinariam. (Cant. ii.)

The King, says the bride, brought me into His wine-cellar. Is not this mystic cellar, into which Thou broughtest Thy beloved, Thine own Heart? for she loved Thee with all the tenderness of hers, and Thou bringest there all who love Thee like her. Is not this delicious wine, with which Thou hast inebriated her, that of violent love, which deprives her of all human feelings, to be conscious only of Thy Divine operations; which causes in the mind a happy alienation of natural reason, that it may reason henceforth only on the supernatural principles with which Thou inspirest it, and which carnal men regard as true intoxication; which extinguishes in the heart all fires kindled by self-love, to inflame it with that of Thy Charity; which makes it perform for Thy Glory bold and extraordinary actions, which the guilty world considers as extravagant? Bring me, Lord, into this Divine Cellar, inebriate me with the precious wine of Thy Love: I shall never have more temperance and more wisdom than when I shall have entirely surrendered myself to the holy inebriation and the wise folly of Thy Love.

SECOND DAY.

Introduxit me rex, &c.

Follow Thy Spouse, O my soul; He will bring thee into His Divine Cellars, to inebriate thee there with His Love. Thou wilt find there exquisite wines of all sorts; and all these different wines increase, sustain, and perfect, love. Choose; it is in thy power: the Spouse will give thee what thou demandest. Wilt thou have the strong wine of constant and noble love? thou wilt find it in this abundant Cellar; thy Spouse Himself first drank of it plenteously when He suffered Death for thee; drink, and thou wilt find the flavour of constancy and strength. Dost thou desire fervent and zealous love? thou wilt find this fiery liquor in the Cellar of thy Spouse. This Cellar is His Heart, and this Heart is burning with zeal for thy salvation. Dost thou thirst for the wine of tender love, full of sweetness, to console thee in dryness and in bitterness? thou wilt find it in abundance, thou shalt be His delights, He shall be thine, and He will inebriate thee with chaste pleasures.

THIRD DAY.

Introduxit me rex, &c.

If thou art so happy as to be brought into the Cellars of the Spouse, O my soul, make good use of this great favour, and come not forth till thou art inebriated with the delicious wine of His Holy Love. Drink deep draughts of this Heavenly liquor, which will fill thee with ineffable sweetness. Be not afraid to be thus inebriated, it is permitted thee, and will do thee no dishonour; be drowned and swallowed up in this Ocean of innocent delights: it is not only a Cellar, it is a vast unfathomable Sea. If thou lovest pleasures, thy Spouse presents thee with the most delightful. Abandon thyself entirely to this holy inebriation. Far from destroying the body, it sustains it; far from blinding the mind, it enlightens it; far from causing the loss of reason, it perfects it; far from carrying corruption into the heart, it purifies and consecrates it.

FOURTH DAY.

Introduxit me rex, &c.

Thou dost not invite me into Thy Cellars till Thou hast entered them Thyself; before pressing me to inebriate myself with Thy love, that which Thou bearest me caused Thee to go out of Thyself in a Divine and Holy way, which is all my glory and all my happiness. It made Thee descend from Heaven to earth to save my soul, and make it Thy bride, notwithstanding Thy Greatness and my low estate; it deprived Thee for thirty-three years of the splendour of Thy Divinity, and clothed Thee with my flesh; it caused Thee to faint while suffering horrible torments for my love; it made Thee die, God though Thou art, to give me life; it made Thee espouse the holy foolishness of the Cross (1 Cor. i. 23) to redeem me from death; it made Thee shed all Thy Blood, to inebriate me with that Sacred Liquor which love drew from Thy Veins; it brought Thee down to me in the Holy Communion, to serve me as food and drink. To what, Lord, can I attribute these extraordinary steps, but that Thy Divine Love overcame Thee? Shall I refuse to do for Thee what Thou hast done for me?

FIFTH DAY.

Comedite, amici, et bibite, et inebriamini, charissimi. (Cant. v.)

Eat, O friends, and drink, said the bride, and be drunken, O beloved. To eat, to drink, to be drunken;

what gross expressions for a man of the world, who has only the polish of the world! But, O my God, what sublime language for a soul that Thou hast carefully instructed in the Divine operations of Thy Love! The carnal man prepares a table of intemperance, the bride one of soberness: he gives material wine in excess, which causes the loss of reason; she offers in Thy Name the spiritual wine of Thy love, which procures true Wisdom: he often falls shamefully; she is supported by her own inebriation, because strength is the inseparable character of the Love which inebriates her: he loses his memory, forgets Thee, and forgets himself; she forgets herself, only because she is entirely occupied with Thee. Receive me, Lord, to that Divine repast where Thou makest Thy nearest friends so blessedly inebriated with the excess of Thy love, until I shall possess that kingdom which Thou hast promised me, where I shall be filled and overwhelmed with the delights of Thy Table throughout Eternity.

SIXTH DAY.

Inebriamini, charissimi.

How is it possible, Lord, to be over-filled with the delicious wine of Thy love, when Thy most perfect lovers are always insatiable, and the more they drink of this Heavenly Liquor, the more they thirst for it? The most exquisite wines at first flatter the senses, while their excess disgusts; but that of Thy love ever excites the thirst of the soul. It is true that a single drop of this sacred wine always procures true pleasures; but I feel also assuredly, that abundance would infinitely increase my thirst and my desire. If this delicious wine of Thy Love entered my heart like an impetuous torrent, it would still desire Thee; if this insatiable heart were plunged, drowned, swallowed up in it as in a vast sea, its thirst would yet be more ardent. But I understand, Heavenly Spouse, that in Thy Love thirst exists with inebriation, and that Thou art never more ardently desired than when Thou art possessed, and when we are entirely filled with the precious wine of sublime charity.

SEVENTH DAY.

Inebriamini, charissimi.

To lose the mind, the memory, and the senses, to say and do extravagant things, are the monstrous consequences of the inebriation of wine; but they are also the effects of the inebriation of Divine Love; and when we go forth from the Holy Table of the Spouse, if it is not so with us, we have failed in our duty, because we have not loved sufficiently. Yes, LORD, I desire to love Thee even to the loss of my mind, I mean this human mind, this worldly mind, which is not in accordance with Thine, that I may think and reason only according to the rules of Thy love; I desire to lose the memory of all sensible things, that I may remember only Thy Goodness and Thy Mercies; I desire to lose, by my inebriation, all sense of pleasure, insults, and amusements, that I may feel henceforth only the ardours of Thy Charity; I desire to speak only the language of Divine Love, and I consent to stammer in all beside; I desire also to undertake, with holy boldness, all that Thy Love shall command me, even if I pass for a madman in the eyes of men: happy and wise madness, for it will proceed only from the inebriation of Thy Love, which is sovereign Wisdom!

Fifty-first Week.

LOVE OF DEATH.

The great Saints who have experienced the mystic Death caused in them by the excess of Divine Love, have carefully described it, in order to awaken in us a desire for it; and the Apostle, who was often in this blessed state, gives an admirable portrait of it when he says of himself: "I live; yet not I, but Christ liveth in me." (Gal. ii.) The first Christians formed by this skilful master had, like him, attained to it; he praises them for it when he says to them, "Ye are dead, and your life is hid with Christ in God." (Col. iii.)

This blessed death, a thousand times more desirable than the most delightful life, occurs, says a holy man (Man. c. 20. ap. St. Aug.), when the soul, by the sweet violence of her love, is so withdrawn from the corporeal senses, that it is no longer conscious of itself, because its exquisite sense of the Presence of God absorbs all other feelings. Attracted, then, says St. Bernard (Serm. lxxxv. in Cant.), by the ineffable sweetness of this love, it flies and escapes from itself; it is ravished and carried away to enjoy The Word in Whom it lives and dwells; it is unable to act, because God acts; it feels its body no more, possesses it no more, because it feels and possesses its God.

But this delightful death pre-supposes another which costs many struggles. The soul must first die to its passions, its attachments, its desires, and itself. This death being passed, says a holy Doctor, charity begins by wounding the heart; being wounded, it binds it strongly to God; being bound, it makes it sicken : at last it gives it this blessed death. (Richard à St. Vict. part. i. de 4 grad.)

The bride had passed through all these stages before she arrived at the mystic death of Divine Love. She says, indeed, to her companions, Stay me with flowers, comfort me with apples ; for I am sick of love : fulcite me floribus, stipate me malis, quia amore langueo. (Cant. ii.) But to prepare herself for this death by that of all her passions, she takes a noble resolution to go to the mountain of myrrh, which is the figure of Calvary, where she must crucify herself with CHRIST : vadam ad montem myrrhæ. (Cant. iv.)

Being dead to herself, the Divine language of the Bridegroom is heard in her heart ; and she so loves it that she says her soul melted and dissolved when He spake : anima mea liquefacta est ut locutus est. (Cant. v.) At length she happily attains this mystic death ; and after having experienced it, she unfolds its mystery, and declares its prodigious effects, when she says, that love is strong as death : fortis est ut mors dilectio. (Cant. viii.)

AFFECTIONS.

FIRST DAY.

Fulcite me floribus, stipate me malis, quia amore langueo. (Cant. ii.)

"Stay me with flowers," says the bride, "strengthen me with apples, for I am sick of love." But, LORD, what flowers and what fruits did this bride desire, but Thine, but Thyself, for she says elsewhere that Thou art the Flower of the fields, and the Fruit-tree of the wood ? If I felt this blessed sickness of the bride, I should be very near this mystic death to which I aspire : but another sickness hinders me from feeling that of true Charity. I am sick, LORD, because I do not love enough, and I should be sick from excess of love. Yet I ask Thy flowers and Thy fruits to cure my sickness; that is, I ask the feelings and the acts of a more ardent love, which may bring upon me the sickness of the bride, and prepare me for the delicious death of Divine Love.

SECOND DAY.

Quia amore langueo.

I know, O my God, said St. Ambrose (hic viii.), explaining the loving swoon of the bride, that to fall sick with excess of holy love is to be occupied only with that which we desire and love; it is to cling to it with all our strength; to desire to leave this mortal body in order to be inseparably united with it; to strive to make a sort of transfusion of ourselves into this Adorable Object, in order to be lost and absorbed in It: that in this sickness, the weaker the soul becomes by its desires and transports, the stronger is it and the more does it find its love increase; that the more it sickens, the more ardent and courageous is it: happy dissolution, says this Father, which tends only to the total destruction of human frailty, that we may be clothed with Divine strength and power! Happy sickness, which sets the bride's heart all on fire, instead of freezing it! Happy agony, which leads this fainting soul to the death it desired so much, only to give it life in the Divine Object That it loves!

THIRD DAY.

Vadam ad montem myrrhæ. (Cant. iv.)

"I will get me," says the bride, "to the Mountain of myrrh:" so true is it, that in the empire of Divine Love we must gather myrrh before we gather the palm; we must die to all creatures and to self, before we can attain to the mystic Death of Holy Love. If this delightful Death is a glorious Tabor, where the soul is transfigured and transformed into God, the other is a Mountain of Myrrh, or a Calvary where it must die to all things. I consent, LORD, I desire to die, in order to prepare myself to die; I desire to die to myself in order to obtain the precious death of Divine Love; I desire to die to my inclinations, my attachments, my self-will, to my own intellect, my desires, my natural affections, my flesh, my self-indulgence, even to all temporal and spiritual joys; and I desire that all my external and internal senses shall bear the image of the death which I shall give myself in order to love Thee better. And to encourage myself to this, I will often secretly go up to Calvary, where I shall see Thee covered with wounds, bleeding, dying for love of me. In this Thy bitter agony, O LORD, Thou shalt be the Divine Model which I will strive to copy well, that I may learn to die to myself.

FOURTH DAY.

Vadam ad montem myrrhæ.

To live and to die with what we love is the character of true friends, who never part without a struggle. I desire to live and to die with Thee, O my GOD! but I cannot do it unless I die continually to myself, and unless I often go up with the bride to the Mountain of Myrrh by mortification and suffering. I desire, also, to die like Thee, if Thou commandest it. This death will be sweeter to me than the most delightful life, for it will unite me eternally to Thee. Ah! I feel, Heavenly Spouse, that my heart has not yet said enough. To live and to die with Thee is not sufficient for my love; I desire, also, to live and to die for Thee, whatever it may cost my self-indulgence; and by this I hope to prove to Thee the strength of my love. Thou hast died for me, Thou Who art innocent, Who art GOD: I should be most ungrateful if I refused to die for love of Thee, I who am guilty, who am a worthless creature.

FIFTH DAY.

Anima mea liquefacta est ut locutus est. (Cant. v.)

"My soul," says the bride, "melted when my Beloved spake." How astonishing is the power of Thy Divine Word, O Heavenly Spouse, above all when Thou speakest the language of Divine Love to a watchful listening soul that loves Thee already! It pierces deeper than the sharpest sword, for it divides asunder the soul and spirit, to give a delightful death to both. (Heb. iv.) Thou speakest to the bride, and instantly her soul melts, it dissolves, and flows out to go in search of Thee; it has no longer any human feeling, it leaves its body to go and live in Thee. Speak to my soul, LORD, and speak to it of Thy love, to inflame it, to separate it, to dissolve it, to melt it by Thy Divine ardour, that it may flow out to Thee. Metals must be long in the most ardent fire to melt; but one of Thy words of fire can produce this effect on my soul: or give to me, as to the Prophet (Ps. xxii.), a heart like wax; I shall feel it melt within me as soon as I hear the sound of Thy Voice.

SIXTH DAY.

Fortis est ut mors dilectio. (Cant. viii.)

"Love is strong as death," says the bride, because, as death separates the soul from the body, and renders it insensible, so Divine love separates them in a manner wholly sublime. When the soul has happily fallen sick with desire of Him Whom it loves; when it has been pierced by this chosen arrow, this fiery arrow of Sacred love, it dies to all which is not GOD, it ceases to animate that in which it was, and goes to live where it was not, because it is far more where it loves than where it animates: with this difference, that natural death is painful, and that the mystic death, which proceeds from the violence of love, is full of delight. The one freezes the heart, the other inflames it; the one destroys the natural man, and makes of his body a frightful carcase, the other destroys the carnal man, and transforms him into God. Thus to die, Lord, is not to die, but it is to begin to live, in order never to die.

SEVENTH DAY.

Fortis est ut mors dilectio.

Cause me, O my God, to feel the Almighty power of Thy Divine love. If it is strong as death to gain victories every where, I have no other ambition than to be its conquest; and, far from resisting it, I will assist it to overcome me, though at the expense of my life. If it requires sacrifices, I make a free-will offering of all that I am; I desire to be its victim, and to receive from it the stroke of death, convinced that this death, far from separating me from Thee, will unite me closely with Thee. If it is armed with a sword, I offer my heart to be wounded; happy if I never recover from my wound, but receive the death which I desire! happy if this sword cuts off and destroys in me all that is carnal! If it is armed with fire to consume all, send it down to my heart to inflame me, and to reduce to ashes all in me which is unpleasing to Thy Eyes.

Fifty-second Week.

LOVE OF UNION.

There is an union with God, which is a gift common to all the just; there is another which He grants only to the most perfect and to His nearest friends. To possess the first, it is sufficient to be in grace and to have charity; but we must have made great progress in the Divine love to obtain the second. The one is contracted when the soul begins to love, the other is the crown and the completion of holy love.

It is in the secret soul that this wondrous union is formed. GOD draws it to Himself or descends into it with unspeakable ardour, light, and joy. It sees, feels, touches Him, is united with Him, cleaves to Him, and embraces Him so closely, that nothing can cause a separation; all its natural powers are raised to a supernatural order; it is unclothed and clothed upon, in the words of St. Paul (2 Cor. v.); unclothed of its own qualities, and clothed upon with those of GOD. All its mortality is swallowed up in life, and that life is love, and that love is GOD. All its fleshliness and earthliness are consumed by this devouring fire, and this fire, also, is love and GOD at once. It now lives only in the life of GOD, because He is life, and this Divine life is within it. It is united with Him, says the learned Gerson, as the graft with the tree in which it is inserted; it is lost and absorbed in this vast ocean of light, of ardour, and of joy; it is changed into Him, as a drop of water put into a large vessel of wine; it receives His ardour as iron receives that of the fire in which it burns; it feels, in a word, that it is in GOD, and that GOD is in it; that He dwells and works in it, and that it possesses Him.

How did the bride seek her Beloved before she attained to this union which she so desired? Carried away by the wise foolishness of her love, she ran to the wilderness to find Him Whom her soul loved, and exposed herself to the mockery and insults of the soldiers: at last, directly she had passed the watchmen of the city, she had the joy of finding Him: paululùm cùm pertransissem eos, inveni quem diligit anima mea. (Cant. iii.) These rude and ignorant watchmen, say the holy Fathers, are figures of our senses; we must pass them by lively faith and by love, detached from all corporeal phantoms, to attain to this union, which is altogether spiritual. She adds, afterwards, that she holds her Beloved, and will not let Him go: tenui eum, nec dimittam. (Ibid.) After tasting the incomparable delight of this chaste and intimate union with GOD, is it possible to depart from Him?

AFFECTIONS.

FIRST DAY.

Inveni quem diligit anima mea. (Cant. iii.)

"At length," says the bride, "I found Him Whom my soul loveth." She sought Thee, LORD, with the eagerness of a lover, and Thou didst hide Thyself: yet she still sought Thee more ardently; it was right that Thou shouldst show Thyself to her. She ran after Thee, and Thou fleddest; yet she continued to run without being discouraged; and Thy goodness led Thee to wait, to spare her weakness, and to crown her noble perseverance. She strove to the utmost to raise herself to Thee, and had not the power; it was fitting for Thy goodness, either to lift her up, or to descend to her, to facilitate the union which she desired so ardently. At length, LORD, she found Thee, and was united to Thee, which proves that, GOD though Thou art, Thou canst not resist our love; that Thou withdrawest Thyself from Thy friends only to lead them to attain more intimate union, by inspiring them with more violent desires; that Thou formest these desires in their hearts, that Thou renderest them efficacious, and that Thou Thyself desirest this union as much as we; O wondrous Goodness!

SECOND DAY.

Inveni quem diligit anima mea.

When I shall be so happy as to find Him Whom my soul loveth, I shall be united with Him, I shall live in Him, and He in me: for there is this difference between knowledge and love, that knowledge in no manner unites a man with that which he knows; he does not go out of himself, but brings the object into Himself; whereas love unites him closely with that which he loves; the heart is carried into it, he cleaves to it, takes its properties, and is transformed into it. If the thing that I love is nobler and higher than myself, it ennobles and elevates me; if not, it lowers me; if I love the earth, I become earth. My Saviour, Who could love nothing above Himself, humbled Himself to love our flesh, and became flesh. Since, therefore, the excess of Thy love, my God, has brought Thee down to me, may I not aspire, by loving Thee with all the tenderness of my heart, to rise to Thee, to be closely united with Thee, and to become a partaker of Thy Divine nature, according to Thy promise?

THIRD DAY.

Inveni quem diligit anima mea.

The bride succeeded in finding her Beloved, and contracting an eternal union with Him, because her love was faithful and fervent. By this, Lord, Thou wouldst teach me, that as long as our love is feeble and transient, Thou hidest Thyself, and we find Thee not; or that Thou art at most to us like a traveller, who passes through the heart without abiding, but, that when our love is heroic and constant, Thou dwellest there, and art closely united with us: then Thou becomest our Lover, Thou contractest with us a chaste union, a heavenly marriage, from whence proceed abundantly fruits of grace and blessings: thence proceed sighs and lamentations; tears of tenderness; burning desires; pure feelings; thence delightful transports toward Thee. Art thou united to thy God, O my soul? Produce, then, the fruits of thy union; otherwise acknowledge, that far from having found thy Beloved, like the bride, thou hast perchance not even sought Him.

FOURTH DAY.

Inveni quem diligit anima mea.

Hope not, O my soul, to find that God Whom thou lovest, without seeking Him with all the ardour of which thou art capable. Though the end of love be union with the God Whom we love, and though thou desirest it, believe that thou hast yet far to go before thou attain it. To be united to God, to live with God, in God, and by the life of God, thou must pass through many hard trials, and sustain many combats. Thou must die before thou canst live; thou must detach thyself; tear thyself away before thou form an union; moreover, the union to which thou aspirest will be completed only in Heaven. The love which leads us to this has its origin, its progress, and its end. The Holy Ghost is its Adorable Origin; Faith, Hope, and Charity its progress; Union completes it. Believe, hope, love, constantly; the crown of love awaits thee in Heaven: thy Spouse will set it upon thy head in this life, and will fix it by an eternal and complete union, in that Blessed abode.

FIFTH DAY.

Tenui eum, nec dimittam.

"I hold my Beloved," says the bride, "and I will not let Him go." To find God, to hold Him, and never to let Him go, these are the degrees of perfect union. What comfort to find God after having sought Him! what happiness to hold Him after having found Him! what faithfulness never to let Him go after having once held Him! This, O my soul, is the whole secret of the union to which thou aspirest. The first step is to seek God in order to find Him. This requires desires, eagerness, and perseverance. The second step, to hold

Him after having found Him; the union is now begun: for this it is requisite to speak to Him, to hearken to Him, to value our happiness, and to cherish it. Never to let Him go, is perseverance in Union; for this we must have strength, attention, and great fear of losing this precious treasure. Seek carefully, O my soul, and thou wilt find thy God; hold thy Spouse firmly when thou hast found Him; and unite thyself with Him so strongly as never to let Him go.

SIXTH DAY.

Tenui eum, nec dimittam.

I have found Thee, LORD; or, rather, by an excess of Love Thou hast come Thyself to find me, and to unite Thyself to me in the Holy Communion. There have I had possession of Thy Heart when It was so near to mine, and It sought only to kindle it, and to be united to it. Can I flatter myself that I have united my soul to Thine, and received and preserved the Divine impression? Ah, LORD! when I have the blessing of finding Thee at the Holy Table, I will hold Thee with all my strength and with all my love; I will unite myself so strongly to Thee, that I shall have but one mind, one heart, and one soul, with Thee. An union so Glorious, and cemented by Thy Adorable Blood, shall never be broken.

SEVENTH DAY.

Tenui eum, nec dimittam.

When a soul has happily attained to union by the perseverance of her love, it is lost in GOD, and never leaves Him. It ceases, says St. Augustine, to possess itself, in order to possess GOD Alone; it cleaves to Him, is swallowed up and absorbed in Him, as in its Centre, and its repose. The Holy fire of Divine love melts and dissolves it, that it may flow into the

Heart of God; of this it takes possession, there it fixes itself, and abides as in its own domain, and never leaves it; there it is inflamed with Divine fire; there it enjoys infinite delights; and is at length transformed into that which it loves. Thus, my soul, is the union of the bride with her Spouse and her God produced. Thou wouldest experience these chaste pleasures, these delightful emotions, and these sacred out-pourings of the Heart of God into Thine; thou canst do it, but first thou must combat, conquer, and die to all which is not of God. Fear not, thou wilt be supported by thy love itself, which will bring thee at last to union in this life, till God crowns in Heaven the complete union which thou wilt enjoy eternally, without alarm, and without fear of separation.

Recapitulation of the Eighteen preceding Weeks.

A PRAYER TO OBTAIN THE LOVE OF GOD IN THE UNITIVE LIFE.

Adorable Spouse of my soul, Only and Divine Object of all the tenderness of my heart, complete in me what in Thy Infinite Goodness Thou hast begun. Thou hast given me the first-fruits of Thy Love, by purifying me from my sins, and lighting me in the paths of uprightness; add to these favours that of a more ardent love, which may give me entrance and perseverance in the unitive life, in which I may feel inviolable attachment (Thirty-fifth Week) to Thee as to the only Object Which I ought to love with all my heart, and with all my soul. Arouse my indolence and sloth by constant fervour (Thirty-sixth

Week). Cure my pusillanimity by heroic Love (Thirty-seventh Week), which will risk all through zeal for Thy Glory (Thirty-eighth Week), and which will blindly undertake all things to make Thee beloved (Thirty-ninth Week), and to cause Thee to reign supremely over all hearts (Fortieth Week). Send me into solitude (Forty-first Week), there speak to my heart, and fill it with true sympathy for Thee (Forty-second Week), that it may follow Thee whithersoever Thou goest; may imitate Thee, that it may espouse Thy sentiments, and take delight in Thee Alone and in that which Thou lovest (Forty-third Week). Grant me the favour of being admitted to Thy familiarity as Thy friend (Forty-fourth Week); consecrate my soul as Thy bride (Forty-fifth Week), that it may love Thee purely and without alloy (Forty-sixth Week); perfectly and unreservedly (Forty-seventh Week). I am Thine, LORD, be Thou mine; I sacrifice myself entirely to Thee (Forty-eighth Week), and I desire henceforth to repose in Thee Alone (Forty-ninth Week). Sacred Love, inebriate me with Thy Divine torrents (Fiftieth Week). I will die to all, that I may live only with Thee, by Thee, and for Thee (Fifty-first Week): happy if this mystic death, to which I aspire, unites me to Thee in time and in eternity (Fifty-second Week).

THE END.

www.ingramcontent.com/pod-product-compliance
Ingram Content Group UK Ltd.
Pitfield, Milton Keynes, MK11 3LW, UK
UKHW041951190726
13854UKWH00005B/1902
9 798869 357625